Collecting
LLADRÓ ®

738.2

Published by

krause publications

700 East State Street • Iola, WI 54990-0001
715/445-2214 • FAX: 715/445-4087   www.krause.com

"Lladró® is a registered trademark of Lladró USA, Inc. and Lladró Comercial, S.A.. All rights reserved. Neither Lladró USA, Inc. nor Lladró Comercial, S.A. is responsible for any information contained in this Guide and neither is affiliated with the book, the publisher nor the author.

All Lladró® figurines and products are copyrighted and protected by the copyright laws of the United States."

The following are copyrighted terms:
- eBay™
- Q-tip™
- NAO®
- Golden Memories®

Cover pictures, counterclockwise: "Girl Student" (#4518M), retired in 1978 and now worth $550-$575; "Swan with Wings Spread" (#5231G), currently retailing at #145; "1993 Limited Edition Egg" (#6083M), first of a series of five limited edition eggs distributed only in the U.S., valued at $240-$300; and "World of Fantasy" (#5943), made for the 1992 World Expo and distributed only in Spain, currently valued at $325-$350.

Please call or write for our free catalog of publications. Our toll-free number to place an order or obtain a free catalog is 800-258-0929 or please use our regular business telephone 715-445-2214 for editorial comment and further information.

Library of Congress Catalog Number:
ISBN: 0-87341-973-1

Dedication

*This book is lovingly dedicated to my parents, Pat and George Whiteneck,
who have, in countless ways, supported my career as a writer and whose example
taught me the joy of collecting beautiful things.*

&

*To Janet Gale Hammer, without whose boundless generosity over the years in sharing
her knowledge and love of Lladró, this book would not have been possible.*

Acknowledgments

I extend my deepest appreciation to all those who have generously supported the preparation of this book and who have eagerly awaited it

In particular, I am indebted to the following persons and companies for sharing their knowledge and expertise in Lladró:

Collectors Brad Welch, Joan [Lewis] Devlin, Dr. Bill Jann; Barbara Bennett, and Deb and Dennis Landis; Janet Gale Hammer of "A Retired Collection" in Longboat Key, FL; Herb Rostand of Rostand Fine Jewelers in Sunland, CA; Francisca Madden of "La Dulcinea" in Memphis, TN; Clark Sanchez of Sanchez Collectibles in Phoenix, AZ; Francisco Nadal of Nadal Collectibles in Woodland Hills, CA.

The following persons and companies provided photographs or venues for photograph-taking: Jane Shelley of Shelley's Auction Gallery in Hendersonville, NC; Frederica Edelman; Judith Kirby; Robert Graves; Felix Hardy; Paulette McNary; Kennedy Brothers, Inc. in Vergennes, VT; Florence DeNagy; The Antiques Collaborative in Quechee, VT; June Seligman; Carole Webber; Stanley and Ethel Cortis; Robert Sobr; The Vermont Antique Mall at Queechee Gorge, VT; Caren Reed; Carolyn Pearson; Joe Uccello; Reed's Antiques and Collectibles in Wells, ME; Phoebe Siemer; Champlain Valley Antque Center in South Burlington, Vermont; Virginia Herzog; Knotty Pine Antique Market in West Swanzey, NH; and Antiques at Colony Mill in Keene, NH.

A very special thanks to William B. Bradley, Jr., whose technical and artistic mastery of the photography medium graces the pages of this book.

And finally, I want to express my deep and abiding appreciation to Acquisitions Editor Paul Kennedy, and Book Editor Tracy Schmidt, at Krause Publications, for the energy, enthusiasm, and unflagging support they have brought to this project. They are a big part of the reason you, dear reader, are able to hold this book in your hands.

Table of Contents

Foreword

Chances are your first piece of Lladró was acquired as a gift or purchased as a memento while on a trip to Spain or perhaps during a cruise to the islands. Whether your Lladró was made in 1960 or as a millennium souvenir, a visit to your library or local bookstore in search of information about Lladró has been pretty much a dead end.

The Lladró Company has published at least three hardcover books. In 1981, there was *Lladró; the Art of Porcelain*. Then, in 1989, came *Lladró; The Magic World of Porcelain*. Most recently, in 1998, it brought out *The Will To Create*. These books provide mostly history about how the porcelain is created, with many beautiful color pictures of finished product anxiously ready for sale. There is much copy written about the many authentic Lladró identification markings and, in the later two books, the creation of the Lladró Society in 1985 with its grant of the exclusive right to buy at least one special figurine every year. More recently, there has been refreshing news of the *Second Generation of Lladró: Rosa, Mari Carmen and Juan Vicente*.

In 1994, the first edition of *The Lladró Authorized Reference Guide* was released, and there have been several updated editions of it since. But when you are reaching beyond that first piece toward a collection of significant value, you want to know more, and you want objective, independent commentary and background. Finally, enter Peggy Whiteneck and a book written from the collector's viewpoint.

In Spain and other European countries, it's considered something of a sin to sell your Lladró for a higher price than you paid. In Europe, Lladró is creative art to be passed on through family generations as an heirloom. Hence, there is little meaningful company recognition of a secondary market for retired pieces, which is seen as something of an American capitalistic anomaly.

I met Peggy in 1995 and was immediately impressed with her intense passion for Lladró and her instinctively inquisitive nature. When combined with her proven credentials as a top-notch writer, it's no surprise that we finally have a book specifically written to satisfy the sincere interest of loyal Lladró collectors.

Collectors often ask me what I think will become the next "Little Pals." The first Lladró Society figurine, "Little Pals" originally retailed in 1985 for $95. As I write this, it is currently available through A RETIRED COLLECTION at only $2,400.00 + shipping—or on eBay.com, with a small chip on the left ear of the right puppy, at only $1,465!

Should my Lladró be signed by Jose Lladró, Hugh Robinson, former Director of Lladró USA (now retired in Bradenton, FL), Herb Rostand, owner of Rostand Fine Jewelers and founder of the Lladró auctions (now semi-retired in Sunland, CA), or Mari Carmen Lladró? Or Mark McGwire? Should it be signed at all? This is a trick question, but if you want to know the real answer, I suggest you read Peggy Whiteneck's book.

Do you want to know how to clean your Lladrós without damaging or breaking them? Is restoration worth doing? Is there really a gray market for retail pieces? Is a figurine with an original box worth more than one without the box? What if the box is damaged?

For me, it has been an honor and a pleasure to be associated with this publication. I am certain collectors worldwide will agree that Ms. Whiteneck has done them an outstanding service.

Janet Gale Hammer
Longboat Key, Florida

Introduction

The allure of Lladró certainly can't be explained by its age: It's a relative upstart in a field dominated by much older, more famous names such as Meissen, Sevres, and Royal Doulton. Nor is it that Lladró is particularly affordable. Many's the day I've asked myself why I couldn't have started collecting something less expensive!

Lladró cannot be distinguished by its attractive glazes, nor its famous muted pastels, nor even the material of which it is made, fine as all may be. So what is it about these figurines and forms that has even people of limited financial means squirreling around to afford yet another addition to their collections?

Lladró's appeal must be found in its less tangible, but more essential, qualities. For one thing, Lladró has, among the famed porcelain-producing houses of Europe, thematic interests unrivalled for their breadth and inclusivity. Royal Copenhagen figures are Scandinavian in both theme and style, and Royal Doultons are quintessentially British. For those who collect them, the national flavor of these products is an important aspect of their attraction. By contrast, Lladró aspires to a more global appeal, at once reflecting and transcending its Spanish origins. As one expression of this global aspiration, Lladró makes figurines to represent nearly every racial, ethnic, and religious grouping on earth. This is especially remarkable, given that the three founding brothers were the poor sons of a farmer with little experience of the world beyond Valencia.

Another vital aspect of Lladró is its bias for the feminine form and personality. The great majority of the human figures in the Lladró corpus are female. The female children are especially well rendered, managing to capture the essence not only of form but of personality—the saucy way girls hold themselves and move and play. This, too, is surprising, given that Spanish culture is noted for its "machismo" and that not only the company's founders but all of its known sculptors are male.

Many Lladró figurines also have a kind of anecdotal appeal—a story quality—about them. The subtle tales a Lladró tells are part of what qualifies it as art and not just fine craftsmanship. Figurine #1248, known in English as "Sweety" or "Honey Lickers" (a title which, from the original Spanish, literally translates "Sweet Tooths") is a good example of what I mean. To the casual observer, this model will appear as a quite charming figurine of a girl dipping her finger into a pot while surrounded by three clamoring Dalmatian puppies. We know the jar in question is a honey pot because the Spanish word *miel* (honey) is painted on the side of it.

An important part of the aesthetic pleasure this figure gives is its multiple intersecting triangles: the arrangement of the puppies, the position of the girl's hair braids in relation to the top of her head, the position of the lower legs, the position of the elbows in relation to the torso. The top two in the triangular placement formed by the three puppies are obviously hoping to get some of that honey being sampled by the girl with the mischievous smile on her face. But the puppy who forms the third anchor of the triangle is much more interested in—and is apparently about to lick—the girl's big toe.

"Sweety" AKA "Honey Lickers" (#1248G), sculpted by Juan Huerta. Issued in 1974 and retired 1990 with a last retail of $350. Secondary market value: $550-$575. (Photo by William B. Bradley, Jr., from the author's own collection.)

The title of the piece could refer to the girl or the three puppies. For the puppies, the sweetness being sampled is obviously the honey, but, for at least one of them, it is also the girl! For the girl, the puppies are as important a part of her experience of "sweetness" as is the honey, but a third dimension of sweetness is evident in the look on her face: the joy of doing something illicit. In the final analysis, it is to the collector that the most varied dimensions of sweetness are reserved: the girl, the puppies, the vicarious taste of honey, and the internal delight evoked by the figurine itself!

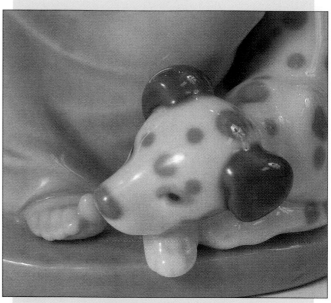

Close-up detailing of "Sweety" showing third puppy's fascination with a toe. Puppies were also sold individually but are hard to find on the secondary market. (Photo by William B. Bradley, Jr., from the author's own collection.)

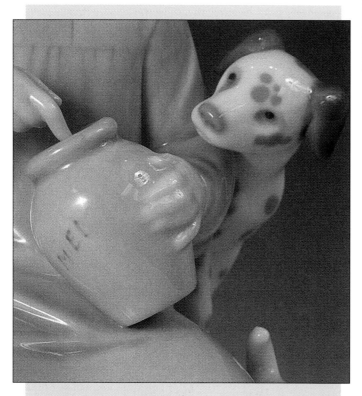

Close up showing detailing of top puppy in the grouping "Sweety" (#1248). (Photo by William B. Bradley, Jr., from the author's own collection.)

Consider also figurine #4915, entitled "Girl with Pigeons." When I first acquired this item for my own collection, I was attracted to the extraordinary tenderness with which the girl holds one of two fantail pigeons against her chest. In the other hand, she holds a small cup with seeds; it is a tribute to Lladró's ingenuity in detailing that one can actually see the seeds modeled in the tiny cup. The girl is dressed in a white kerchief and apron, Lladró's symbolic "cues" that the girl is a peasant—a shepherd or a farm worker.

But what's this? What are those elegant cuffs on her sleeves? What is that flouncy, lace-trimmed petticoat ostentatiously swishing beneath her skirt? And what, above all, is that fancy dress shoe with the bow on it—thrust toward the viewer so as not to be missed? What is that doing on the foot of a peasant girl?

Is this a peasant girl "dressing up," pretending to be a lady of the manor? Or is this a bored young lady of the manor "dressing down" to play the part of a shepherd? In art, as in life, there's more going on than meets the casual eye. The process of discovering the story in a Lladró is a satisfying way of communing with the artist—a sort of shared joke between sculptor and collector that enhances the pure pleasure of Lladró collecting.

The constant mystery, surprise, and unpredictability of its work are an important part of what makes Lladró so fascinating and so interesting to collect. In the final analysis, we collect Lladró because it is a work of art that can stand on its own merit. It doesn't need high-blown marketing hype or elaborate promotion strategies. All it needs is the discerning eyes of all those who will ever love it.

"Girl with Pigeons" (#4915G), sculpted by Salvador Debón. The pigeons are fan-tails, similar to doves. Issued in 1974 and retired in 1990. Secondary market value: $350-$400. (Photo by William B. Bradley, Jr., from the author's own collection.)

For the sake of clarity and to address what I believe is a significant collector confusion about what is and what is not a Lladró product, I want to acknowledge at the outset that NAO® by Lladró, a NAO predecessor called Zaphir, and Golden Memories® are all brand names for additional Lladró products. Whether they are still active, as in the case of the NAO collection, or have been withdrawn from production, as in the case of Golden Memories, these brands are considered by the company to be quite separate from its "core collection." While I recognize the growing collector interest in these other Lladró brands and hope to be able to address it in future writing, the focus of this particular book is exclusively on the core collection (i.e., on those products identified by the Lladró name with no other brand names attached).

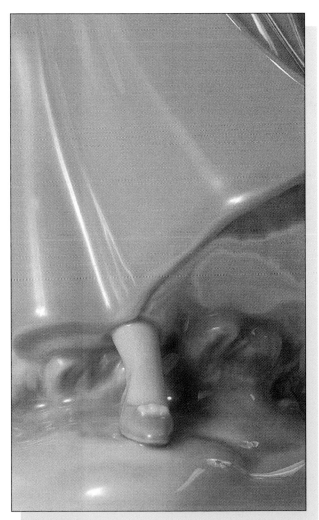

Detail from "Girl with Pigeons." Note the flouncy petticoat and fancy dress shoe—on a peasant girl!

"Cinderella" (#4828G/M) graced the cover of the first-ever edition of Lladró's Expressions magazine. Cinderella has become, along with Don Quixote, a sort of "signature character" for the company. This model was issued in 1972 and retired relatively recently in 1998 at a last retail price of $245. Expect to pay $275-$300 for her today. (Photo courtesy of Lladró USA, Inc.)

Lladró Porcelains: A Historical Timeline

1941 — Jose and Juan Lladró Produce the Oldest of Extant Works, consisting of very rare, one of a kind painted files.

1951 — The Brothers Build First Backyard Kiln capable of achieving the temperatures required to fire ceramics.

c1952-53 — Brothers Build a Better Kiln capable of vitrifying porcelain.

1953 — Lladró Company Officially Founded First of Extant Vases is modeled by Vicente Lladró and painted by older brothers Juan and Jose (rare item from company museum).

1954 — Earliest Protoypic Figurines are produced; these figurines have decimal point serial numbers and, for the most part, predate factory production. (In extremely limited quantities, "decimal-pointed" works were made through the mid 1960s.)

1955 — First Retail Store opened in Valencia.

1958 — "Foundation is Laid" for Lladró factory at Tavernes Blanques, eventually to become known as "Porcelain City".

c1962 — Factory becomes fully operational.

1963 — Artisan's Workshop Established at Porcelain City for the training of new Lladró artisans.

c1963-1966 — Lladró Acquires the Zaphir Collection, Renames it "NAO".

c1964-1965 — First Factory-produced and Exported Figurines from the core collection, including Salvador Furió's "Clown with Concertina" (#1027) and Fulgencio García's "Sad Harlequin" (#4558).

1970 — Gres Series Debuts in core collection and NAO. First Lladró Limited Editions from core collection, both in Gres: #2016 "Girl with Guitar," #2018 "Madonna with Child".

c1970 — First Blue Backstamp and Logo Debuts, with an error in spelling that leaves the accent off the *o* in Lladró.

1971 — First non-Gres Limited Editions from core collection, "Othello and Desdemona (#1145) and "Antique Auto" (#1146).

c1974 — Second Blue Backstamp adds trademark sign to name and restores accent too.

c1975 — Third Lladró Backstamp with © DAISA added.

1977 — Fourth Lladró Backstamp adds copyright date to mark.

1982 — Norman Rockwell Collection Introduced.

1983	Crystal Collection Debuts, a collaboration with the famous French glassmaking company Daum Nancy.
1985	Lladró Society Founded in the United States. First Edition of Expressions Magazine for Lladró Society members. First Lladró Society Figurine, "Little Pals" (#7600).
1988	Lladró Museum Opens on W. 57th Street in New York City, with displays including the rare early works of the three brothers. Goyesca Series Debuts.
1989	First U.S. Exclusive Lladró Auction, sponsored by Rostand's Fine Jewelers, held in Universal City, California.
1990	Contemporary Backstamp Introduced with streamlined logo and typeface to increase legibility. Expressions Published in Japanese to accommodate a growing number of Lladró Society members in Japan.
1991	Capricho Series and Most of Core Collection's Matte Corpus Retired. *Expressions* Finally Printed in Native Language of Company Founders! (Published in the U.S., the English language edition was formerly shipped to Valencia, where Spanish-language inserts were added.) *Lladró Collector's Catalog* Debuts, essentially a loose-leaf compendium of color pictures of every figurine in the corpus to that date, with

captions describing the piece and identifying the sculptor.

c1991-92	Outlet Store Opens in Williamsburg, VA.
1992	First East Coast Lladró Auction, sponsored by Thalheimer's Auction Gallery, held in Florida. Disney Collection Introduced with Tinkerbell (#7518). Golden Memories Collection Debuts and production of NAO is suspended to accommodate GM's retail run.
1994	Fulgencio García, Great Early Lladró Sculptor, Dies. Golden Memories Permanently Closed and NAO brought back on line.
1996	Last West Coast Lladró Auction to be sponsored by Rostand.
1997	Last East Coast Lladró Auction to be sponsored by Thalheimer's.
1999	Gaudi Series Debuts, based on the mosaic style of famous Spanish architect debuts in Spain and Japan.
2000	The Legend Collection Debuts, consisting of cherubs and other fantasy creatures heavily accented in gold and other precious materials. The Fantasy Collection Debuts, consisting of winged fairies and other fantasy figures surrounded by large, lush flowerwork. The Lladró Society is Phased Out at the end of this, its 15th year.

A mint condition example of Juan Huerta's "Charlie the Tramp" AKA "The Eternal Poet" (#5233G), issued in 1985 and retired in 1991. As a "cross-collectible," mint examples fetch big bucks on today's secondary market, with typical prices ranging from $700 to over $1,000. Last retail price in 1990 was only 245! (Photo by William B. Bradley, Jr., from the author's own collection.)

Chapter 1

HISTORY, MARKS, AND MANUFACTURE

The Lladró company's accounts of its own history often make it seem effortless and inevitable—very much a Cinderella story. We do know, however, that a company and its art don't really evolve in the twinkling of an eye or a dubbing of the fairy godmother's wand. In Lladró's case, corporate history is not so easily extracted from a complex product history. This chapter explores that history in detail. (Those wanting a more concise, bird's-eye view of the history of Lladró from its founding to the present may wish to consult the historical timeline that follows the Introduction to this book.)

Production History of the Core Collection

The Lladró company was formally incorporated in the year 1953. By 1955, the three brothers, Juan, Jose, and Vicente, had established their own retail shop in Valencia, where they sold some of their earliest wares (those which today would be considered rare). At this time, the brothers had only a single kiln consistently capable of achieving the temperatures necessary to vitrify porcelain. (Their very first kiln had been built in 1951 and was apparently only rarely capable of achieving such temperatures.)

The "foundations were laid" for the present Lladró factory in 1958—and all Lladró sources are careful to repeat this precise phrasing. It is, therefore, unlikely that the factory was fully operational much before the early to mid-1960s. Lladró began exporting figurines shortly after the factory came into full production.

Lladró refers to its basic collection of figurines (those whose brand name is simply the family name) as its "core collection." At almost 4,000 pieces, the sheer magnitude of the core collection is astonishing. Each year, in spring and fall, the company introduces new figures and retires several others to make room for the new issues in company inventory.

Earliest items have been assigned a decimal point serial number. For the most part, these items date from the mid-1950s to early 1960s, though a few of them date to the early 1970s. Decimal-numbered items were made in very limited quantities and are today considered extremely rare.[1] Not all of these have yet been discovered and catalogued. (See "A Gallery of Rare and Unusual Pieces" for some of these rarest items not found in the Lladró reference books.)

Unless the item in question is a limited edition, it is virtually impossible to find out precisely how many of any particular open issue figurine in the core collection are made in a year's time. The company does know, however, that only 100 copies of the decimal-numbered "Spain-USA" (#347.13) were ever produced.[2] Considering the tens of thousands of collectors who would give their eye teeth to have one of these decimal-numbered items in their collections, 100 copies is not very many! Moreover, "Spain-USA" was a fairly late example of a decimal-numbered item. It was issued in 1973, after the company had full production capacity. It is probably safe to extrapolate from its tiny production run that certainly no more than 100 copies were made of the even earlier decimal-numbered items from the 1950s and early 1960s.

Company publications usually give 1969 as the first year of issue for the oldest, non-rare items in the core collection, which are identified with whole serial numbers. This date may be too late by as many as five years. An article in an early edition of *Expressions*, the magazine of the Lladró Society in the U.S., notes that "Sad Harlequin" (#4558) had already been marketed "with great success" as early as 1965.[3] As late as the *Expressions* of summer 1990, a short article focusing on the activities of sculptor Salvador Furió mentions that "his very first figurine made for Lladró in 1964 was 'Clown with Concertina' (L1027)."[4]

Beyond the early decimals, the product history of the company cannot be traced chronologically merely by using serial numbers. In numerical order, the first non-decimal, whole number that appears in core collection lists is #1001, "Shepherdess with Goats." However, we

Lladró's very rare "Woman with Traditional Dress" (#1157) issued in 1971 and retired in 1975. Sculpted by Julio Fernandez, the form and style are unusual for Lladró. First issued at $25, she brought $600 at one of the exclusive Lladró auctions held in the early 1990s. (Photograph by Francisca Madden from her private collection.)

Sculptor Salvador Furió's famous "Clown with Concertina" (#1027G/M), first issued in the mid-1960s and retired in 1993 at a last retail of $735. Prices on the secondary market are in the $800-$875 range. (Photo courtesy of Lladró USA, Inc.)

also know that one of the first-released non-rare figurines from the core collection was the aforementioned "Sad Harlequin," with a serial number in the 4000s (#4558). At the same time, the 2000 numbers were being reserved for the Gres series, the first item of which was introduced as early as 1970. What this means is that the company has been using, ever since it started using whole serial numbers, four-digit numbers in three series of 1000s, 2000s, and 4000s pretty much simultaneously.

In fact, the oldest items in the 4000 series were originally issued as three-digit numbers without the "4."[5] The 4000 number series started with #4501, "A Basket of Goodies," whose issue date the company gives as 1969. That figurine was originally issued as #501. "Sad Harlequin" was originally issued as #558, and so on. Therefore, collectors with items serial numbered in the low 1000s should not assume their items are older than some others that are serial numbered in the 2000s or 4000s.

How a Lladró Piece Is Made

The Lladró factory, known to most collectors as "Porcelain City," is located in the town of Tavernes Blanques, just outside Valencia, on the eastern Mediterranean coast of Spain. The term "factory" could

give collectors in industrialized nations a false impression, since it evokes for most of us the image of machine tools and assembly lines—precisely the wrong image for what happens at Lladró.

In contrast to items that are made from what we normally envision as factory molds, no two examples of the same Lladró figurine will ever be exactly alike because each will bear the marks of having been hand-worked by human artisans. There will be subtle size and color variations in the same figure caused by how different batches of porcelain and paint interact with the kiln's fire. There will be slight differences in facial expression; a kitten whose expression appears merely curious or quizzical in one example of a figurine may look downright mischievous in another example of the same model.

The first part of the creation process begins with a number of design drawings. Some are produced by the three Lladró brothers and others by the various sculptors working for them. These drawings are examined by the Lladrós themselves. Those they deem promising as Lladró figurines are made by Lladró sculptors into three-dimensional models about a third larger than the final figurine (to allow for shrinkage in the kiln). The figure is further analyzed and, if need be, revised until it is in a production form that is approved by the Lladró family—which today includes second-generation members, as well as the three founding brothers.

"Sad Harlequin" (#4558G) was sculpted by the great Fulgencio García. Identified by Jose Lladró as the seminal figure in the elongated style that would come to be seen as characteristic of "old Lladró," it was issued sometime in the mid-1960s and retired in 1993. It commands $650-$850 on today's secondary market, well above its last retail of $510. (Photo courtesy of Lladró USA, Inc.)

Despite what might appear to be a high serial number, "A Basket of Goodies" (#4501G) was one of Lladró's earliest issues; her original number was 501. On the retail market from the mid- to late 1960s through 1985, her Lladró auction price range was $300-$475, and her secondary market price today is about $400-$450. (Photo courtesy of Lladró USA, Inc.)

A copy of the original sculpture is then cast in a hollow plaster form that can be cut up into several parts to form molds. The number of distinct molds required to make even one figurine will be multiple; the exact number depends upon the number of projecting parts in the figure. According to the company Web site (www.lladro.com), as many as fifteen to twenty individual molds are required on average to make a figure, although more complex figures may require more than 200.

To give a more precise sense of the range, nine distinct molds were required to make the fairly uncomplicated "All Aboard" (#7619), the 1992 Lladró Society members-only figurine.[6] At the other end of the spectrum, the fabulous "18th Century Coach" (limited edition #1485, and at current retail of $31,000, the most expensive thing Lladró ever made) takes 350

individual molds to make.[7] New molds must be made as often as required to retain the sharpness and precision of detail in the original sculpture. Each of these multiple molds has a life of only about forty to fifty castings before new molds have to be created. No wonder "18th Century Coach" (shown on page 18) is so expensive!

Through the centuries, the porcelain formulas used by famous companies have always been an arcane matter. Lladró maintains its own chemistry department, and the secret of its porcelain formulas (the formulas for Gres and Goyesca being different from the formula for the rest of the core collection) is likewise carefully guarded. This liquid porcelain (called "biscuit" or "slip") is injected into the moistened molds (which consist, for each part, of at least two pieces held together by large rubber belts). The porcelain is allowed to dry, and then the mold is separated to extract the new part.

Next, the parts are manually polished to eliminate rough edges so that the joinings in the final figurine will be seamless. The parts are reassembled using liquid porcelain to adhere the joints.

The bodies of the figurines are then hand-painted with the appropriate colors in Lladró's palette of over 5,000 different tones. In order to reduce the amount of unacceptable variation between figurines from the same molds, painters specialize in certain figures. The process is prevented from becoming tedious for the artisans by the annual retirement of some older figurines and the yearly addition of brand new ones.

At this stage in the production, colors will look quite a bit different from their final form. The raw paints when first applied will be more vivid, even gaudy, than the softened colors that emerge from the kiln after firing. Thus, Lladró painters are required not only to be artists, but technicians as well, knowledgeable of how various pigments will interact with the kiln's fire.

"All Aboard" (#7619G), the Lladró Society figurine for 1992, issued at $165 and trading on today's secondary market at $300-$325. Even this relatively uncomplicated model required nine separate molds to produce. (Photo courtesy of Lladró USA, Inc.)

At its current retail price of $31,000, "18th Century Coach" (#1485) has the distinction of being the most expensive thing Lladró ever made. (Small wonder the edition size was only 500!) First issued in 1985, it would have cost you a lot less then—only $14,000. (Photo courtesy of Lladró USA, Inc.)

Parasol production is likewise labor-intensive. The parasols feature lace and tulle dipped in porcelain, beneath which the fabric disintegrates in the kiln, leaving behind only the porcelain image of the lacy pattern. These design elements must usually be sewn together in their cloth forms in order to make such things as ruffled trim before the item is anywhere close to being converted to actual porcelain. The parasol panels are also made from cloth panels cut out and assembled together to form the parasol. The porcelain-

"Valencian Girl" (#4841G) was issued in 1973 and is still retailing at $240. She is particularly interesting not only for her traditional Valencian costume, but also for the orange of the fruit—a color seldom seen on a Lladró. (Photo courtesy of Lladró USA, Inc.)

At times, collectors have observed interesting variations in the painting of the same figurine. A picture of the detail from "Duck Seller" (#1267, below) shows one of these enhancements. The figure is most often painted plain, but, in this case, there are groups of three tiny, pale green dots of raised paint on the scarf. The girl's skirt has a similar pattern of groups of four dots of pale pink. The overall effect is of tiny rosettes. Broker Janet Gale Hammer has observed this variation on other figures as well.

Similarly, some of the angels in the child angel series (#s 4536-4541, pictured on page 194 have little paint-dotted accents along their hem and collar lines, while others are simply plain. The uniformly pale green foliage on my "vintage" "Koala Love" (#5461, seen on page 20) is quite different from the variegated darker green and white leaves that I have seen on a version of it with a later mark. The figurines "Soccer Player" (5200) and "Special Male Soccer Player" (#5200.3) are, as the serial numbers imply, essentially identical models, but they are painted in entirely different colors.

After painting, decorative accents such as parasols, and separately modeled leaves and flowerwork will be applied through the manipulation of tiny pieces of flexible, moist porcelain with the color already in the porcelain itself. The flower-making process is a creative endeavor all its own, and there are Lladró artisans dedicated exclusively to this work. The task of adding these famous flowers to a figure is minute, time-consuming, and painstaking as each leaf, stamen, stem, and petal is individually modeled and applied. Therefore, the addition of flowerwork to a figure usually adds considerably to its retail price.

Detail from "Duck Seller" showing variant of little dots of paint in design configurations of four in pale green on the girl's head-shawl; a similar pattern of three pale pink dots is on the skirt. (Photo by William B. Bradley, Jr., from the author's own collection.)

dipped parasol is then fired around a domed frame that helps it retain its shape and can be removed when the item emerges from the kiln.[8]

At this stage in the production process, a matte figurine will be essentially ready for firing. For glazed figurines, however, there is one more step. Lladró specializes in *bajo cubierto* ("painting under glaze"). The glaze in question is a thin varnish that will be

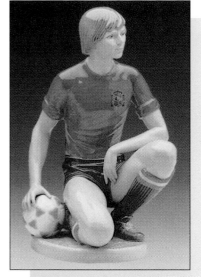

"Male Soccer Player" (#5200G) had a retail run of 1984 through 1988 and trends on the secondary market at $450-$500. (Photo courtesy of Lladró USA, Inc.)

"Special Male Soccer Player" (#5200.3G) is a color variant of #5200 and had the same retail years. It trends slightly higher on the secondary market at $525-$600. (Photo courtesy of Lladró USA, Inc.)

"Oriental Forest" (#6396G) cuts a stunning figure. The parasol would have been a challenge to make just in itself. Issued in 1997, this beauty retails at $565. (Photo courtesy of Lladró USA, Inc.)

sprayed evenly over the entire painted figure. This is an important stage of the process for a glazed figurine. Too little glaze or an uneven application of it will fail to bring out the already subtle colors in the figure and/or will retract, leaving spots of exposed matte, ranging in size from pinpricks to patches, where the glaze should be. Too much glaze will fill in delicate, sculpted features, especially around the face. Lladró artisans are unusually skilled in the application of this glaze; by contrast, some famous porcelain companies that also use *bajo cubierto* apply the glaze so thickly that modeling details are lost, and the eyes of large animal figurines develop "glaze blisters" which can later break and cause a most unsightly effect.

The final stage of production is firing of the figures in large kilns, each of which contains shelves to accommodate groups of several figurines for firing at

"Koala Love" (#5461G) issued in 1988 and retired in 1993. A paint variation observed on a model with a 1990s backstamp featured dark green leaves with white borders. The mark on this particular item, whose leaves are a uniform light green, shows it was fired in the 1980s. Value today: $275-$300. (Photo by William B. Bradley, Jr., from the author's own collection.)

"Koala Love" showing facial detailing. Note how the artists have captured the look of anxiety on the mother's face. A skilled application of glaze is required in order not to obscure the features. (Photo by William B. Bradley, Jr., from the author's own collection.)

Legitimate Marks of the Core Collection

The evolution of the core collection's mark is complex and sometimes confusing to collectors. The blue backstamp is certainly the mark collectors would be most likely to encounter on the secondary market—and it is the only mark they would encounter on today's retail market.

Unfortunately, even some of the company's own marketing copy seems to imply that any mark that isn't a late-issue backstamp is a potential fake. This has led some collectors routinely to pass over older Lladrós with perfectly good marks because they assume that anything not sporting the more recent and familiar backstamp is either a "second" or a forgery.

For the record, the oldest marks collectors may be lucky enough to find on the secondary market are not the blue backstamps but several variations of earlier

one time. The figures will be "batched" according to the temperature and number of hours required to fire them. As an example of the time and temperature requirements for even a smallish figurine, each "All Aboard" (#7619) was fired for 12 hours at 1,320° C.[9]

Lladró is thus handmade in every sense that counts. These kiln shelves and the artisans' personal workbenches and tables are the closest thing to an assembly line to be found at the Lladró factory!

marks incised right into the porcelain of the underbase. Genuine marks for the core collection, with captions indicating their approximate years of use, are shown at the back of this book; I have deliberately overlapped the ends of the ranges because two marks were often used simultaneously during periods of transition from older to newer marks. Also included are examples of variations of the core collection backstamp for members-only Society issues and for Special Events figurines.

There are a few marks even older than the two incised marks pictured, but these are unlikely to be found outside Spain. Those who would like to see examples of these old marks can find them on the company Web site at www.lladro.com under the section entitled "History of the Logotype" or in some of Lladró's own book publications (see list of References in the Appendices).

According to Lladró USA, Lladró did not mark some of its earliest figures at all, and at least one long-time collector/dealer to whom I have spoken has a known early and authentic Lladró limited edition in his own collection that is unmarked. Collectors are advised to avoid the wild goose chase. Unless there was an early buying trip to Spain involved, the chances of finding an unmarked Lladró are probably equal to the chances of finding any other rare one.

The logo the company developed for the core collection is a stylized amalgam of the Spanish bellflower and an ancient alchemical symbol and is meant to represent the marriage of art and science in the creation of Lladró porcelain. The earliest blue backstamp on which the logo appears was introduced sometime between 1971 and 1974 and omits the accent over the *o* in the family name; there is no trademark or copyright sign. The omission of the accent may seem minor, but it actually constitutes a misspelling leading to today's widespread mispronunciation of the name, even among Spanish-speakers. Without that accent, the normal stress would be on the first syllable, in Spanish as well as in English. Perhaps as a result of "porcelain migration patterns" secondary to tourist travel, I have found and purchased many examples of this oldest misspelled backstamp in Northern New England.[10]

Fairly early on, Lladró began to experience pirating of its mark by unscrupulous manufacturers. The company took legal steps in the mid 1970s to protect the integrity of its mark by trademarking the name Lladró and copyrighting individual figurine designs. The images of the core collection mark published here are intended to provide as comprehensive a

picture as possible of legitimate variations in the mark as a help to collectors in distinguishing legitimate products from the bogus ones. (For more on counterfeit marks, including a picture of one, see Chapter 4.)

"Boy with Dog" (#4522G/M). Issued in 1970 as #0522, it later became #4522. Retired in 1997, its secondary market value is $200-$250. This particular example features the first blue backstamp with the misspelling of the name Lladró. (Photo by William B. Bradley, Jr., from the author's own collection.)

The name "DAISA," in Lladró's copyright notice often causes confusion to new collectors. It is neither (to address two of the more common misconceptions) the name of the girl figurines on which it appears nor a "rival company" of Lladró! DAISA is the acronym for the umbrella company that holds the intellectual and design property rights for the Lladró company; it stands for Designos Artisanos Industriales, SA. (The last two letters stand for Sociedad Anónimo and serve much the same function as the abbreviations "Inc." in the United States and "Ltd." in Great Britain). In 1977, a copyright date was added to the mark. This date is usually, though not always, the year before the actual issue date. (This, too, gets confusing because Lladró eventually backdated later firings of older open issues. For example, a figurine first issued in, say, 1969 may contain a 1977 copyright date if the example in question was actually fired in 1978 or after. Many people unfamiliar with Lladró mistakenly believe that the copyright date is an indicator of age. However, because an issue may remain open for several years, during which time the copyright date will remain the same, that date is of little or no help in determining when a given figurine was actually fired.)

By this time, the mark appeared quite busy and cluttered, an effect exaggerated when the blue of the mark "bled," as it often did. The company designed the 1990s mark to introduce more space and crisper lines into the logo and lettering. The logo was

This unusually tall piece is not marked and was purchased by the owner's father in Spain in the 1970s along with a few smaller pieces that were marked and identifiable as Lladró. The woman carries a closed parasol under her arm. Lladró did not consistently mark its very earliest pieces, nor has it captured in its catalogs every last early item ever produced. While this item is not shown in any Lladró catalogue, it has all the aesthetic hallmarks of a Lladró. Estimated value: $1000-$1500. (Photo by William B. Bradley, Jr., from the private collection of Mark Hayes.)

simplified so that only a remnant of the original alchemical symbol—the part that looks like the "leaves" and stem of the flower—remains.

"Seconds" will be discussed at greater length in Chapter 4. Suffice it to say for now that any blue mark that has the logo scratched off is either a "second" from the factory in Spain or a purchase from the Lladró outlet store in Williamsburg, Virginia (also discussed in Chapter 4).

Around the mid-1980s, the company began incising the four-digit serial number into the base of the figurine (as visible in some pictures of the mark shown at the back of the book). Prior to that time, the serial number was to be found only on the original box, which if lost made it difficult for collectors to identify their figurines.

Novice collectors sometimes confuse the serial number with various other artisans' numbers on the base of the figurine. The incised serial number will always have four digits and will usually be larger than any of the other marks on the base, thereby making it clear that it is, in fact, the serial number. Several other, smaller incised marks are also found on the base; most of these are the marks of various artisans who worked on the piece (painters, decorators, etc.). According to the company, these marks cannot be interpreted for collector information purposes and are simply in-house codes used to track production for quality assurance.

Mention might be made of one set of small number-letter codes that began to appear on the base of figurines sometime in the early to mid-1970s. This code consists of a letter of the alphabet followed by a dash, a number, and an additional letter. An example might be F-20E. In a pattern too remarkable to be purely coincidental, the middle numbers all range from 1 to 31 (the maximum number of days in a month) and the last letters all correspond to the initial letter or letters of the Spanish names for months of the year:

E	= Enero (January)
F	= Febrero (February)
M	= Marzo (March)
A	= Avril (April)
MY	= Mayo (May)
J	= Junio (June)
JU	= Julio (Julio)
AG	= Agosto (August)
S	= Septiembre (September)
O	= Octubre (October)
N	= Noviembre (November)
D	= Diciembre (December)

"Josefa Feeding Her Duck" (#5201G), issued 1983 and retired in 1991. Colors are quite vivid for Lladró, especially the deep teaberry pink in the skirt. Secondary market value $325-$375. Most of the firings of this model would have been late enough to have the serial number impressed into the base's underside. (Photo by the author, from her personal collection.)

In the example F-20E, then, the item would have been manufactured on the 20th of January.

Knowing this does little good, of course, in the absence of a year symbol, the presence of which would allow us to date to the day and year the time when all but our oldest figurines were actually manufactured—and wouldn't that be fun! I have tried a variety of combinations in an effort to make sense of this first letter as a code for year of manufacture; while several of my attempts made substantial sense, none of them was able to account for all the items even in my own collection. There would always be one or two that didn't "fit"—i.e. that came out with a production date too far prior to what I already knew to be the issue year or that came up with a manufacture date too long after the item had already been retired.

It may be that this first letter was simply a batching code rather than a year of production—in which case the code is essentially meaningless to collectors. On the other hand, it would indeed be an odd oversight hadn't someone at the company given thought to dating the items manufactured, as virtually all the other great porcelain houses of Europe have done. (Royal Doulton, Royal Copenhagen, and Wedgwood, for example, can all be year-dated by codes on their bases.)

Three Kinds of Finish

Lladró core collection figurines can appear with three types of finish: glazed, matte, and Gres. The most common and popular is the high-gloss glaze often associated with Lladró as one of its defining characteristics—although I personally don't know how the

23

average naked eye would distinguish the Lladró glaze from any of a number of high-gloss glazes produced by other manufacturers of fine-quality porcelain.

Less commonly seen are pieces in the matte finish (i.e., those that are not glazed), including a few in a totally white finish known as "bisque."[11] Lladró produced many of its pre-1991 core collection figurines in both matte and glazed forms. However, the majority of open-issue matte figurines were retired in 1991 because of unreliable retail sales. (See Chapter 5 for more on "matte vs. glaze.") The company retained some extraordinarily popular items in both finishes (e.g., the series of six child angels, #s 4536-4541), but it has been introducing far fewer new mattes since 1991.

Sculptor Fulgencio García's "Girl with Pig" (#1011G/M), one of the smallest human figurines Lladró has made. Issued in the mid- to late 1960s, this matte version was retired in 1991 along with much of the rest of the matte corpus. While the glazed version still retails for $95, the matte can command $150. (Photo by William B. Bradley, Jr., from the author's own collection.)

Figurine finish is distinguished in company catalogs, dealer stock, and price lists in one of two ways. In older lists, a "G" after the number stands for "glazed" while an "M" means the finish is "matte." "G/M" after a serial number means the item was produced in both forms. In 1992, the company dropped the letter suffixes and began using the numbers "0" and "1" as serial number prefixes, with "0" indicating glaze and "1" indicating matte. This system is confusing, since the company also uses the number "1" to refer to Gres finish figurines, which are not matte in the traditional sense. The addition of extra numerical digits to serial numbers is also complicated for the eye. For these reasons, I have chosen to stay with the original G/M codes for listings in this book, except where I make it obvious that the item in question is Gres or Goyesca, in which case the finish letters do not apply, and I have simply left them off. While many inventory lists use the suffix "M" for matte to denote Gres items, I have avoided that usage in this book because I think it makes it difficult for collectors to know when a figurine was made in traditional matte and when it was made in Gres.

The Gres finish is unique in texture and surface appearance. Many Lladró items produced in the glazed finish are also made in Gres, but there are some figures that are only made in Gres, including several large limited edition groupings.

The material of Gres figures appears to the eye to be more similar to stoneware or pottery, but it is porcelain. Gres porcelain has a terra-toned pigment in the porcelain itself and is usually left unglazed on exposed skin surfaces while enamel paint is used to define clothing and other non-skin elements; the

painting often has a mottled appearance. In general, the enamel painting does not have the subtle detailing that can be found in twin models with the more familiar glazed finish, and this gives Gres a more rustic appearance.

The Gres formula is, like the knowledge of all Lladró's porcelain formulas, a closely guarded secret. According to the company, Gres took twenty years of experimentation to develop. Lladró was looking for a formula that would allow greater versatility in item size than porcelain normally offers. (You may have noticed that, in general, porcelain does not lend itself to works of monumental proportion.) A number of the Gres figures range in height from 15 to 25 inches.[12] The life-size figures in traditional Valencian costume that grace the entryway to Porcelain City are also Gres; for sheer size, they would be hard to imagine in traditional porcelain!

Gres also lends itself to greater versatility in ethnic expression, as it is much easier to define non-Caucasian features with a darker-hued porcelain. I personally prefer the Gres treatments of religious themes involving various members of the Holy Family, for instance, because I find them more authentic.

"Playing Cards" (#1327) is a tableau made in the Gres porcelain formula—a rustic effect for what looks like a rough group! Issued in 1976, it currently retails at $6600. (Photo courtesy of Lladró USA, Inc.)

Gres achieved popularity in Europe much sooner than in the United States. Until very recently, many authorized dealers in the U.S. did not even carry it. The company has been aggressively promoting its Gres exports to collectors looking for a more versatile decorating alternative than offered by the muted pastel colors of the rest of the core collection. More recently, Gres appears to be catching on in the United States.

"Camel" (#2027), an early Gres issued in 1971 and retired in 1975. Lladró has made relatively few animal figurines in this earthy porcelain formula. This one is quite large at 18" in height, and although it last retailed at $210, it'll cost you roughly ten times as much today. (Photo courtesy of Lladró USA, Inc.)

One measure of Gres' growing hold on the hearts of U.S. collectors is the interesting case of "Scheherazade" (#7678). This first-ever Society members-only Gres limited edition featured the famous muse reclining semi-nude and playing her mandolin. Issued in 1999 at $950, her edition size of 1,000 took all of two weeks to sell out worldwide! It is estimated that, as a result of Gres' slow market maturity in the States, only 200 of these were ever sent here—about half of the usual U.S. allotment for a limited edition of this subscription size. This was bound to create an instant shortage should the model prove popular, and—you guessed it—U.S. collectors are now so frantic to acquire her that she was selling on the secondary market for a cool $2,500 by midway into the year 2000. (By the way, the first two limited editions Lladró ever fired were both Gres: "Girl with Guitar" [#2016] and "Madonna with Child" [#2018].)

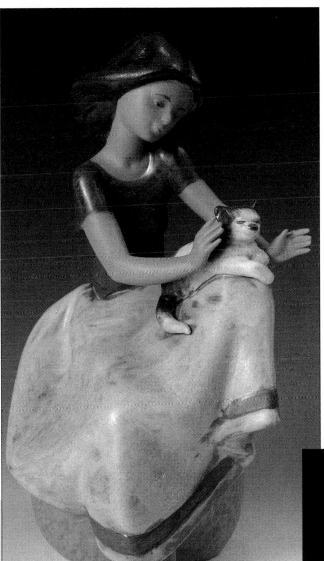

"Repose" (#2169), a good example of the earthy surface of a Gres figurine. Note dark skin tones. Still active and retailing at $210. (Photo by William B. Bradley, Jr., from the author's own collection.)

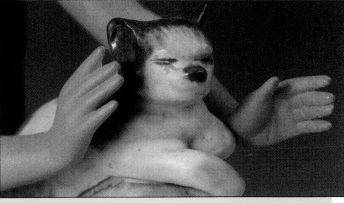

Detail from "Repose" showing rustic painting on kitten. (Photo by William B. Bradley, Jr., from the author's own collection.)

This 16" Gres head of a "Woman from Guadalupe" (#4768) would make a fabulous table centerpiece. Unfortunately, she was issued in 1971 and retired by the end of 1973, so she would be difficult to find today. I don't know anyone who has her for sale right now, but it would not surprise me to see her priced at $600-$900. (Photo courtesy of Lladró USA, Inc.)

Core Collection Sculptors

Of the three brothers themselves, only the youngest, Vicente, was trained as a sculptor. Juan, the oldest, and the middle brother, Jose, are painters. Various artists and artisans collaborate with the Lladrós, including a group of extraordinarily gifted sculptors, of whom I will mention here only a few of the oldest and best known. At any given time, the company has a dozen or more sculptors working on the core collection.

Salvador Furió, Fulgencio García, and Juan Huerta are among the oldest and most celebrated of the sculptors associated with Lladró. All are of advanced age. In fact, García died in 1994 at the age of seventy-nine; as nearly as I can determine, the very last issue that bears his name is a tall (17" high) model of the Virgin titled in English "Heavenly Prayer" (#6145), released the year he died. Some of the other models he created are also still active issues.

As much as any early sculptor still working at Lladró by the 1990s, García had a hand in shaping that elegant, elongated, almost ethereal El Greco "style" that would come to be recognized as quintessentially "old Lladró." He sculpted, for instance, the model for the earlier-mentioned "Sad Harlequin," which Jose Lladró has identified as the seminal figure in this style.[13] García's name is attached to many of the very earliest Lladró pieces, even those rare ones with decimal point serial numbers made in very limited quantities in the 1950s. The first known rare Lladró he sculpted, "Bunny" (#55.04), dates from 1954.

Salvador Furió became famous among veteran Lladró collectors for his work on historical and literary

"Scheherazade" (#7678), the Lladró Society's first-ever Gres limited edition. Her small edition size of 1,000 worldwide has created a situation of unfilled demand which accounts in large part for her secondary market price of $2700-$3250 today. (Photo courtesy of Lladró USA, Inc.)

figurines, including most of the Lladró treatments of Don Quixote and associated characters, Sancho Panza and Dulcinea. As late as 1990, the aging Furió was still making special events tours at which he was doing on-site sculpting for the delight and amazement of collectors![14]

Furió did not go in very much for domestic animal figurines, the items #4642, titled simply "Dog" (shown at lower left) and #4643, "Skye Terrier" being two notable exceptions. He preferred hunting themes, especially those featuring packs of dogs bringing down deer. To this day, I cannot imagine having the scene "Fearful Flight" (#1377) sitting in my living room (even if I could afford its $18,000 price tag!), not to mention various other Furió tableaux of equally graphic subject matter. My own tastes notwithstanding, the Furió hunting scenes are highly sought after worldwide, especially among male collectors. There is no doubt that Furió is an artist's artist in the sense that he did not linger long over sentimental topics and was unafraid to explore the darker, more elemental aspects of life.

Juan Huerta is the sculptor responsible for many of Lladró's most popular figures featuring children, animals, and children with animals or birds. Huerta had a habit of weaving hidden stories into his sculptures; "Honey Lickers" (#1248), pictured in the introduction to this book, is his. As of this writing, Huerta is still sculpting.

"Heavenly Prayer" (#6145G) was the tall (over 17") but ethereal-looking Madonna that may have been the last creation of the great Lladró sculptor Fulgencio García, who died at the age of 79 the year this was issued, 1994. This item was retired in 1997 and has a secondary market value of $750-$775. (Photo courtesy of Lladró USA, Inc.)

Lladró encourages its artists in a variety of ways, but most especially to "push the envelope" of innovation and to stretch their individual talents to include themes they might not otherwise explore. If for Furió this encouragement led to the creation of a couple of domestic dog figurines now famous among Lladró collectors, in Huerta's case it meant, among other things, exploring the theme of a famous person, a camp usually held by Furió. The Huerta figurine resulting from this excursion was a fabulous "cross-collectible" figure of Charlie Chaplin, entitled in English "Charlie the Tramp" (#5233) but accurately translated from the literal and more elegant Spanish as "The Eternal Poet." Issued in 1985 at a retail price of $150, this figurine was only on the retail market for six years before its retirement in 1991. Someone lucky enough to buy it at the time of issue would have substantial equity in it now, as it is seen on the secondary market at prices ranging from a low of $700 to a high of $1100.[15]

Other older sculptors include Antonio Ramos, a miniaturist, and Salvador Debón. Both these sculptors enjoy working in tightly confined spaces with a maximum of decorative detail molded into the porcelain itself as opposed to being added as accessories. Ramos did many of the animal miniatures in the Lladró corpus, as well as the popular sets featuring three miniature Christmas ornaments. Even in his larger pieces, such as "In the Garden" (#5416), a fondness for miniature detail is evident.

"Fearful Flight" (#1377) is a famous scene by Salvador Furió, who specializes in the "hunt" for his themes involving animals. While this would not be my cup of tea for living room décor, it has plenty of takers, even as the price keeps going up. As recently as 1998, it was retailing at $18,000; if you waited until 2000 or later to buy it, it'll now cost you $20,600! (Photo courtesy of Lladró USA, Inc.)

"Dog" AKA "Llasa Apso" (#4642G), a "domestic animal" sculpted by Salvador Furió, who much preferred hunting scenes. Secondary market value range: $395-$500. The Spanish title for this is most descriptive, literally translating as "Moustaches." (Photo by William B. Bradley, Jr., from the author's own collection.)

Debón, for his part, favors Japanese themes and bird groupings. For example, the marvelous series of bird and flower groupings, #s 1368-1371. His figures of Japanese women such as "Nippon Lady" (#5327, illustrated on page 30) are characterized by amazing detail in the flowery decorations sculpted right into the kimonos. He was also responsible for the 1994 event piece, "Little Riders" (#7623, as seen on page 51), notable for its almost miniature detail.

Unless your tastes are quite eclectic, you'll find that your collection tends to favor one or two sculptors, and it is fun to discover who they are. In my own collection, for example, the work of García and Huerta predominates.[16]

The next chapter continues our exploration with a consideration of the diversity in the Lladró corpus that results in a number of distinctive series within the core collection.

"Charlie the Tramp" AKA "The Eternal Poet" (#5233G), issued in 1985 and retired in 1991. (Photo by William B. Bradley, Jr., from the author's own collection.)

Detail from Huerta's "Charlie the Tramp." (Photo by William B. Bradley, Jr., from the author's own collection.)

"In the Garden" (#5416G/M), sculpted by Antonio Ramos, most noted for his miniatures and miniature detail. Issued 1987, retired 1996, this model fetches about $400 on today's secondary market. (Photo by William B. Bradley, Jr., from the author's own collection.)

Close-up of "In the Garden" showing miniature detail and the anecdotal secret of the piece, as the girl looks over her shoulder to catch a small bird pecking at the fringe of her shawl. (Photo by William B. Bradley, Jr., from the author's own collection.)

Salvador Debón's "Nippon Lady" (#5327G), issued in 1985 and retired in 2000. Last retail price: $595, but she's already pulling in secondary market prices of $625-$650. Lladró's figures of traditional Japanese women appreciate rapidly on the secondary market. (Photo by William B. Bradley, Jr., from the author's own collection.)

Detail from "Nippon Lady." Flowers on fan and kimono are sculpted right into the porcelain and are individually painted. (Photo by William B. Bradley, Jr., from the author's own collection.)

HISTORY, MARKS, AND MANUFACTURE

Notes to Chapter 1

1 These should not be confused with later Lladró decimals, which used a .3 to distinguish a white version or a reduced size version of a particular model. For instance, #4602 "Doctor" has a reduced size version numbered 4602.3, and #4922 "Sea Breeze" has an all-white version numbered 4922.3.

2 Lladró Museum column, "Tribute to Friendship," *Expressions* (Summer 1992), 8:2, 4.

3 "Lladró: Rights of Passage", *Expressions* 1:2 (Summer 1985).

4 Special Events column, *Expressions* 6:2 (Summer 1990): 11.

5 Cf. "This and That," *A Work of Art* 1:1 (Fall 1990): 12. (This periodical, which was issued on a quarterly basis before it ceased publication a few years later, was begun by broker/collectors Brad Welch, Joan [Lewis] Devlin, and David Lewis as a means of informing collectors about retired figurines and the evolution of the Lladró secondary market. *A Work of Art* performed a valuable service in those years as virtually the only reliable published source of Lladró secondary market information and in-depth analysis of retired figurines.)

6 "Tracking the Arrival of All Aboard," *Expressions* 8:1 (Spring 1992): 5.

7 For a fascinating account of this mammoth undertaking, see "The 18th Century Coach," *Expressions* 4:1 (Spring 1988): 19-23. The article contains a folded insert picturing this fabulous work—which is probably about as close to it as most of us will ever get!

8 For a complete description of the fine art of Lladró parasol production, see "Accent on Accessories: Parasols," *Expressions* 2:1 (Spring 1986): 17-19.

9 "Tracking the Arrival of All Aboard," 5.

10 For the record, the correct pronunciation of the name is Ya-dro', with the Spanish double-L pronounced as a y and the stress on the second syllable.

11 The term "bisque" is sometimes used casually to refer to any matte surface. Its technical meaning, however, and the sense in which it will be used in this book, refers to a white matte only.

12 "Classical Treasures for Today's Collector: Gres," *Expressions* 2:2 (Summer 1986): 6.

13 "The Favorite Figurines of Jose Lladró, "Sad Harlequin," *Expressions* 13:1 (1997): 4.

14 *Expressions* 6:2 (Summer 1990): 11

15 Here is an example of the volatility that yet characterizes some Lladró secondary market pricing; there is quite a lot of distance between the ends of this range. However, what is perhaps more telling of the abiding appeal of this particular model is the distance between even the lower end of this range and the last retail price.

16 Collectors wishing to know the names of all the Lladró sculptors and/or to identify the sculptors of their particular figurines are referred to the *Collector's Catalog*, published by the company itself and available through any authorized dealer. This four volume set provides the only nearly complete photographic record in color of the entire core collection from the earliest days through 1994 and includes sculptors' names in all the descriptive captions. The original company plan was to update the volumes every two years, but the project was behind schedule as of this writing.

A Gallery of Rare and Unusual Pieces

Due to the extraordinary rarity of the items pictured in this section, I do not give price ranges for them. The values given are those set by A Retired Collection of Longboat Key, Florida, from whose courtesy these photos were provided.

A word also needs to be said here about definitions for the terms "pre-production" and "prototype." Pre-production pieces were developed and distributed in very tiny quantities, almost as "market testers," and were never brought into full distribution, at least in the core collection. A "prototype," on the other hand, is a true experimental piece, a "one-of-a-kind."

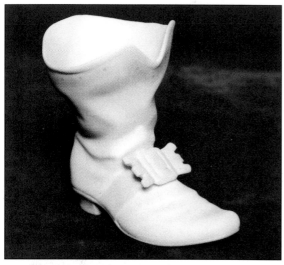

"Small Boot—Warrior" (matte finish), a Lladró pre-production piece valued at $800. (Photo courtesy of A Retired Collection in Longboat Key, Florida, from the private collection of Dr. Bill Jann.)

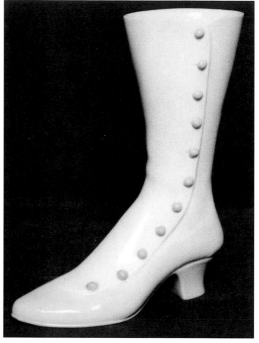

"Dress Boot" a Lladró-marked pre-production piece from the 1950s. Bet you haven't seen one of these kicking around on the generic secondary market! Valued at $2400. (Photo courtesy of A Retired Collection in Longboat Key, Florida, from the private collection of Dr. Bill Jann.)

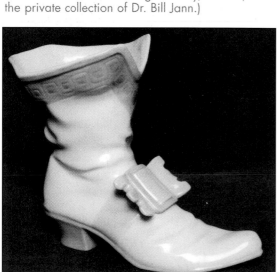

"Boot, Warrior," a pre-production Lladró made in very limited quantities and never sold outside Spain. Valued at $1600. It is distinguished from the "Small Boot-Warrior" not only by size, but by the decorative trim at the top of the boot. All of the pre-production pieces pictured here date from the late 1950s. (Photo courtesy of A Retired Collection in Longboat Key, Florida, from the private collection of Dr. Bill Jann.)

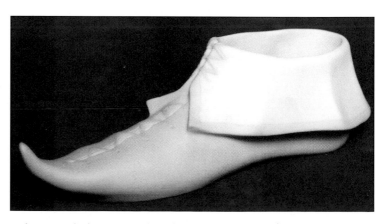

"Shoe," a Lladró pre-production piece. Valued at $1200. (Photo courtesy of A Retired Collection in Longboat Key, Florida, from the private collection of Dr. Bill Jann.)

"Swan Bending Neck," a matte pre-production piece marked Lladró, from the 1950s. The mate to "Swan, Neck Up." Valued at $1500. (Photo courtesy of A Retired Collection in Longboat Key, Florida, from the private collection of Dr. Bill Jann.)

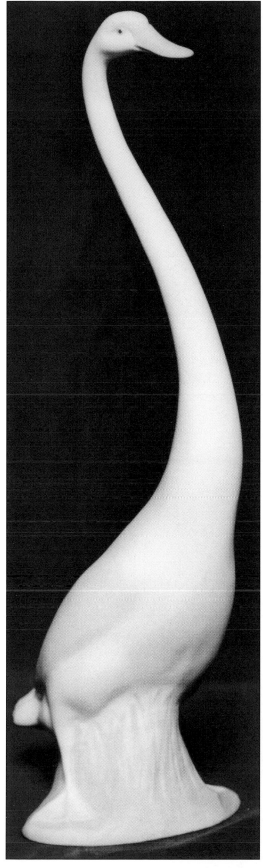

"Swan, Neck Up," a Lladró-marked piece dating from the 1950s that never went into production in the core collection. Valued at $1500. (Photo courtesy of A Retired Collection in Longboat Key, Florida, from the private collection of Dr. Bill Jann.)

A set of pre-production stylized "Doves" from the 1950s, all marked Lladró but never marketed in the core collection. Valued at $650 apiece. (Photo courtesy of A Retired Collection in Longboat Key, Florida, from the private collection of Dr. Bill Jann.)

33

"Contemplation," a matte pre-production piece from the late 1950s. Valued at $2400. (Photo courtesy of A Retired Collection in Longboat Key, Florida, from the private collection of Dr. Bill Jann.)

"Seated Harlequin," a matte pre-production piece. Valued at $5000. (Photo courtesy of A Retired Collection in Longboat Key, Florida, from the private collection of Dr. Bill Jann.)

"Dog Sitting" pre-production piece, marked Lladró, from the late 1950s. Valued at $1875. (Photo courtesy of A Retired Collection in Longboat Key, Florida, from the private collection of Dr. Bill Jann.)

"Seated Cellist," a Lladró pre-production piece made in such limited quantities you won't find him in any Lladró catalog. Valued at $1850. (Photo courtesy of A Retired Collection in Longboat Key, Florida, from the private collection of Dr. Bill Jann.)

"Mother/Child," a matte pre-production piece, still bearing an old Lladró sticker on the skirt. (Also marked on base.) Vintage and classical Lladró, and you won't find her in any catalog. Valued at $1850. (Photo courtesy of A Retired Collection in Longboat Key, Florida, from the private collection of Dr. Bill Jann.)

"Vase," a pre-production piece by Jose Lladró himself. Valued at $3500. (Photo courtesy of A Retired Collection in Longboat Key, Florida, from the private collection of Dr. Bill Jann.)

"Little Duck" is actually a pre-production piece that looks a lot like one of the ducks that went into production as #s 4551-4553. The difference is the beak in the pre-production piece rests a little further forward of the wing, and there is an upsweep on the wing's end that is not present in the design that went into production. Value of the pre-production piece: $1000. (Photo courtesy of A Retired Collection in Longboat Key, Florida, from the private collection of Dr. Bill Jann.)

A pre-production "Furniture" suite, consisting of a couch and two chairs. Bet you never saw any Lladro like this before! Value of the couch: $800. Value of the chairs: $750 apiece. (Photo courtesy of A Retired Collection in Longboat Key, Florida, from the private collection of Dr. Bill Jann.)

"Jockey," a one-of-a-kind prototype with trophy. Value unknown. (Photo courtesy of A Retired Collection in Longboat Key, Florida, from the private collection of Dr. Bill Jann.)

"Girl's Head with Shawl," a matte prototype valued at $1750. The shawl is made from porcelain-dipped tulle. (Photo courtesy of A Retired Collection in Longboat Key, Florida, from the private collection of Dr. Bill Jann.)

"Girl's Head Decorated," a matte prototype valued at $1750. The headgear and necklace are shaped with porcelain-dipped tulle accented with porcelain flowers. (Photo courtesy of A Retired Collection in Longboat Key, Florida, from the private collection of Dr. Bill Jann.)

"Blue Egg with Lace and Flowers," a Lladró prototype valued at $1000. An unusual design quite unlike any of the several porcelain eggs Lladró has produced since. (Photo courtesy of A Retired Collection in Longboat Key, Florida, from the private collection of Dr. Bill Jann.)

"Girl in Chair and Pedestal" prototype. Valued at $1875—a real bargain when you consider that, as a one-of-a-kind, it is essentially priceless! (Photo courtesy of A Retired Collection in Longboat Key, Florida, from the private collection of Dr. Bill Jann.)

"Tall Blue Flower Basket" prototype. The basket has been wrapped in porcelain-dipped tulle and lace. Valued at $1875. (Photo courtesy of A Retired Collection in Longboat Key, Florida, from the private collection of Dr. Bill Jann.)

A medley including some of Lladró's most special and hard-to-find pieces. Back row, left to right: Salvador Furió's "Don Quixote" (#1030G), one of the most famous Lladró figures ever created, first issued in the mid- to late 1960s and still retailing at $1450; the limited edition "Car in Trouble" (#1375G), edition size 1500, first issued in 1978 and retired in 1987, value today: $5500-$7500; and the Gres "Chinese Farmer with Staff" (#2065), first issued in 1977 and retired in 1985, value today: $1800-$2200. Front, left to right: "Peruvian Girl with Baby" (#4822G/M), retail span of 1972-1981, value today: $600-$775; the famous "Little Pals" (#7600G), first Lladró Society member-only figurine issued in 1985 and valued today at $2200-$2500; "Bird Watcher" (#4730G/M), issued in 1970 and retired in 1985, valued today at $300-$400; "Playful Piglets" (#5288), issued in 1984 and retired in 1998, value today: $185-$200; "The Cart" (#1245G), issued in 1973 and retired in 1981, valued at $550-$650; "Little Traveler" (#7602G), second Lladró Society figurine issued in 1986, value today: $1150-$1350; and "Gypsy Woman" with her trained bear (#4919G), issued in 1974 and retired in 1981, today worth $1100-$1500. (Photo by Jane Shelley, courtesy of Shelley's Auction Gallery in Hendersonville, NC.)

Chapter 2

SPECIAL SERIES, SCULPTURES, AND STUDIES

s described in Chapter 1, most of the items produced by Lladró have one of three recognizable surfaces: glazed, matte, or Gres. These various finish types provide a foundation for diversity in the enormous core collection. That diversity is further elaborated by several series within the core collection, which have distinctive names based on other factors: aesthetic style, subject matter, the unique materials used to make them, or the market to which they are targeted. This chapter deals with these several series or sub-collections within the core collection.

The terminology here can get confusing, as the company often refers to these various series as "collections." They are more precisely referred to as series in order to distinguish them from brand name collections by Lladró.[1] For purposes of this particular chapter, the term "collection," as used by the company, refers to smaller series within the core collection.

Some of these special categories, especially later ones, may seem somewhat artificial or arbitrary from a collector's perspective—more marketing categories than discrete collecting categories. However, several of them do provide consumers with options for specialization. This may be helpful for most of us, since, with a corpus as huge as Lladró's, we obviously can't adopt the collection strategy of our childhood's cereal box premium days and "collect them all!"

Capricho

his series, now mostly retired, consists of flowers and porcelain-dipped lace incorporated into such items as baskets; arrangements of flowers; and miniature models of ladies' hats, masks, and ballet shoes. Caprichos were so delicate that they shipped poorly; it was not uncommon for large portions of a shipment to arrive broken at their destination despite the company's notoriously careful packaging. Unable to surmount this vulnerability, the company withdrew most of the series from production in 1991.

"Leopard Butterfly No. 12" (#1684M) is one of several butterflies of various shapes and decorations that were produced in the Capricho series. All of them were issued in 1989 and went the way of all Caprichos in their en masse retirement in 1991. This one's last retail price was $195. Secondary market value is $225-$250. Later in the 1990s, Lladró began to make sturdier butterflies out of regular porcelain molds, and these are still available on the retail market. (Photo courtesy of Lladró USA, Inc.)

Porcelain lace at Lladró (on its early ballerina tutus as well as in Capricho flower arrangements and on accessory parasols for other core collection figurines) has been made in the time-honored tradition pioneered by older manufacturers such as the various Dresden companies in Germany. The lace itself is dipped in porcelain, molded to the figurine, and then fired. Under the influence of the kiln's heat, the underlying cloth lace burns away, leaving behind the porcelain image of it. Small wonder such delicate material would be especially brittle! Some old Dresden "china lace" seems to disintegrate merely upon touch, and much of the lacework in rare decimal-numbered Lladró figures made in the 1950s shows signs of similar damage.

Because of their delicacy and comparative rarity, mint examples of Capricho usually command high prices on the secondary market. One of the most extraordinary Capricho arrangements ever created was "Orchid Arrangement" (#1541), retired in 1989. Brad Welch, East-Coast collector, and at that time a broker of retired Lladró, once hand-delivered one of these mint condition arrangements to a West Coast customer so as to avoid risking it to a shipper. Having sold the item to the customer for $1800, Brad flew from New York to Denver, Colorado "on a Saturday night…with ORCHID ARRANGEMENT safely in his hands; grabbed a few winks of sleep at the airport; met Sunday morning with the collector who had purchased the piece; waited for her to inspect it very carefully; then got right back on a plane and flew home in time for work the next day."[2] Only a collector that passionate would be a seller that considerate!

In 1993-1994, the company issued a series of whimsical cups and saucers and sugars and creamers featuring animals, birds, and flowers cavorting around the rim, handle, or saucer. The company sometimes also referred to these in its marketing brochures and catalogues as "Capricho," but they bear little resemblance to the lacy, ethereal Caprichos of the earlier years. All of these non-utilitarian table whimsies were retired in 1999 and 2000.

Goyesca

"Orchid Arrangement" (#1541) may be the most elaborate Capricho flower arrangement ever made. Not surprisingly, this wasn't around on the retail market for very long: 1988-1990. The technical challenges of creating it were a cinch compared to the technical challenges of shipping it. A mint example will be awfully hard to come by and will cost you $1800-$2000. (Photo courtesy of Lladró USA, Inc.)

The artistic inspiration for the familiar elongated style of many core collection figures is said to have been El Greco (1541-1614). The Lladró brothers coined the name "Goyesca" for another series within the core collection whose aesthetic reminded them of the artist Francisco Goya (1746-1828). The sculptor for the entire series of Lladró Goyescas, which were first released in 1988, is E. San Isidro, whose name is not associated with anything else in the core collection.

"The Champion" (#1746) is, to date, the only stand-alone animal model in the Goyesca series. The detail is extraordinary. Issued in 1991 and retired in 1994, this beauty will run $2250-$3000 on the secondary market. (Photo courtesy of Lladró USA, Inc.)

While "Iris Arrangement" (#1542M) was not as elaborate as "Orchid Arrangement," it certainly ranks with it as the two most exquisite representatives of the Capricho line. Issued in 1988 and retired in 1990 at a last retail price of $800, its secondary market price range is $1100-$1500. (Photo courtesy of Lladró USA, Inc.)

The porcelain used in Goyescas is unusually elastic and pliable, allowing manipulation of pre-hardened materials by hand to make lines and creases in faces and garments. Consequently, these features will literally bear the imprint of the artist's fingers. While most of the core collection achieves its colors through painting, the Goyescas are made with colored porcelain, i.e. with the color integrated right into the material itself. This necessitates many additional mold changes to accommodate different colors, making Goyesca

"Gypsy Dancers" (#1770) is an extraordinary work by any standards. Done in the Goyesca formula, it is so dynamic that it looks as if it were moving when the picture was taken. The technical and artistic balance in the figurine illustrates why competitors can't hold a candle to a real Lladró. Its last issue price was $2500, and it is already trending on the secondary market at $3500-$4000. (Photo courtesy of Lladró USA, Inc.)

production especially complicated and time-consuming. Consequently, Goyescas are made in small-run limited editions that are expensive to purchase yet quickly subscribed. Texture in clothing is often obtained through impressing cloth patterns onto the malleable porcelain before it is hardened.

Goyescas are unique and extraordinarily expressive. A few are among the "darker" creations in the Lladró corpus, not only because of the materials used but also because of the treatment of subjects. Sculptures such as "Little Boy" (#1696, whose Spanish title is more aptly translated "Addled Child") and "Mayoress" (#1729, the ultimate "crone") are unforgettable in their impact—at once chilling yet deeply moving.

"Mayoress" (#1729), the quintessential crone, is one of the Goyesca models. Issued in 1989, she was retired in 1991. Expect to pay $1000-$1200 for her if you can find her today. Her companion piece is "The Mayor," issued some years before her in 1981 but retired the same year as she. (Photo courtesy of Lladró USA, Inc.)

The Elite Collection

For collectors who may have pondered the rhyme or reason for inclusion of an item in the Elite series, price is generally the determining factor. The series title is a company marketing category applied to very high-end limited edition groupings that run into the many thousands of dollars on the retail market. (At those prices, another distinguishing feature of the Elite series is that many of them are still active, including some issued in the late 1970s.)

And what a "Garden Party" (#1578) it was! Issued in 1988 in an edition size of 500, its first retail price was $5500. It sold out in 1999 at a last retail price of $7250—and you can already tack $500 or so onto that if you want it today. Those amazing floral arches, the tallest of which measures almost 23", would have represented an extraordinary production challenge—not to mention the packaging and shipping challenges! (Photo courtesy of Lladró USA, Inc.)

For the record, the most expensive Lladró item at the time of initial marketing is the Elite grouping "Cinderella's Arrival," which entered on the market at $25,950 and is currently retailing at $26,400. Its massive size (at two feet high and several inches longer than that) coupled with delicate detailing would make it a particular display challenge. I always imagine it under glass in the middle of a European great hall, with few other furnishings in the surrounding décor!

"Celestial Journey" (#1848) is an Elite series limited edition of 1500 issued in 1999 and currently retailing at $3900. It measures 14 1/2" x 19". The price is a bargain for an Elite item, especially considering the number of separate elements and the elaborate detail of the piece. (Photo courtesy of Lladró USA, Inc.)

The most expensive item in the corpus at current retail, however, is "18th Century Coach" (#1485, previously pictured on page 18). It was issued in 1985 in an edition of 500 at a retail price of $14,000; today it will cost you a staggering $31,000 retail. As with "Cinderella's Arrival," the display challenges posed by this marvelous antique coach tableau probably account as much as its price for an exceptionally lengthy retail run on an edition size of only 500.

Those who prefer something a tad more modestly priced might consider the Elite series "Outing in Seville" (#1756) at a retail price of $24,500 or "Fearful Flight" (#1377, pictured on page 27) at a mere $18,000!

Over the years, there has been speculation in Elite Lladrós by wealthy collectors using them as an alternative form of investment. Organizers of Lladró-only auctions held in California and Florida in the early 1990s sometimes had difficulty finding enough pieces, especially these large limited editions, to make such auction events worthwhile for those attending. Many collectors seemed to have unrealistic expectations of the appreciation potential of limited editions and would not consign them when auction estimates did not match the figure of their dreams.

In one of the most interesting articles ever to be published in *Expressions* magazine, auction sponsor Herb Rostand lamented that "60-70% of [collectors who have old pieces] will say, 'I thought it was worth $25,000, but if I can only get $2000 to $3000 I don't want to sell.'[3] Such attitudes were not, it appears, entirely unfounded; in general, the more expensive an item is at time of retail purchase, the more vulnerable it will be in retaining its equity. (For more on this subject, see Chapter 5.)

Other Numbered Limited Editions

There are two ways in which a Lladró gets to be a limited edition: by time limit and by edition size. Lucky for most of us, Lladró has produced a number of limited editions that are not "elite" in the sense that you'd need to mortgage the ranch to buy them. Some limited editions sell for a few hundred dollars, and some of the time-limited editions can be purchased for under $300 at time of issue.

The Gres "Madonna with Child" (#2018) shared with "Girl with Guitar" the distinction of being the first limited editions ever produced by the Lladró company. The edition size for 2018 was small, at 300, and it was fully subscribed by 1974. It is quite tall, at 29", and it is likely that some of these went to churches to grace their sacred space. While she only cost $450 back in 1974, brokers with access to her price her at $1800-$2800 today. The sculptor was Antonio Ruiz. (Photo courtesy of Lladró USA, Inc.)

Lladró's very first numbered limited editions were produced in 1970: "Girl with Guitar" (#2016) and "Madonna with Child" (#2018), both in Gres.

They were followed in 1971 by "Hamlet" (#1144), "Othello and Desdemona" (#1145) and "Antique Auto" (#1146). At issue, you could buy "Hamlet" for a mere $250 and "Othello and Desdemona" for $275. "Antique Auto" was a bit pricier at $1,000. Retail price increases were usually initiated every year or two that a limited edition was open.

Sculpted by Vicente Martinez, "Girl with Guitar" (#2016), a Gres, shared star billing with another Gres, "Madonna and Child," to become, in 1970, Lladró's first-ever limited editions. The edition size for "Girl with Guitar" was 750, which sold out in 1982 at a retail price of $1265. Its secondary market price range today is $1800-$2750. Considering its historic importance, which may not be known to many collectors, it is probably undervalued. (Photo courtesy of Lladró USA, Inc.)

"Othello and Desdemona" (#1145), sculpted by J. Ruiz, shared with "Hamlet" the privilege of being the first-ever limited editions in the regular porcelain formula. Its edition size was 750, which, like Hamlet's edition, sold out by the end of 1973. It runs $2500-$3700 on the secondary market. (Photo courtesy of Lladró USA, Inc.)

Some of the earliest made limited editions took ten years or more to be fully subscribed ("18th Century Coach" is still open fifteen years after issue). "Young Oriental Man" (#2021) took eleven years to sell out, despite its relatively low edition size of only 500. Between year one and year ten, his retail price had more than doubled! Since going off the market in 1983, his appreciation rate has been more modest, but still notable. He brought $1850 at one of the Rostand-Thalheimer auctions, against a last retail of $1100. The lesson is clear; those who have the best equity in this piece are those who bought it at its first issue price of $500.

Numbered limited editions come with certificates of authenticity that give the name of the figure, its issue size, and the series number of the particular figure or grouping purchased. In the "old days" of limited edition collectibles, these issue-run numbers were more important than they are for Lladró, where new molds are made for approximately every fifty copies. Therefore, a copy numbered 2076 in a Lladró edition size of 3000 isn't likely to be any fuzzier in its detail than those numbered one through fifty.

Inasmuch as they certify the legitimacy of very expensive items, certificates of authenticity are important. Collectors are encouraged to make photocopies and store them appropriately. If the original copy ever becomes lost or damaged, the company will be able to replace it as long as the replacement information is accessible. A photocopy will best enable the company to replace your certificate, although it can also work with information supplied from a photograph of the base.

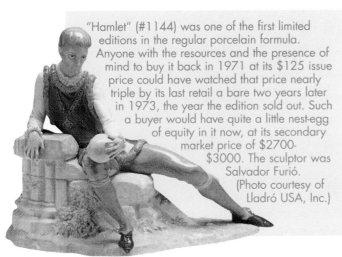

"Hamlet" (#1144) was one of the first limited editions in the regular porcelain formula. Anyone with the resources and the presence of mind to buy it back in 1971 at its $125 issue price could have watched that price nearly triple by its last retail a bare two years later in 1973, the year the edition sold out. Such a buyer would have quite a little nest-egg of equity in it now, at its secondary market price of $2700-$3000. The sculptor was Salvador Furió. (Photo courtesy of Lladró USA, Inc.)

The company has produced some numbered limited editions which were available to Lladró Society members only. These have included "Jester's Serenade" (#5932, edition size 3,000), "Guardian Angel" (#6352, edition size unknown); "Garden of Dreams" (#7634, edition size 4000), "Where Love Begins" (#7649, edition size 4000), the first and only Gres Members-only limited edition "Scheherazade" (#7678, edition size 1000), and "Enchanted Lake" (#7679, edition size 4000).

"Guardian Angel" (#6352G), a time-limited edition available to Lladró Society members only and only for the year 1997. An unusually tall figurine at 20", its last retail price in 1997 was $1300. It could already be worth somewhere between $1700 and $1825. (Photo courtesy of Lladró USA, Inc.)

"Enchanted Lake" (#7679G) was issued in 1999 as a limited edition of 4,000 worldwide for Lladró Society members only. That year was a banner year for the Society limited editions (which also included the enormously popular "Scheherazade"), and this one sold out rapidly, so that, within a few short weeks there was nary a one found anywhere! Issued at $1,225, she has little trouble fetching $1600-$1700 on the secondary market. (Photo courtesy of Lladró USA, Inc.)

"Where Love Begins" (#7649G), Lladró Society limited edition of 4,000, issued in 1996 and sold out the same year. Its last retail price was $895, but you'd be hard-pressed to find it for less than $1100 on today's secondary market, and it could run as much as $1500. (Photo courtesy of Lladró USA, Inc.)

Collectors of more limited means should remember that items with very short retail runs may be considered de facto limited editions even if they are not officially intended as such. We would all love to know just how many of each open-issue figurine are made in a year so that we could calculate how many items of a particular short-run open edition might have been made in the year or two it was on the market. Unfortunately, this information has proven elusive, as the company only keeps track of production numbers on numbered limited editions. Given what we know about the labor-intensity of production, however, it is unlikely that more than a very few thousand of an open issue can be produced in a given year. This process of becoming "a limited edition by default" can also happen with items that were retired in the 1970s, before as many people knew about Lladró and wanted to buy it as there are today—and also, presumably, when the company had less staff and production capacity.

Members-Only and Special Event Pieces

For each of the fifteen years of the Lladró Society's existence, Lladró issued premiums, limited editions, and annual Society figurines that were, theoretically at least, available only to members of the Society. The reason I qualify this statement is because the advent of the Internet auction (discussed at greater length in Chapter 5) has pretty much blown apart the members-only exclusivity of these figures by making them available to all comers on the secondary market. Still, the supply is limited by the fact that only members had initial access to the figures. Although anecdotal evidence suggests that this system did occasionally get "scammed" by unscrupulous buyers, it was generally reliable in ensuring a limited supply of these items.

"Little Traveler" (#7602G), the second Lladró Society figurine, continued with the clown motif. Issued at $95 in 1986, his Lladró auction range was $1100-$2100, but he can usually be found at prices at and sometimes just under that range's lower end. (Photo courtesy of Lladró USA, Inc.)

The "New Member" package from the Lladró Society: the famous Lladró Society plaque, a special edition of *Expressions* magazine with some of the best articles from former issues, and a small leather key-case with a porcelain medallion of the Lladró logo. (Some collectors may not be aware that the ever-diversifying Lladró company also makes luggage!) One practical use of the membership plaque is for comparison purposes in identifying signatures on other signed pieces. (Photo by the author.)

As with any limited edition series, the first issue in a members-only series is the most desirable—not necessarily because of some premium of quality or aesthetics, but just by virtue of its being the first. The first annual Lladró Society figurine was the now-famous "Little Pals" (#7600), a clown in full dress carrying a poodle puppy in each pants pocket. Back in 1985, when the Society first started, there would have been relatively few members to buy him, and this accounts for the stellar prices of $2400-$4500 he has achieved at various times on the secondary market. (His issue price, by the way, was a paltry $95!) Speculative trade in this piece has been brisk.

The second Society figurine was "Little Traveler" (#7602), also a clown figure. General price range on the secondary market is $1150 to $1350, although at a 1999 Lladró auction held in Florida, he was not able to reach above $750.

Subsequent annual Society figurines suffer from a certain "sameness" that makes several of the girls in long dresses with flowers difficult to distinguish from one another. Generally, these do not appear to appreciate more rapidly on the secondary market than retired open issues of comparable price and theme.

Occasionally, the members-only items achieve a "breakthrough" with a particularly appealing figure. The

1998 figure, for instance, aptly entitled "It Wasn't Me" (#7672), features a small Cocker Spaniel next to an overturned pot of flowers. This was the only stand-alone animal figurine featured in the members-only annual series. "It Wasn't Me" (pictured on page 51) is sufficiently appealing in its own right that it seldom appears on the secondary market and already commands prices in the $325-$350 range when it does.

"Pals Forever" (#7686G) was the year 2000 Fifteenth Anniversary figurine for members of the Lladró Society. It admirably reprises the theme of the first Lladró Society figurine, "Little Pals," without succumbing to the temptation to reissue the original. (Photo courtesy of Lladró USA, Inc.)

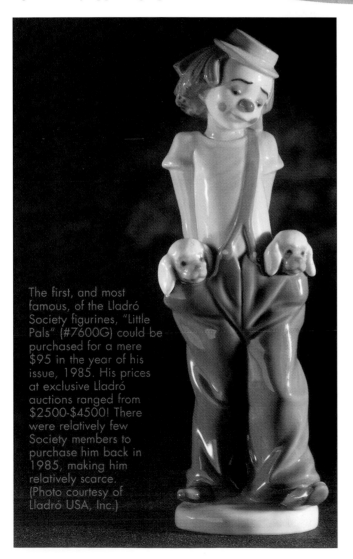

The first, and most famous, of the Lladró Society figurines, "Little Pals" (#7600G) could be purchased for a mere $95 in the year of his issue, 1985. His prices at exclusive Lladró auctions ranged from $2500-$4500! There were relatively few Society members to purchase him back in 1985, making him relatively scarce. (Photo courtesy of Lladró USA, Inc.)

"Destination Big Top" (#6245G) was a time-limited "event" piece in the ever-popular clown motif, issued and retired the same year, 1997, at a last retail price of $225. Secondary market prices in the $475-$650 range, an atypically high appreciation for an event piece. (Photo courtesy of Lladró USA, Inc.)

Salvador Debón's 1994 Event Figurine, "Little Riders" (#7623G). An example of a "late bloomer" on the secondary market, it has only recently been fetching prices of $325-$400 after struggling for the past few years to get above its last retail of $250. (Photo by William B. Bradley, Jr., from the author's own collection.)

"It Wasn't Me" was supposedly part of a marketable series of three, the other two of which appeared either side of it: 1997's "Pocket Full of Wishes" (#7650) and 1999's "A Wish Come True" (#7676). The thematic connection between the three is tenuous at best, consisting largely of flowerwork in each. No interaction is implied among the stand-alone figures, and it is likely that the "series of three" idea was a marketing afterthought more than a design intent.

The year 2000 (15th Society anniversary) figurine, "Pals Forever" (#7686), laudably reprises the theme of "Little Pals" without succumbing to the temptation to reissue the original. "Pals Forever" is likely to be popular with actual collectors as well as with market speculators. As it happens, this model was the last in the Lladró Society series; the society was discontinued in the year 2000.

The so-called "Special Event" (or simply "Event") figurines are issued at retail sales events sponsored by authorized dealers in various locations.

"It Wasn't Me!" (#7672G), the Lladró Society members-only piece for 1998. Take away its flowers and it would still retain its charm. Issued at $295, it was already selling at prices in the $325-$350 range a year or two post-retirement. (Photo by William B. Bradley, Jr., from the author's own collection.)

These are time-limited editions that do not, in general, appreciate as highly or as rapidly as the Society figurines, nor do they necessarily command higher secondary market prices than particularly popular retired issues from the open collection.

The first of these Event figures was "Garden Classic" (#7617), featuring a woman in old-fashioned dress, carrying an open parasol and a basket of flowers, with a small puppy at her feet—all together, a typical Lladró presentation. Issued in 1991 at a retail price of $295, her going price on today's secondary market is $450-$500, although she did fetch "auction fever" prices of $600-$1150 at some of the Rostand-Thalheimer Lladró-only auctions (for more about which see Chapter 5). It is interesting to note that the more modest secondary market prices "Garden Classic" commands today are equivalent to the prices commanded by the 1995 event figurine, "For a Perfect Performance" (#7641), which features a more popular ballerina theme.

"Pick of the Litter" (#7621G), a Lladró time-limited "event" piece was issued and retired in 1993. Its secondary market price range today is broad, from $400 (just a little over its last retail) to $700. (Photo courtesy of Lladró USA, Inc.)

My personal favorites among the Event figurines are the two with the most "depressed" appreciation rates, "Pick of the Litter" (#7621) from 1993 and "Little Riders" (#7623) from 1994. In some places on the secondary market, "Pick of the Litter" hasn't tottered much above $400 on a last retail of $350, and "Little Riders" has only recently found its stride on the secondary market after balancing for years just under the $300 mark against a last retail price of $250. The appreciation problems experienced by "Pick of the Litter" may be related to its relatively high initial price. With a number of separately modeled parts, it would have been expensive to make, which would account in large part for its initial retail price of $350.

The acquisition lessons for collectors of Event pieces are, first, to buy only the ones they really like and, second, not to expect Event pieces to appreciate at rates better than those for popular retired items in the open collection.

Commissioned Works

The United States may well be Lladró's largest and most lucrative export market, so it is not surprising that Lladró produced a couple of series commissioned by American companies and designed to appeal to American popular taste and culture. One of these was the Norman Rockwell collection. At various times, Rockwell's work has been denigrated as mere commercial art, but it has repeatedly proven to be not so easily dismissed. Right now, his work is enjoying a resurgence of popularity for its nostalgic iconography of optimism in small-town American culture during the mid-20th century.

The Lladró Rockwell series consisted of seven porcelain groupings (#s 1405-1411) based on Rockwell paintings. All of these groupings were released as limited editions of 5000 in 1983 and were distributed through David Grossman Designs of New York. While it had potential to be a popular cross-collectible, this series was felt by many collectors to be too expensive at retail and sales were slow; it is doubtful that all were ever fully subscribed.

The irony is, of course, that the secondary market has its own laws and dynamics, and each of these pieces now trades at prices far higher than their original retail. True to the trend elsewhere in the corpus for more modestly priced retail items to appreciate farthest and fastest on the secondary market, the most expensive pieces today are the two that had the lowest retail prices. "Young Love" (#1409), which retailed at $450, goes for as much as $1350 today and "Daydreamer" (#1411), which also retailed at $450, is the most expensive of this series on today's secondary market, able to command as much as $1500.

A display of "Snow White and Half a Dozen Dwarfs!" Missing when photo was taken: Sneezy (#7535G), often among the missing for this lot. Value of "Snow White" (#7555G): $600-$650. Value of the Dwarfs (#s 7533-7539): $300-$350 ea. (From the private collection of Francisca Madden of "La Dulcinea.")

Marks on this collection are somewhat variable. The first ones issued were numbered on the bottom by hand and were accompanied by a certificate of authenticity. Those still on the inventory shelves when the series ceased production were marked "Norman Rockwell by Lladró" and were not numbered.

No logo flower occurs above the Lladró name on any of the Norman Rockwell pieces, which may confuse some collectors as to their authenticity. Normally, a missing logo would indicate a second or outlet purchase. The difference is that the logo has been scraped off in the case of a second, with the scraping usually clearly visible, while the Rockwell Lladró figures apparently never had the logo to begin with. (For more information on "seconds", see Chapter 4.)

The other U.S. "pop culture" inspiration for Lladró was Disney characters. Beginning in 1992, Lladró made thirteen (13) Disney figurines which were distributed exclusively through Disney's own retail venues. Themes included Snow White (#7555), each of the seven Dwarfs (#s 7533-7539), Snow White's Wishing

"A World of Love" (#6353G) was created for UNICEF. First issued in 1997, it went off the retail market in 1999. Its last retail price was $475, and its secondary market price is $650-$675. In a way, it's almost a shame to have these works commissioned for nonprofit organizations retired because, of course, the organization achieves no benefit from the secondary market trade. (Photo courtesy of the author from her own collection.)

Well (#7558), Peter Pan (#7529), Tinkerbell (#7518), Cinderella and her Godmother (#7553), and Sleeping Beauty dancing with her prince (#7560). The Snow White pieces were all distributed as open issues, while the Peter Pan, Tinkerbell, Cinderella and Godmother, and Sleeping Beauty pieces were limited to edition sizes ranging from 1500 to 2500.

With the exception of the Cinderella with Godmother and Sleeping Beauty figures, which originally retailed for $875 and $1280 respectively, the figures were relatively modestly priced at retail compared to other Lladró limited editions. The 1992 figure of Tinkerbell was fully subscribed in her issue year at a price of $350 but today commands prices ranging from $2000 to $3000. (The highest price she ever fetched at a Lladró auction was $3800.) The "star" of the original tale, Peter Pan, trades somewhat lower, even though he, too, was fully subscribed in his issue year and retailed higher than Tinkerbell at $400. (He had a larger issue size, however, at 2000 pieces.) His highest Lladró auction price was $3400, but his asking price on today's secondary market is usually under $2000.

As the Disney series illustrates, it's always a good idea to complete your sets early on in their retail run, as there is no guarantee you'll be able to fill in the gaps later with what shows up on the secondary market. Secondary market brokers have long waiting lists of anxious people looking for one or more of the Seven Dwarfs to go with their Snow White. Apparently, it's not all that much fun to have "Snow White and a Half-Dozen Dwarfs!"

Other companies that commissioned works by Lladró included Ford Motor Company (#s 7504, 7507, 7508, 7017, a series of models of Ford automobiles made as Spanish subsidiary company giveaways to dealers and/or VIPs); and two liquor bottles commissioned by Spanish companies, the "Carlos I Liquor Bottle" (#7505 for Pedro Domeq, SA) and the "Liquor 43 Bottle" (#7516 for Diego Zamora, SA). A "Carlos I Imperial Plaque" (#7506) was also made for Pedro Domeq, SA. and a "Liquor 43 Brooch" (#7519, a flowering brooch which is, to my knowledge, the only porcelain brooch ever produced by Lladró).

Lladró produced three items for exclusive distribution by the Franklin Mint: the "Lladró Thimble" (#7500M), "Miniature Plate" (#7501), and "Miniature Vase" (#7502). The thimble, a time-limited edition released and retired in 1983, is much in demand. It features embossed designs around its circumference, including the Lladró logo. It can go for as much as $300 on today's secondary market.

The miniature vase, last of the three in the consecutive number sequence of Franklin Mint pieces by Lladró, is less than three inches tall. A time-limited edition released in 1988, its value is about $300-$350. Its bisque relief work features a young shepherd playing the flute to his flock.

The miniature plate commissioned by the Franklin Mint (as pictured here) is seldom seen on the secondary market. It was part of a series of mini-plates produced by the Mint under the series name

"Miniature Plate" (# 7501) is, at 3 1/4" in diameter, the smallest plate Lladró ever made, and was distributed exclusively by the Franklin Mint as part of its tribute series entitled "World's Great Porcelain Houses." Issued as a time-limited edition for one year only in 1990 at a retail price of $19.50, it is seldom seen on the secondary market. Its value to a Lladró collector interested in unusual items would be in the range of $50-$65 today. (Photo courtesy of the author, from her own personal colection)

"World's Great Porcelain Houses." (Fine porcelain companies that contributed a plate to this series included, among others, Haviland, Wedgwood, Hutschenreuther, Royal Doulton, Zsolnay, and Royal Worcester.) The center bisque relief on the Lladró plate features a seated harlequin playing mandolin for a ballerina seated on a tall stool. At 3.25" in circumference, it was the smallest miniature plate

Lladró ever made (its other miniatures reaching 4" in circumference). The *Lladró Authorized Collection Reference Guide* gives its date of issue as 1990, but at least one other source dates it a decade earlier, to 1981-1983,[5] which would be consistent with the dating on the thimble and the chronological sequence of the serial numbers. First issued at $19.50, the value of this plate today is $50-$95.

Lladró also made commissioned figures for nonprofit groups, including "A World of Love" (#6353), made for UNICEF in 1997 and still active; "Starting Forward" (#7605) for the Rotary Club, also still active; and several figures for Special Olympics (#s 7513-7515 and 7522), all of which were retired in 1996.

Of these commissioned works, only the Ford autos are not pictured in the *Lladró Authorized Collection Reference Guides*. Collectors wishing to know more about them are referred to the Sanchez Collectibles Web site at www.primenet.com/~sanchcol.

Special Theme Collections

The "Days of the Week" series (#s 6011-6024) features a set of boy figures and a set of girl figures that are thematically-based on the famous nursery rhyme: "Monday's child is fair of face, Tuesday's child is full of grace," etc. The glazed-only series was issued in 1993 and retired in 1997. This is another Lladró series with a certain built-in inducement to "collect them all." For this series, today's secondary-market chase is made more interesting by the relatively short retail run.

The girl figure from "Tuesday's Child" (#6014G), featuring a small ballerina seated on a hassock looking down at a cat while she raises her foot in the air to tie on a ballet slipper, seems to be the hardest to find. However, this figure is thematically very similar to "Can I Help?" (#5689), which features a differently posed ballerina girl also seated on a hassock looking down at a cat. The two are also similar enough in size that collectors needing this one figurine to fill out their "Days of the Week" series may find #5689 a suitable substitute until they can find #6014.

"Tuesday's Child, Girl" (#6014) is the most expensive of Lladró's "kids of the week" series on the secondary market because it is the hardest to find. The items in this series, seven boys and seven girls corresponding to the days of the week, were all issued in 1993 and retired in 1997. The general price range for these is $250-$350, but "Tuesday's Child, Girl" will run $335-$375. The sculptor for the series was Juan Huerta. (Photo courtesy of Lladró USA, Inc.)

An interesting sidelight on this series relates to "Wednesday's Child" (#60616), pictured below. Whether the company found the original nursery rhyme too dark and adapted it or was working from an alternative version, collectors accustomed to hearing that "Wednesday's child is full of woe" will be confused by the appearance of Lladró's Wednesday's children. In the version from which Lladró was working, however, "Wednesday's child knows no woe"—which accounts for these figures' distinctly unwoebegone demeanor.

"Wednesday's Child, Girl" (#6016G). Doesn't look too "full of woe," does she? Apparently finding the rhyme too dark at this point, Lladró changed the line to "Wednesday's child knows no woe." Issued 1993, retired 1997. Value: $300-$325. (Photo by the author, from her own collection.)

The several Zodiac figures mentioned here were all issued in 1995 and retired in 1997. Each features a figure (some male, some female) in a long white robe with a conical-shaped hat on which is embossed the appropriate sign. Each stands on a globe on which the name of the sign is also embossed. This one is "Libra" (#6220G), one of the more expensive on today's secondary market at $255-$300 over a last retail of $210. (Photo by William B. Bradley, Jr., from the author's own collection.)

"Can I Help?" (#5689G) was issued in 1990 and retired in 1997. Its secondary market trend is $400-$450. It has the virtue of being similar in size and very similar in theme to "Tuesday's Child, Girl" (#6014) and can substitute for it in a pinch. Sculptor was Francisco Catalá. (Photo courtesy of Lladró USA, Inc.)

"Dragon" (#6715G) is the first in a series of planned models taken from the symbols of the Chinese Zodiac. Released in 1999, he retails at $395. (Photo courtesy of Lladró USA, Inc.)

Another special series with a short retail life was Lladró's first Zodiac series—not to be confused with the Chinese Zodiac series recently begun with "Dragon" (#6715 issued in year 2000). The twelve figures in this first Zodiac series (#s 6214-6225) consist of children, each in a wizard's gown and wearing a tall, conical hat adorned with the appropriate Zodiac sign. Each figure is standing on a globe of the world and holding his or her respective horoscope symbol. The name of the particular Zodiac sign is also embossed on the globe's base.

This series was out for only two years, from 1995-1997. The tallest of the figures, "Libra" (#6220), is over a foot in height. The limited style of the series and the sheer size of it may dampen, for at least some collectors, the incentive to acquire the whole group.

The Black Legacy Collection

By 1990, Lladró had begun to recognize that affluent African Americans are a powerful consumer constituency, and the company responded by creating a number of African American models. While there are marketing brochures dedicated to it, the Black Legacy Collection is not separately identified in the *Lladró Authorized Reference Guides* published by the company, wherein African-American themes are pictured interspersed with the rest of the corpus.

This series was originally named the Black Heritage Collection. In late 1990, the company made the decision to rename the collection after some collectors felt the term "heritage" smacked too much of the history of slavery.[6]

Among the most popular Black Legacy figurines are Dr. Martin Luther King, Jr. (#7528); and two sequences of jazz musician figures: Jazz Clarinet (#5928), Jazz Drums (#5929), and Jazz Duo (#5930) issued in 1992 and Jazz Horn (#5832), Jazz Sax (#5833), and Jazz Bass (#5834) issued the prior year. The collection has family groupings (e.g., "Family Roots" [#5371]) and figurines of African American children, including a sequence of three African American children in sleepwear (#s 6463-6465). The collection also features a series of angel figurines (#s 6490-6493) and a series of elegant young women in contemporary formal gowns (#s 6180-6182).

"Daddy's Little Sweetheart" (#6202G) was first issued in 1995, but it has no trouble achieving its issue/current price of $595 on the retail market. There are many more items featuring mothers with children than fathers with children in the Lladró corpus, so the models of fathers tend to be especially valued. (Photo courtesy of Lladró USA, Inc.)

"Family Roots" (#5371G). First issued in 1986, this large and lovely grouping from the Black Legacy Collection currently retails at $935. (Photo courtesy of Lladró USA, Inc.)

"Jazz Duo" (#5930G), first issued in 1992, has wide cross-collectible appeal because of the popularity of jazz. The jazz series of which this grouping is a part has been a solid seller for Lladró, even at its current retail price of $900. (Photo courtesy of Lladró USA, Inc.)

"Jazz Drums" (#5929G), one of a series of popular figurines of jazz musicians in similar costume produced for the Black Legacy Collection. It was first issued in 1992. Consumers are undeterred by its $610 retail price tag. (Photo courtesy of Lladró SA, Inc.)

The Crystal Collection

For this little-known series, Lladró teamed up with the prestigious Daum Nancy Company of France to produce several Lladró designs in both frosted and clear crystal. Lladró's part of the collaboration seems to have been design only; Lladró does not make glass, and these figures were actually manufactured in France.

The Crystal series is not listed in the company's *Collection Reference Guide* or its 4-volume *Collector's Catalog*. To confuse matters, the serial numbers assigned to this series (#s C4500-C4514) are numerical duplicates of those assigned to items in the porcelain line and, to avoid confusion in reference, should always be preceded by that capital letter "C."

These figurines were made of 24% lead crystal. Subjects for the series were a wedding bell, several bears in frosted and clear crystal, frosted angels, and frosted geisha girls. The least expensive item at the time of initial retail was the wedding bell at $35. The retail range for the figurines was $165-$230. All of

these items were produced for one year only, in 1983, and today are difficult to find on the secondary market, where the figurines command prices in the range of $300 to $450 apiece.

The Legend Collection

Launched in late 1999, this series features angels and fantasy figurines such as elves, each accented in gold and semi-precious stones. As a very recent launch, the appeal of this series to collectors has yet to be tested. For those who like the effect, gold accenting on fine porcelain has a long and venerable tradition, in the Orient as well as in the West. The Legend Collection will not be to everyone's taste, however, as many collecting purists prefer their porcelain unadulterated even by the most precious of added materials. Even those who like "a little gold" outlining their porcelain may find the total envelopment of hair and wings a bit "over the top."

For most of us, preference will be a moot point, as we will have a rather limited opportunity to acquire these pieces in any case. They are said to be extraordinarily pricey, and, as of this writing, their U.S. distribution is limited to Lladró Centers in the three glitz-and-glamor capitals of the nation—New York City, Beverly Hills, and Las Vegas. (Lladró Centers, for those unfamiliar with the concept, are not just authorized dealerships, but chunks of actual real estate and buildings owned by Lladró. They are located in great cities throughout the world.) Those wishing at least to see what the Legends look like could find them in a special presentation on the company's Web site (www.lladro.com) as of the year 2000.

Toward the end of the millennium that closed with the 20th century, there appears to have been a certain aesthetic shift in the preoccupations of Lladró artists. Beginning in the 1990s, a plethora of fantasy and millennial figures was created for the core collection (elves, fairies, and other fantastic creatures). This development is reminiscent of the spiritualism of the late-Victorian era that closed out the 19th century. The Legend Collection appears to be one expression of that *fin de siecle* preoccupation with the occult and fantastic. It is certainly a far cry from the earthy pastoral and animal themes that dominated the Lladró collection at mid-twentieth century.

The Fantasy Collection

This series was issued just before the Legend Collection, and it, too, partakes of *fin de siècle* themes: elves, fairies, cupids, and other fantastic creatures. If gold and other precious non-porcelain materials are the most salient feature of Legend, then extraordinary flowerwork, often including large, lush blossoms, is the hallmark of the Fantasy Collection. "Wings of Fantasy" (#6651) and "Lilypad Love"[7] (#6645) feature winged fairy creatures next to large water lilies. Other items in the collection include "Lakeside Dream" (#6644), "Butterfly Fantasy" (#1846), "Fairy of the Butterflies" (#1850), and the quite elaborate "Celestial Journey" (#1848) featuring Pegasus hitched to a fantasy chariot loaded with flowers and escorted by four cherubs. Also associated with this series was a special limited edition "The Enchanted Lake" (#7679), available to Lladró Society members only and fully subscribed within weeks of its issue.

Primarily due to its extraordinary flowerwork, the items in this collection are not cheap. Some sample retail prices: $495 for "Lilypad Love" and "Lakeside Dream" and $775 for "Wings of Fantasy."

"Wings of Fantasy" (#6651G) is one of the pieces in the Fantasy Collection. Its retail price of $775 is due in no small part to that enormous water lily, each petal and stamen and leaf separately modeled and applied by hand. (Photo courtesy of Lladró USA, Inc.)

Gaudi

In just about every nation where Lladró has major interests, there are Lladró items produced and retailed specifically for that country. For example, a set of five limited edition eggs produced between the years 1993 and 1997 and pictured here were distributed solely in the U.S. Another example, Gaudi, also has a geographically limited product distribution.

The Gaudi Collection was inspired by the Modernist architect Antonio Gaudi, whose work is featured in Barcelona's public parks, including the Guell Park and the Casa Mila in Barcelona. Undulating forms with mosaic surfaces characterize Gaudi's work. Lladró's tribute to this architect is a series of five figurines available (as of this writing) only in Barcelona and Japan, where the architect Gaudi is hugely popular.

Lladró's Gaudi collection features traditional Lladró elements such as birds, kittens, puppies, and girls, perched on undulating mosaic forms of bright primary colors to contrast with the Lladró pastels. Collectors anxious to have one of these should be advised that they will not be readily available in the United States. Prices at one Internet retail source where the handful of Gaudis were offered ranged from a low of $255 to a high of $2,465.

Sculptures and Studies

Although Lladró classifies the material of most of these as Gres, the visual impression created by Lladró sculptures and studies is more akin to that produced by bronzes. All the sculptures discussed here were limited editions, and most were released in very small edition sizes of 125 to 300, though a few were issued in editions of 500 to 750. They include a number of female nudes, Art Deco-style sculptures, and models of

Five limited edition eggs, time-limited, all matte and all sold only in the United States from 1993 through 1997. Each had an issue price of $150. (These are individually pictured and priced elsewhere in this book.) The bas-reliefs feature parent birds and animals with babies. (Photo by William B. Bradley, Jr., from the author's own collection.)

heads and torsos. The majority of the sculptures were executed by Huerta, Debón, García, Ramos, Furió, and other sculptors with whose names collectors would already be familiar as they appear elsewhere in the core collection.

The sculptures are a fruit of the company's constant encouragement of its artists to expand into new territory. Some sculptors took to this particular invitation with evident zest, others with less. Sculptors Vicente Martinez, Francisco Catalá, Salvador Debón, and J. Puche produced several sculptures, Juan Huerta and Salvador Furió relatively few.

In art, "studies" is a term used to refer to several similar, often nearly identical, versions of the same subject—as when,

"Bather" (#3551) was one of the few sculptures done by Juan Huerta—and perhaps he thought no other sculptural statement was needed of him after creating this beauty. Standing at over 23" tall, its limited edition of 300 sold out the year it was issued in 1983. Its last retail price was $950, and, at the $1250 secondary market price I have seen in one broker's inventory, is probably undervalued on the secondary market. (The Lladró sculptures may be an entirely different market from the figurines of the core collection.) (Photo courtesy of Lladró USA, Inc.)

J. Puche was the sculptor for the amazing "Plenitude" (#3542), a work in the Art Deco tradition. Its tiny limited edition of 50 sold out the year it was released (1983) at a retail price of $1000. Anyone who has it today can probably name his own price! (Photo courtesy of Lladró USA, Inc.)

"Nude Kneeling" (#3030) was a limited edition of 300 issued in 1995 and retired in 1998 at a last retail price of $975. Its retail value today would be $1100-$1200. (Photo courtesy of Lladró USA, Inc.)

"Indolence" (#3003) is a limited edition Lladró sculpture issued in an edition size of 150, which sold out the year of issue in 1983. Despite its retail popularity, its price achieved at the one Lladró auction at which it was offered was $1000—well below its last retail price of $1465. (Photo courtesy of Lladró USA, Inc.)

Sculptor Pablo Serrano's "Don Quixote" (#3006.2) was part of a series of four color studies of this bust, each of which was a limited edition of only 200. Released on 1986 and retired in 1988, it last retailed at $1575. Serrano was a well-known artist in his own right, and I am unable to estimate the value of this piece today. (Photo courtesy of Lladró USA, Inc.)

Pablo Serrano's "Don Quixote" (#3011.6) was issued in 1986 and retired in 1988 at a last retail price of $1125. It was one of four studies of Quixote's head, different from the 3006 series. Note the famous missing chunk from the legendary dreamer's hat. The 3011 series last retailed at $1125; I have seen one for sale on the secondary market offered at $1500. (Photo courtesy of Lladró USA, Inc.)

group effort of the company's Decoration and Design Department, a prolific and creative team that seems often to be given free rein not just to "decorate" the work of others but to develop works of its own. The Capricho series was also largely the work of this team.

Items in what may be called the "3000 studies" were all sculpted by Pablo Serrano, now deceased, who made his mark as an artist independent of Lladró and whose abstract sculpture has been exhibited in major European and American museums. His several series for Lladró consisted of consecutive treatments of the same subject identified by a decimal-pointed number (e.g. 3008.1, 3008.2, etc.). The 3006 series was a study of busts of Don Quixote wearing his famous "chewed" hat. The 3007 series consisted of busts of Quixote's creator, the author Cervantes. The 3008 series was a bust of Don Quixote with Sancho Panza done in various colors. The 3009 series was unusual and even bizarre, consisting of a large, surreal owl model executed in various colors. The 3010 series featured a saint known in the series title as "Isabela la Católica." The 3011 series circles around again to the head of Don Quixote, done with a slightly different expression and in a different size than the 3006 series.

The extent to which these Serrano studies represented a departure from the style usually associated with Lladró again highlights the unpredictability of the company, its constant artistic innovation, and its willingness to give its artists full freedom to explore the artistic impulse and the limits of material and form. Lladró seems always to be pushing the medium of porcelain itself, exploring its fullest potential and experimenting to see how far that material might be stretched beyond the limits set for it by artisanal tradition.

for example, an artist does a series of drawing studies to master the form preparatory to committing the subject to canvas or clay. As works of art in themselves, otherwise identical items in a study will often show variations of size and/or color to differentiate them from one another.

As the next best thing to actually seeing them, the color photos in the Collector's Catalog give a good idea of what Lladró artists are about in conducting these studies. Items #5977 to 5984, for example, are studies of male and female torsos. As it happens, this particular series was a

This highly-stylized Serrano "Owl" (#3009.9) was one of five color studies in this abstract form, issued in 1986 and retired in 1988, each in a limited edition of 400. Its last retail price was $1575, and, because Pablo Serrano was a noted sculptor, even apart from his association with Lladró, I am unable to estimate its value today. (Photo courtesy of Lladró USA, Inc.)

Notes to Chapter 2

[1] Brand name collections would include NAO by Lladró and Golden Memories, a short-lived collection from the early 1990s.

[2] Lewis, Joan, "A Special Delivery," *A Work of Art* 4:1 (Winter 1992/93): 17.

[3] "Primer on the Secondary Market," *Expressions* 6:2 (Summer 1990): 4-6.

[4] Brad Welch, "Norman Rockwell Figurines…by Lladró???" *A Work of Art* 2:2 (Spring 1991): 3.

[5] Rinker Enterprises, *The Official® Price Guide to Collector Plates* (New York: The Ballantine Publishing Group, 1999): 258.

[6] Society Director's Column, *Expressions* 6:4 (Winter 1990): 3.

[7] English titles for Lladró pieces are usually not literal translations from the often more descriptive Spanish. A penchant for English-language puns and alliterative titles is something serious collectors may find irritating. At their worst, the English titles are downright misleading, as in the case of the limited edition grouping #1597. This grouping represents Lladró's three-dimensional treatment of a famous painting by the Spanish master Diego Velasquez entitled "Las Meninas." The Spanish title for the Lladró piece is translated "Ladies of the 18th Century Court" (a title which is itself a century off the mark, since the Velasquez painting dates from 1654). The "equivalent" adopted for English-speaking audiences is "Southern Tea," a particularly unfortunate cultural misappropriation not only centuries but continents removed from its original inspiration.

An Exhibit of Lladró Special Collections, Sculptures, and Studies

Capricho

The Capricho "Violet Fan with Base" (#1546G) was out only during 1987. Because of this extremely limited retail distribution and also because fans are such a collecting category in their own right, Lladró fans accented in porcelain-dipped lace command strong prices on the secondary market: $1000-$1600. Lladró also made a "White Fan with Base" (#1546.3) with the same issue/retirement year. Both fans retailed at $675 back in 1987. (Photo courtesy of Lladró USA, Inc.)

"Basket of Dahlias" (#1545M) was issued in 1988 and retired in 1991, the year most of the Capricho series went off the market because it was just too delicate to ship safely. Its last retail price was $695; its secondary market value today would be not much above that at $725-$750. (Photo courtesy of Lladró USA, Inc.)

"Soft Lace Hat" (#1569M) is a confection from the Capricho series. Issued in 1987, it was retired in 1991 along with the rest of the Capricho series. Last retail price was $75; secondary market price is $175-$200. (Photo courtesy of Lladró USA, Inc.)

Elite Limited Editions

"Car in Trouble" (#1375) is one of Lladró's several tableaux featuring antique automobiles. It was issued in an edition size of 1500 in 1978, at a first retail of $3000—which had become $4100 by the time the edition sold out in 1987. Price never appears to have been an object with this model as Lladró auction-goers bid it up to a range of $5500-$8500 for winning bidders. Typical secondary market prices have not been that far off the auction mark, either, at a range of $5250-$7250. (Photo courtesy of Lladró USA, Inc.)

Before there was "Cinderella's Arrival," there was this: "At the Stroke of Twelve" (#1493), issued in 1986 in an edition size of 1500 and sold out in 1982. Its last retail price was $7500, but Lladró auction prices in the early 1990s never reached that level, hovering in a narrow range of $6250-$6500. Most sellers today are looking to get $7250-$8500 for it. (Photo courtesy of Lladró USA, Inc.)

"Ducks at the Pond" (#1317) has been claimed by Juan Lladró as being one of his favorite figurines (*Expressions* magazine, vol. 13, no. 2, 1997). A limited edition of 1200, it was issued in 1974 and retired in 1984 at a last retail price of $6100. Its secondary market value today would be in the $7500-$8500 range. (Photo courtesy of Lladró USA, Inc.)

"Floral Offering" (#1490) is a limited edition of 3000 depicting the floral tributes that are part of Valencia's major festival, "Las Fallas," celebrated in March. First issued in 1986 at a cost of $2500, this lush grouping currently retails at $4450. (Photo courtesy of Lladró USA, Inc.)

"Circus Parade" (#1609) was issued in 1989 in an edition size of 1000 that was fully subscribed in 1998, at which time its last retail price was $6550. It'll probably cost $6500-$7000 on the secondary market. (Photo courtesy of Lladró USA, Inc.)

"Oriental Garden" (#1775) is part of the Elite series of Lladró limited editions. The edition size for this one, first issued in 1993, is 750, and it is still retailing at its whopping issue price of $22,500. (Photo courtesy of Lladró USA, Inc.)

Salvador Furió's "Desert People" (#3555), a limited edition of 750, was open only a few years, from 1982 to 1986. It went out at a last retail of $3100, but, perhaps due to the specificity of theme, was not able to sustain that price at Lladró auctions, where it got gaveled down to a range of $2400 to $3000—just a camel's whisker under its last retail. It has been doing a little better lately on the secondary market, at prices in the $3500-$3700 range. (Photo courtesy of Lladró USA, Inc.)

"Eagle's Nest" (#3523) had a small edition size of 300 for one of the tallest of Lladró creations, at over 30". The edition was open from 1981 to 1994, at which time it was retailing at $11,500. The secondary market has seemed to deem that expensive enough for the moment and has been reluctant to let it rise above $12,500. (Photo courtesy of Lladró USA, Inc.)

"Easter Fantasy" (#1810) is an active limited edition of 1000 first issued in 1996 and retailing at $3500. (Photo courtesy of Lladró USA, Inc.)

Other Numbered Limited Editions

"Young Mozart," limited edition #5915G came with a Certificate of Authenticity identifying him as #1746 of an edition size of 2500. The entire edition sold out. Mozart is so young his feet don't begin to touch the floor! Secondary market value today would be $1500-$1600. (Photo by Francisca Madden of "La Dulcinea" from her private collection.)

"Peace" (#1202G), limited to a very small edition size of 150, was open for one year only, 1972 to 1973. It is very tall at 24". Mint examples of this rare and delicate early limited edition can run $7500 to $9000 on today's secondary market. (Photo courtesy of Lladró USA, Inc.)

"Don Quixote and Sancho Panza" (#1318G) was a limited edition of 1000 first issued in 1976 and fully subscribed by 1983, at which time the elaborate grouping of men with their respective animal mounts was already retailing at $3100. The secondary market value today is $4500-$5400. (Photo courtesy of Lladró USA, Inc.)

Sculpted by the great Fulgencio García, "Soccer Players" (#1266G) was limited to an edition of 500, first issued in 1974 and fully subscribed by 1983 at a price of $1000. Today, it will cost you several times that much at secondary market prices ranging from $6500 to $7500. Its sheer dynamism makes it a good example of a Lladró that looks as if it may come to life at any moment. (Photo courtesy of Lladró USA, Inc.)

This Gres "Group of Eagle Owls" (#1223) was a limited edition of 750, on the retail market from 1972 to 1983. It went out at a last issue price of $1150 and has struggled to retain its equity since, at secondary market prices in the $1000-$1300 range. (Photo courtesy of Lladró USA, Inc.)

"Watusi Queen" (#3524), a limited edition of 1500, was made in the Gres porcelain formula and is an example of Lladró's commitment to a global focus in its products. It was open from 1981 to 1994. With a last retail price of $3050, this is an example of the inverse market dynamics that tend to prevail in late purchases of expensive limited editions. Bought at first issue, this grouping would have cost $1875. Today's secondary market trend of $2800-$3000 would have been a nice appreciation over that. But if you paid full retail for it in 1996, you'd have paid above what the secondary market will bear, at least currently. (Photo courtesy of Lladró USA, Inc.)

"Turkey Group" (#1196) was a relatively small limited edition at 350, but it was still on the retail market for ten years between 1972 and 1982. Its last retail price was $2850, and the secondary market has been reluctant to support that price since, fine though this piece may be. (Photo courtesy of Lladró USA, Inc.)

"Mother Kissing Child" (#1329) was a Gres limited edition of 750, first issued in 1976 and sold out by the end of 1978. Its secondary market price today would be somewhere in the neighborhood of $1700-$1900. (Photo courtesy of Lladró USA, Inc.)

"Proud Warrior" (#3572) was a limited edition of 3000 first issued in 1995 and retired in 1998 at a last retail price of $995. Its secondary market price is not yet much above $1100. (Photo courtesy of Lladró USA, Inc.)

"Partridge" (#1290) is a retired limited edition of 800 that was on the retail market from 1974 to 1976. These early limited editions tended to sell our early and to appreciate in value over time. The secondary market price on this one is $1200-$2400 over a last retail price of $925. (Photo courtesy of Lladró USA, Inc.)

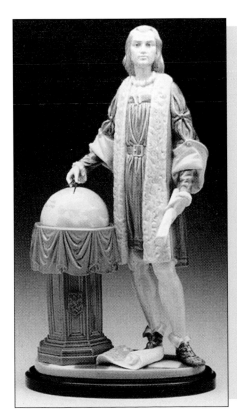

"Columbus" (#1432) was one of several models of the explorer produced by the Lladró company. This one was a limited edition of 1200 issued in 1982 and fully subscribed in 1988. While its highest Lladró auction price was $1800, its more typical secondary market range has been $1100 to $1350. (Photo courtesy of Lladró USA, Inc.)

Measuring over 21" tall, "Moses and the Ten Commandments" (#1811) cuts a commanding figure. It was issued in 1996 in an edition size of 1200 and is still active at $1950. (Photo courtesy of Lladró USA, Inc.)

For a bust, "Gentle Moment" (#3564) is an unusual theme exquisitely rendered. Its edition size of 1000 is still active as of this writing. Retail price is $1835. (Photo courtesy of Lladró USA, Inc.)

"Thoroughbred Horse" (#5340M) was a limited edition of 1000 first released in 1995 and fully subscribed in 1993. Its last retail price was $1050, and it trades on the secondary market at $1150-$1450. (Photo courtesy of Lladró USA, Inc.)

"Oriental Horse" (#2030) is a Gres limited edition of only 350—which probably accounts in part for why it costs $4000-$5000 to buy it on today's secondary market. But I like to think it costs that much mostly because of its undeniably great form, which is reminiscent of the equine statues found in ancient Chinese tombs. The edition was open from 1971 to 1983. (Photo courtesy of Lladró USA, Inc.)

The 18" tall "Pegasus" (#1778) is here featured with "son of Pegasus." A limited edition of 1500 first issued in 1994 and still on the retail market, it is, at $1950, not expensive as Lladró limited editions go. (Photo courtesy of Lladró USA, Inc.)

"Violin Sonata" (#1804G) was a limited edition of 3000 first issued in 1995 and retired in 1999. Its last retail price was $815, but it is already achieving prices of $900-$925 on the secondary market. (Photo courtesy of Lladró USA, Inc.)

First issued in 1995, "To the Rim" (#1800) is a currently-active limited edition of 1500 that can be purchased for $2475. (Photo courtesy of Lladró USA, Inc.)

"Portrait of a Family" (#1805) is an active limited edition of 2500. First issued in 1995, it costs $1975. (Photo courtesy of Lladró USA, Inc.)

"Playing the Blues" (#3567) is a limited edition of 1000 first issued in 1996. Its current retail price is $2160. (Photo courtesy of Lladró USA, Inc.)

"Three Graces" (#2028) was a limited edition of 500 on the market from 1971 to 1976. This model is very tall, at 29.5." Right now, its value is about six times its last retail price, at a range of $6000 to $6500. Fulgencio García was the sculptor. (Photo courtesy of Lladró USA, Inc.)

Society Members Only

Special Theme Collection, Zodiac

"My Buddy" (#7609G), released in 1989, marked the first time a boy was featured as a Society figurine. Issued at $145, his Lladró auction range shows much more volatility than older Society figurines, with a range of $345-$1150. He can be found on today's secondary market at prices in the $400 to $600 range. (Photo courtesy of Lladró USA, Inc.)

"Capricorn" (#6222G) from the Zodiac series. Value today: $250-$275. (Photo by the author, courtesy of Paulette McNary and Kennedy Brothers, Inc. in Vergennes, VT.)

"Mystical Garden" (#6686G), a limited edition available only to Lladró Society members, released in year 2000 in an edition size of 5,000. Note the lush flowerwork. Retail price: $1100. (Photo courtesy of Lladró USA, Inc.)

"Scorpio" (#6225G) from the Zodiac series. Value today: $250-$300. (Photo by the author, courtesy of Paulette McNary and Kennedy Brothers, Inc. in Vergennes, VT.)

"Virgo" (#5215G) from the Zodiac series. Value today: $250-$300. (Photo by the author, courtesy of Frederica Edelman and Kennedy Brothers, Inc. in Vergennes, VT.)

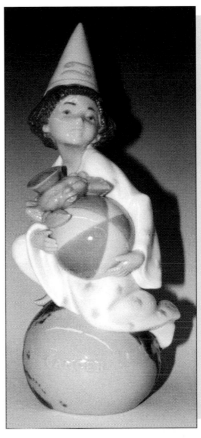

"Cancer" (#6224G) from the Zodiac series. Value today: $250-$300. (Photo by the author, courtesy of Frederica Edelman and Kennedy Brothers, Inc. in Vergennes, VT.)

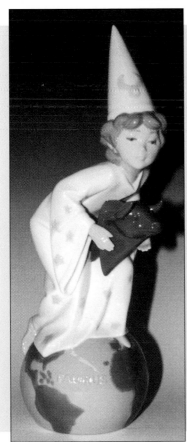

"Taurus" (#6218G) from the Zodiac series. Value today: $250-$275. (Photo by the author, courtesy of Frederica Edelman and Kennedy Brothers, Inc. in Vergennes, VT.)

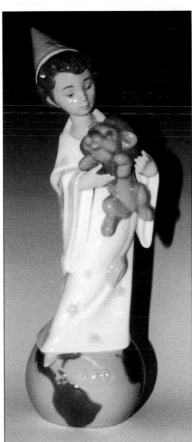

"Leo" (#6214G) from the Zodiac series. Value today: $265-$285. (Photo by the author, courtesy of Frederica Edelman and Kennedy Brothers, Inc. in Vergennes, VT.)

Black Legacy Collection

"School Chums" (#5237G), issued in 1984 and retired in 1996. It had a relatively hefty last retail price of $485, as is consistent with figurines involving more than one element (in this case, two boys). Secondary market price range: $500-$550. (Photo courtesy of Lladró USA, Inc.)

"Sharing Sweets" (#5836G), issued in 1991 and retired in 1997. Its last issue price was $245, and the secondary market price has been slow to appreciate since then, hovering in the $265-$285 range. (Photo courtesy of Lladró USA, Inc.)

"Children's Games" (#5379G), issued in 1986 and retired in 1991 after a relatively short retail run. Its last retail price was $480, and its secondary market range has been volatile since then at a wide range of $585-$750. (Photo courtesy of Lladró USA, Inc.)

"I've Got It" (#5827G), issued in 1991 and retired in 1995 at a last retail price of $180. It is a "sleeper" on the secondary market at prices ranging from its last retail to $230. (Photo courtesy of Lladró USA, Inc.)

"All Dressed Up" (#5909G), a classic pose for a growing boy feeling stiff in his formal attire in a formal chair. On the retail market from 1992 to 1997, its last retail price was $450. Secondary market range is $475-$525. (Photo courtesy of Lladró USA, Inc.)

"Meet My Friend" (#5994G) was out for four years only, 1993-1996. Its secondary market price of $700-$725 has not appreciated much beyond its hefty last retail of $695. In general, models with more than one major element (two or more figures) tend naturally to be more expensive on the retail market because they require additional molds and are more labor-intensive to produce. (Photo courtesy of Lladró USA, Inc.)

"Wanda" (#6182G) has been on the retail market since 1996 and retails currently at $205. This is a tall figurine at over 12" high. Some collectors orient their collections entirely around Lladró's figurines of elegant ladies. (Photo courtesy of Lladró USA, Inc.)

"Finishing Touches" (#6104G), recently retired in 1999 after a retail run of five years, had a last retail price of $285. While the current secondary market trend is modest at $300-$325, Lladró ballerinas have traditionally appreciated very well over the long term. (Photo courtesy of Lladró USA, Inc.)

"Velisa" (#6181), another of the elegant ladies from the Black Legacy series, was first issued in 1995 and currently retails at $185. (Photo courtesy of Lladró USA, Inc.)

"Soft Meow" (#5995G) was issued in 1993 and retired in 1998. Last retailing at $515, it has been holding its own on the secondary market in a price range of $550-$575. (Photo courtesy of Lladró USA, Inc.)

"Gardening Buddies" (#6472G), first issued in 1997, is bargain-priced at $195 current retail. (Photo courtesy of Lladró USA, Inc.)

Special Collections Price List

Capricho

#1291M	Flower Basket #1 (flowers in handled basket) Ret.1983	$200-$225
#1296M	Flower Basket #6 (many small roses in handleless basket) Ret. 1983	$200-$250
#1540M	Pink Ballet Slippers Ret. 1991	$450-$475
#1540.3M	White Ballet Slippers (Ret. 1991)	$450-$475
#1549M	Square Handkerchief with Flowers (Ret. 1991)	$325-$350
#1550M	Round Handkerchief with Flowers (Ret. 1991)	$325-$350
#1551M	Small case with Iris (Ret. 1991)	$500-$525
#1555M	Pink Flower Basket (holding 3 camellia flower heads) (Ret. 1991)	$210-$225
#1559M	Small Pink Flower Basket [folded over basket with handles] (Ret. 1991)	$150-$200
#1559.3M	Small Blue Flower Basket [same model as 1559] (Ret. 1991)	$150-$200
#1635-1645	Various Masks (this series of intricate, lacy eye masks is impossible to differentiate with verbal description) (Ret. 1991)	$675-$1200 ea.
#1649-1659	Various Crosses (flower and lace-decorated crosses, likewise difficult to differentiate in) verbal description] (Ret. 1991)	$200-$525

Goyescas
(Limited and Open Editions)

#1696	Little Boy [head of a child with hat, Spanish title more literally translated as "Addled Child"] (Ret. 1991)	$500-$600
#1744	My Only Friend [boy with hat and cape holding small dog on knee, edition size 200] (Ret. 1991)	$2000-$2100
#1752	Apple Seller [figure of boy in cap and scarf holding apple in right hand, edition size 300] (Ret. 1993)	$1100-$1200
#1763	Trusting Friend [figure of seated boy in overalls holding puppy on lap, edition size 350] (Active)	$1200
#1774	A Treasured Moment [figurine of seated mother holding small girl on lap, edition size 350] (Active)	$965

Elite

#1492	Three Sisters [3 young ladies in long hoop skirts and carrying parasols, limited edition of 3000 issued 1986] (Active)	$3250
#1510	A Sunday Drive [old-fashioned couple in horseless carriage with 2 dogs on road, limited edition of 1000] (Active)	$5250

#1605	Kitakami Cruise [Japanese scene of several people aboard a covered boat, issued 1989 in an edition size of 500] (Last sold in 1993)	$7000-$8000
#1758	Circus Time [amazing grouping of seated kids watching circus clowns under the "big top," limited edition of 2500 first issued in 1992] (Active)	$6500
#3504	The Rescue [a Gres picturing several seamen rowing a rescue boat over rough seas, boat angled upward navigating a wave, with young boy and dog in the bow, limited edition of 1500 issued in 1978] (Sold out in 1987)	$4500-$5000
#5911	Presenting Credentials [old-fashioned enclosed stagecoach with two coachmen and pulled by a team of two horses, issued 1992 in edition size of 1500] (Last sold in 1999)	$18,000-$20,000

Other Limited Editions

#1338	Shakespeare [balding bard with quill in hand seated in chair, edition size 1200] (Ret. 1985)	$1500-$1700
#1510	A Sunday Drive [couple in horseless carriage, dog on ground at side, edition size 1000] (Active)	$5250
#1523	A Happy Encounter [people in antique auto stop to talk to man on horseback going in opposite direction, edition size 1500] (Active)	$4900
#1615	Jesus the Rock [unique crucifix with body of Christ as if carved into rock ledge, ltd. ed. of 1000, active from 1989 to 1994]	$1850-$2100
#1732	Venice Vows [wedding party seated in gondola, oarsman standing, edition size 1500] (Active)	$4100
#1801	Young Bach [young musician seated at pipe organ, edition size 2500] (Active)	$850
#1807	A Dream of Peace [blind-folded lady justice stands behind a small boy in a war helmet breaking a toy gun, limited edition of 2000, first issued in 1995 and last sold in 1997]	$1300-$1400
#1815	Young Beethoven [young musician standing at antique keyboard, edition size 2500] (Ret. 1999)	$900-$1000
#1817	The Burial of Christ [grouping of two apostles and two Marys holding body of Christ near an arch of stone, limited edition of 1250] (Open)	$5300
#1826	On the Balcony [two Spanish ladies in mantillas and holding fans, one seated, one standing, on latticed balcony decorated with flowerwork, limited edition of 1000] (Active)	$3000
#1829	Flowers of the Sea [conch shell with coral "garden" in mouth, edition size of 300] (Ret. 2000)	$950-$975
#2176	Christopher Columbus [Gres limited edition bust, chart in one hand, two fingers raised on other, edition size of 1000, first released in 1987 and last sold in 1994]	$1400-$1450
#3562	Indian Brave [Native American in traditional garb standing next to pony, edition size 1500] (Ret. 1998)	$2300-$2400

#3571   At the Helm [Gres bust of seaman at ship's wheel, edition size 3500] (Active) $1495

#3573   Golgotha [3/4 bust of Christ wearing robe and crown of thorns with hands tied in front of him, limited edition of 1000] (Open) $1650

#3574   Test of Strength [pair of Sumo wrestlers, edition size 1000] (Active) $950

#3578   A Soft Refrain [Gres reclining harlequin with long-necked mandolin, edition size of 1000] (Active) $1300

#5602G   Freedom [single standing eagle with wings raised and partially open, limited edition of 1500 issued in 1989 and sold out the following year] . . . . $1100-$1250

#5847G   The Voyage of Columbus [group of three children tracing Columbus' route on a large globe, limited edition of 7500, first released in 1992 and sold out the following year] . . . . $1400-$1700

#6385   Royal Slumber [adult servant with scepter standing at attention next to small throne with sleeping child king, edition size of 750] (Ret. 2000) . . . . $1475-$1550

#6473   Romantic Gesture [pair of woman's hands extending upward from lacy cuffs, holding rose, edition size of 2000] (Active) $990

#6478   The Pelicans [nesting pair, limited edition of 1000] (Ret. 2000) . . . . $1000-$1100

#6507   A Mile of Style [very elongated clown holding coat on floor with one hand, flower in other; Vanguard exclusive, time-limited] (Ret. 1998) . . . . $400-$450

#6520G   Fourth of July [limited edition of 2000 first issued in 1998] (Open) $700

#7575G   George Washington [ltd. edition of 2000] (Open) $1390

#7563G   Statue of Liberty [ltd. edition of 2000] (Open) . $1620

#7554G   Abraham Lincoln [ltd. edition of 2500] (Open) . $2190

Lladró Society Member Figurines

NOTE: In this section, I am departing from my usual procedure of not listing items that are already pictured with their price captions because I think there is some additional value to collectors in seeing the Members Only figures listed all together in one place.

#7600   Little Pals (1985) . . . . $2500-$4500

#7602   Little Traveler (1986) . . . . $1100-$2100

#7603   Spring Bouquets (1987) . . . . $550-$750

#7604   School Days (1988) . . . . $500-$700

#7607   Flower Song (1988, Lladró Museum Commemorative) . . . . $350-$700

#7609   My Buddy (1989—first boy in series!) . . . $450-$600

#7610   Can I Play? (1990) . . . . $325-$425

#7611   Summer Stroll (1991) . . . . $375-$400

#7612   Picture Perfect (1991, 5th Anniversary figurine) . . . . $450-$475

#7619   All Aboard (1992) . . . . $325-$350

#7620   Best Friend (1993) . . . . $300-$325

#7622   A Basket of Love (1994) . . . . $300-$350

#7635   Ten and Growing (1995, 10th Anniversary figurine) . . . . . $450-$500

#7636   Afternoon Promenade (1995) . . . . $300-$350

#7642   Now and Forever (1995, another 10th Anniversary figure!) . $550-$600

#7644   Innocence in Bloom (1996) . . . . $275-$350

#7650   Pocket Full of Wishes (1997) . . . . $400-$450

#7672   It Wasn't Me (1998—first stand-alone animal in series!) . . . . $325-$350

#7676   A Wish Come True (1999) . . . . $375-$395

#7686   Pals Forever (2000, 15th Anniversary figurine) last retail $350

Black Legacy

#5699G   Sitting Pretty [small girl seated in chair and holding dog on lap] (Ret. 1998) . . . . $350-$375

#5828G   Next at Bat [small boy in baseball cap and wearing shirt with no.1 holds bat across shoulders and behind neck] (Ret. 1998) . $225-$250

#5833G   Jazz Sax [seated boy in striped pants and bowler hat holding saxophone] (Open) $315

#5834G   Jazz Bass [boy in striped pants and bowler hat leaning against standing bass fiddle] (Open) . . . $425

#5835G   "I Do" [bride and groom] (Open) $190

#5837G   Sing with Me [little girl lying on stomach looking at bird perched on hand] (Ret. 1997) . . . . $265-$295

#5908G   Just a Little More [little girl seated in formal chair feeding puppy in lap] (Ret. 1997) . . . . $425-$450

#5928G   Jazz Clarinet [boy with striped pants and bowler hat walking with clarinet under arm] (Open) $295

#5986G   Sunday Sermon [robed preacher standing in front of pulpit] (Open) $425

#6103G   Beautiful Ballerina [ballerina girl seated, looking off to her left] (Ret. 1999) . . . . . . $300-$325

#6471G   My Pretty Flowers [young girl holding basket of flowers low in front of her] (Open) . . $165

#6492G   Your Special Angel [girl angel, shading eyes with hand and looking down] (Open) $95

#6493G   Filled with Joy (boy angel with hands on chest] (Open) $95

#6494G   Onward and Upward [boy graduate in robe and mortar board holding rolled diploma] (Open) . . $170

#6495G   The Road to Success [girl graduate in robe and mortar board holding rolled diploma] (Open) . . $155

#7528G   Dr. Martin Luther King, Jr. [standing figure with right hand and index finger raised] (Open) $375

"Birds and Chicks" (#7007), Mother's Day Plate for 1972. All the other 8" plates in this series feature human mothers and children. Secondary market value: $125-$150. (Photo by William B. Bradley, Jr., courtesy of Florence DeNagy and The Antiques Collaborative in Quechee, VT.)

Chapter 3

"UTILITARIAN WARES"

One of the things differentiating Lladró from other fine porcelain companies is its primary focus on figurines. Many of its utilitarian wares (listed under the heading "Functional" in the *1998 Authorized Reference Guide*) are composed more for whimsy than utility. Lladró has made at least one set of table china, not available for retail purchase in the United States and little known among collectors. Other Lladró plates are, as is typical of collector plates, purely decorative; one wouldn't risk putting a spoon to the matte bas-relief designs on their surface.

The most functional among Lladró's utilitarian items are its multiple vases; even most of these are of sufficient fancy and expense that most collectors would be hard-pressed to allow themselves the indulgence of putting live flowers and water into them.

This chapter takes the reader on a tour of various functional or utilitarian items (for lack of better terminology) in the core collection.

Lladró Vases

Lladró vase styles range from Art Nouveau to Art Deco to traditional Oriental, and come in multiple sizes and shapes and in forms from traditional to fantastic. Glazes and decoration include everything from matte bas relief to *bajo cubierto* to a mottled glaze more like that found on some types of art pottery. Most of the vases are very difficult to find on the secondary market and, during their retail lives, are not usually seen at smaller authorized dealerships. Several have the same or similar names and/or feature the same patterns in different sizes. Consequently, they are difficult to describe or differentiate without accompanying pictures.

"Ricinus Palm Vase" (#1592) is a taller version of the vases in this pattern, at 10.25". Also available on the retail market in the years 1988 to 1993, it last retailed at $550 and runs $625-$650 on the secondary market. (Photo courtesy of Lladró USA, Inc.)

"Ricinus Palm Vase" (#1598) was one of several vases of various heights and shapes that Lladró made with this Ricinus Palm pattern. This one was 7" high and retailed from 1988 to 1993 at a last retail price of $630. Today, it would be valued at $725-$750. (Photo courtesy of Lladró USA, Inc.)

Among favored themes for *bajo cubierto* vases are peacocks (#1137 Paradise Vase, #1761 Oriental Bird Vase No. 2, #1620 Peacock Vase, #1200 Peacocks Floral Vase); dragons (#1116.3 Blue-White Dragon vase, #1120.3 Dragon Vase, #4696 Dragon Tibor Jar, #4690 Yellow Dragon Vase, #4690.3 Jug Decorated); the Ricinus Palm (#1589, #1590, #1591, #1592, all called "Ricinus Palm Vase," executed in various sizes and shapes); and various flowered vases (e.g., #5916 Oriental Peonies Vase, #5917 Oriental Peonies Vase # 2, #4740 Cylindrical Floral Vase, and several "Chrysanthemum Vases" of various shapes and sizes).

"Floral Vase" (#1191) was a limited edition of 150 issued in 1972 at $465 and retired in 1982 at a last retail price of $1900. Despite its undeniable beauty, the secondary market has not supported a price much above $2000 since. (Photo courtesy of Lladró USA, Inc.)

The most affordable vases are the series of mottled, non-figural art-pottery-like vases in the smaller sizes, issued in 1988 and retired in 1991. Several of these had a modest last retail price of under $100 (e.g., #1692 Small Vase, #5527.5 Topaz Vase No. 16, #1693 Round Vase, #5226.4 Silver Vase No. 14, etc.).[1] The glaze is not immediately recognizable as Lladró, but all these items are marked with the blue backstamp.

Perhaps the most famous and elaborate Lladró vase ever created was the Elite Series #1536, "Japanese Vase," issued as a limited edition of 750 in 1988 and last sold in 1990. It features a number of Japanese figures surrounding the outside wall of the vase and done in three-quarter relief. Its last retail price was $3000 and it would be worth at least $3500 to $4000 today.

"Japanese Vase" (#1536), one of Lladró's limited edition vases, may be the most famous and elaborate one it has ever made. Its face features three-quarter sculpted figures of Japanese people. It was issued in 1988, but by 1990 its extraordinary artistic value had already been recognized by upscale buyers who had little trouble plunking down the $2600-$3000 it cost in those retail years. (Photo courtesy of Lladró USA, Inc.)

Although it ranks among the most striking of the vases, "Japanese Vase" is not the most expensive, as will be evident from the short price list of limited editions below. Most of the Lladró vases were produced as open issues, but the several limited editions produced include:

#1619 Bird Vase (16" tall, issued in 1989 in an edition size of 300 and last sold in 1998 at $3995)

#1137 Paradise Vase (19.25" tall, time-limited edition issued in 1971 and retired in 1972)

#1138 Rooster Vase (19.25" tall, time-limited edition issued in 1971 and retired in 1972)

#1191 Floral Vase (19.25" tall, issued in 1972 in an edition size of 150 and retired in 1982 at a last retail of $1900)

#1192 Red Mango Vase (19.25" tall, issued in 1972 at 150 and last sold in 1982 at $2750)

#1197 Floral Vase (19.75" tall, issued in an edition size of 150 in 1972 and retired in 1982 at a last retail of $2000)

#1200 Peacocks Floral Vase (28.75" tall, edition size of 150, first issued 1972 and retired in 1978 at $2200 with a later auction price of $2350)

#1362 Pheasant Vase (29.25" tall, issued in an edition size of 750 in 1978 and retired in 1987 at a last retail of $8500)

#1617 Swallow Vase (20.5" tall, limited edition of 300 issued in 1989 and retired in 1998 at a last retail price of $3075)

#1620 Peacock Vase (20.5" tall, issued in 1989 in an edition size of 300 and retired in 1998 at a last retail of $3150)

#1621 Pheasants and Mums Vase (20.5" tall, issued in 1989 in an edition size of 300 and last sold in 1998 at a retail price of $3300)

#5916 Oriental Peonies Vase No. 1 (20.75" tall, edition size of 300 issued in 1992 and still active at $7500)

#5917 Oriental Peonies Vase No. 2 (same size, edition size and issue year as 5916, also still active at $8000)

#5918 Fanciful Flight Vase (19.25" tall. edition size of 300, first issued in 1992, still retailing at $4800)

Two things are immediately evident from even a cursory analysis of this list. The first thing is that the limited edition vases are all quite large, ranging in height from nearly 20" to almost 30" in height. (The average range for the vases in the open corpus is 6" to 20", with the tallest being a very rare "Vase No. 7," whose slender trumpet neck tops out at an astonishing 39 inches.) This accounts in part for the second point evident in a review of this list, that these limited edition vases are by and large beyond the means of collectors with modest incomes.

"Oriental Bird Vase No. 2" (#1761) is very tall at almost 21" and was issued, along with its companion piece "Oriental Bird Vase No. 1" (#1760, featuring the bird in flight), was issued in 1992 in a limited edition size of 300. Each of these vases retails at $7,000. (Photo courtesy of Lladró USA, Inc.)

"Don Quixote Vase" (#4770) retailed from 1971 to 1975. You could have bought it for only $25 when it was first issued and only $40 the year it went off the retail market. Expect to pay $650-$750 for it today. (Photo courtesy of Lladró USA, Inc.)

What is a bit less obvious from the information given above is that these very expensive items may have difficulty retaining their equity, at least this early in their secondary market life. Precious few of these are available on the secondary market, so any conclusions from current broker stock lists or auction records must be drawn with caution. Still, it is worth noting that #1191 and #1192, fairly early retirements in 1982, have had difficulty sustaining even their last retail prices. Auction records for the quite early, time-limited Rooster Vase (#1138) show it gaveling down in the $900-$1000 range, a decent enough appreciation over its last retail of $355 but a far cry from the thousands of dollars commanded by vases of comparable size and style that are still active. The trend is fairly consistent across those items for which secondary market sales data exist.

Lladró's vases are nonetheless artistically important to the extent that vases are among the traditional and classical indicators of a fine porcelain company's artistic mettle. Quite simply, one doesn't "do" porcelain without doing vases. Urns (two-handled vases) were among the very first items ever produced by the three brothers. These were done in the classic European style of Sevres and Meissen, with rococo handles and pastoral or courtly scenes. Early on, the brothers and their artistic collaborators abandoned this imitative style for the more innovative and avant-garde Lladró styles produced later. Despite the historic importance of vases for porcelain in general and Lladró in particular, the only items still active on the retail market are the few items still open in the limited editions listed above.

"Coral Vase" (#2050) has wonderful pastel color combinations. Issued in 1973 and retired in 1979 at a last retail price of $265, it would be worth $600-$650 today. It is quite tall at over 13". (Photo courtesy of Lladró USA, Inc.)

"Blue Empire Vase" (#1199) was a limited edition of 300 issued in 1972 at the then weighty price of $610 and last retailed in 1982 at $2750. A color variant also called "Blue Empire Vase" (#1198) was issued in the same year but retired in 1975; it has no white accents and is, along with a third "Empire Vase" (#1193), today considered rare. (Photo courtesy of Lladró USA, Inc.)

Part of the problem here may well be the limited exposure of the vases relative to other, better-known items in the corpus. One of the market laws of collecting is that a demand cannot be generated for that to which collectors have had too little exposure. Lladró is best known for its figurines, and most collectors have rarely, if ever, seen one of the vases except in pictures.

Lamps

Many of the Lladró lamps were produced in geometric shapes or with bases that resemble vase forms. Perhaps the most popular and striking of the lamps, however, were those produced with figural bases. In many but not all cases, these models were taken from the existing Lladró figurine corpus. There are, for example, lamp counterparts for five of the six popular child angel figurines: Angel with Horn lamp #4543, Chinese Angel Lamp #4544, Black Angel Lamp #4545, Thinking Angel Lamp #4546, Praying Angel Lamp #4547. (All of these five angel lamps were issued in the late 1960s and retired by the mid-1970s. The earliest retired was the Chinese Angel Lamp in 1970 and the latest the Thinking Angel Lamp in 1976.) Other well-known figurines also incorporated into lamp bases were Girl with Lamb (#4505, which became, in lamp form, Shepherdess with Lamb, #4728) and Boy with Goat (#4506, in lamp form Shepherd with Kid, #4727).

Lladró started making lamps very early on. The rare lamps dating from the mid-1950s to mid-1960s include Young Flutist Lamp (#88.06), Hunting Lamp (#76.05), Giraffe Lamp (#355.13), Fawns Lamp (#307.13), Young Shepherd Lamp (#365.13), Young Shepherdess Lamp (#366.13), The Hunter Lamp (#86.06), Girl with Flower Basket Lamp (#87.06), Gazelle Lamp (#350.13), Horses Lamp (#351.13), and La Tarantella Lamp (#1124).

Lladró decided at some point to get out of the lamp business almost entirely, at least for its core collection. The only two core collection lamps still being made are the "Nymph" lamp (#1607) and "Pierrot's Proposal" (#6508), which was first issued as late as 1998. Both are expensive, at current retail prices of $1795 for "Nymph" and $1450 for the more recent "Pierrot's Proposal."

Check out the fabulous lines on this "Ballet Lamp" (#4528G/M), one of Lladró's several figural lamps made in the earlier years of the company. Issued in 1969 and retired in 1985 at a last retail price of $475, it was made in both matte and glazed versions. Mint examples can run $950-$975 on the secondary market. (Photo courtesy of Lladró USA, Inc.)

The necessity of turning lights off and on as well as of bulb and shade maintenance would obviously render figural lamps of this delicacy especially vulnerable to damage. It will be difficult, though not impossible, for collectors to find mint examples on the generic (non-brokered) secondary market.

"Horse Rearing Lamp" (#4592G) was issued around 1969 and retired in 1972 at a mere $70. Be prepared to ante up $1100-$1200 for it today! A companion lamp, should you want a set, features "Horse Bucking" (#4593). (Photo courtesy of Lladró USA, Inc.)

"Violinist Lamp" (#4527G/M) was one of several figural lamps produced in the earlier years of the company. Did I own this wonderful piece, I'd live in mortal terror every day of damaging those delicate lines! This lamp was issued in 1969 and retired in 1985 at a last retail price of $325. The secondary market has been generous to it since, with mint examples commanding $875-$950. (Photo courtesy of Lladró USA, Inc.)

Clocks

Since 1989, Lladró has made almost two dozen quartz clocks, featuring the clock face surrounded by a porcelain case. Several of these are still active as of this writing, including: Diamond Clock (#5655.3), Two Sisters Clock (#5776), Swan Clock (#5777), Pierrot Clock (#5778), Time for Love (#5992), and Angelic Time Clock (#5973).

The richly figural "Angelic Time Clock" (#5973) is 11" tall at its tallest points and is one of the most expensive Lladró clocks ever made. First released in 1993, it retails at $1100. (Photo courtesy of Lladró USA, Inc.)

"Swan Clock" (#5777) is one of several Lladró clocks featuring figural elements. First released in 1991, it is still active on the retail market at $555. (Photo courtesy of Lladró USA, Inc.)

Most of the clocks still in active issue are figurals; i.e., figurines are incorporated into the base. Another active issue, Moongate Clock (#7541) is sold exclusively in Bermuda. Once again, "clock" is not a word that comes immediately to mind in association with the name "Lladró," and these are seldom seen in smaller authorized dealership displays or on the secondary market.

"Bow Clock" (#5970) is a very recent retirement—year 2000. First released in 1993, its last retail price was $245. (Photo courtesy of Lladró USA, Inc.)

"Pierrot Clock" (#5778), released in 1991, is still open on the retail market at $475. (Photo courtesy of Lladró USA, Inc.)

Candleholders

Lladró has made about a dozen different candleholders or candelabra, none of which are currently active. Among the more interesting figural items are Mermaid Candleholder (#1110), Male Candelabra (#5226, featuring a reclining nude with garland stretched between the two candleholders), Female Candelabra (#5227 featuring a reclining female nude with garland), Angel with Lyre Candleholder (#5949), Angel with Tambourine Candleholder (#5950), and an elaborate centerpiece called "Oriental Candelabra" (#5225) in the shape of a pagoda flanked by two praying figures seated in the lotus position.

"Oriental Candelabrum" (#5225) would make a fabulous centerpiece for a home decorated in an Asian motif. It measures over 17" at its tallest point. Out on the retail market for a short time only, in 1984 and 1985, its last retail price was $685. At this writing, A Retired Collection had one available for $1800. Good luck finding this one in mint condition without the aegis of a broker! (Photo courtesy of Lladró USA, Inc.)

In 1997 and 1998, the Lladró Society membership premiums consisted of a bisque (i.e., white matte) vessel about the size and shape of a custard cup but identified by the company as votive candle holders. "Sailing the Seas" (#7657) featured sailing ships in its motif and #7658 was called "Dolphins at Play." These are pretty enough for those who like bisque relief, but they are somewhat impractical for their identified purpose, as one might well hesitate to burn wax candles in a matte votive candleholder.

Two Lladró Society votive candleholders, left to right: "Dolphins at Play" (#7658M) and "Sailing the Seas" (#7657M), membership premiums for 1997 and 1998 respectively. One might well hesitate to burn candles in these bisque holders! The value of each of these today would be in the $25-$50 range. (Photo by William B. Bradley, Jr., from the author's own collection.)

Collector Plates

Painted plates were among the oldest and most frequent forms actually worked by the Lladró brothers themselves in their earliest forays into art. The oldest of these (unlikely to be found outside the Lladró museums) date from the early 1940s.

Closer to the present, Lladró made two series of eight-inch collector plates featuring bisque relief surfaces surrounded by glazed rims in *bajo cubierto* light blue with a thin gold highlight around the inner and outer rims. These series might be called "occasion plates": the Christmas Plates (featuring the word "Navidad" with the year of issue on the rim) and the Mother's Day Plates (featuring the words "Día de la Madre" and the year of issue on the rim). The choice of these two occasions was probably a function of tradition in other great porcelain houses. For example, the esteemed Danish firms of Royal Copenhagen and Bing & Grondahl are both famous for their Christmas and Mother's Day plates.

At times, Lladró artists seem to undertake certain forms just to prove that they can, before they move on fairly quickly to other realms they find more interesting or that are more lucrative for sale. While the Danish plates mentioned above sustained decades of annual issue of Mother's Day themes, using the infinite variety in mother-offspring combinations provided by the bird and animal kingdoms, Lladró made only ten of the Mother's Day Plates, all but one of which features human mothers and children. The only non-human scene is that featured in plate #7007 called "Bird and Chicks" (see photo on page 78). Each of the Christmas and Mother's Day Plates is a time-limited edition, issued and retired in the same year.

Lladró also made several 4" miniature plates. A number of them were open issues featuring children engaged in various activities such as swinging and apple picking. Three of them featured birds: ducks, flamingos, and turtle doves. None of the miniature plates have writing on the rim as the larger plates do.

Three of the miniature plates were special issues. One, called simply "Miniature Plate" (#7501) was a time-limited edition issued in 1990 exclusively for the Franklin Mint, which used a series of these miniature plates to celebrate the great porcelain houses of Europe (as mentioned in the previous chapter). At 3.25 inches in circumference, it was the smallest plate Lladró ever made. (A photo of this item can be seen in Chapter 2 under "Commissioned Works".)

The second of these miniature plates was called "Christmas Melodies" (#6184) a four-inch time-limited edition plate (see photo below) made in 1994 essentially as a promotional piece for the figurine of the same title (#6128) issued that same year. The plate features the figurine model in miniature bisque bas relief.

"Christmas Melodies Plate" (#6184), a time-limited edition issued and retired in 1994 as a promotional piece for the figurine "Christmas Melodies" (#6128). Value range: $35-$45. (Photo by the author, from her own collection.)

While "Great Voyage" (#5964) was not billed as a special issue or even a limited edition, it has the unique distinction among Lladró collector plates of having a colored bas relief. Released in 1993 as an open issue but soon retired in 1994, the plate features the famous three ships of Columbus in all their full-masted glory (see photo below).

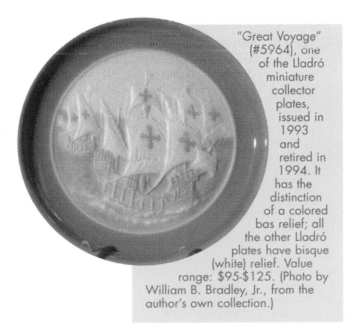

"Great Voyage" (#5964), one of the Lladró miniature collector plates, issued in 1993 and retired in 1994. It has the distinction of a colored bas relief; all the other Lladró plates have bisque (white) relief. Value range: $95-$125. (Photo by William B. Bradley, Jr., from the author's own collection.)

All Lladró collector plates, of whatever size, have been retired.

Bowls and Centerpieces

Lladró created a number of bowls and bowl-like table centerpieces, many of which were figural or quasi-figural. Some of these seem to have been in the nature of "studies"—the same model made in different sizes and colors. This was the case, for example, with the 4-inch "Fruit Bowl(s)" (#4737 and 4737.3) and "Star Centerpiece(s)" (#s 4724, 4724.3, 4736, 4736.3), all of which were in the form of a starfish folding up its "arms" to form a bowl. Pedestaled versions of this model were made as "Star Cups" (#s 4734, 4734.3, 4735, and 4735.3). The same starfish motif would be repeated in multiple-level centerpieces: two level (#4738 and 4738.3) and three-tiered (#s 4739 and 4739.3).

"Star Cup" (#4735.3M) was one of several single- and multiple-tiered centerpieces made in this pattern, all of which were issued in 1970 and retired in 1972. The motif is a starfish accented by seahorses on each of the ridges, and it makes an especially arresting visual statement on the multi-tiered items. The single bowls were made with and without pedestals and retailed for about the same price either way, with the yellow-blue combination (#4735, without the decimal point) being only slightly more expensive than the blue-white. Secondary market prices for these single bowls, with or without pedestal, would be $500-$750. (Photo courtesy of Lladró USA, Inc.)

"Star Three-Level Fruit Bowl" (#4739M) was made in three tiers of graduated sizes. (A two-tier version was produced as #4739.3M with the blue-white version numbered as 4738.3.) These three-tiered items retailed at about twice the price of the single-level bowls, so I'm going to hazard a secondary market range of $1000-$1500 for the three-tiered models—assuming they can be found! (Photo courtesy of Lladró USA, Inc.)

The company made a series of peacock bowls (#4766 and 4766.3, both called "Decorative Peacock" and #4767, called "Royal Peacock"), which, strictly as a matter of superficial form and presentation, are not unlike the figural peacock planters made by other ceramic companies famous and non-famous. The most interesting of the Lladró figural "bowls" include Mandarin Duck (#4695), Little Mermaid Bowl (#1111) and Decorative Pheasant (#4693).

Most Gres centerpieces feature girls' heads in which a scooped-out portion in the top of the head forms the "bowl". They include #2041 and 2042 (both called "Girl's Head"), and Byzantine Head (#1106). All of the bowls and centerpieces mentioned here are retired.

"Girl's Head" (#2046) is a 14-inch centerpiece which can readily accommodate fruit or flowers in the basket atop the girl's head. I have actually seen this piece on the secondary market (with one braid repaired) and it is quite large; what I remember most about it, though, was how bright the eyes seemed! Issued in 1971 and retired in 1975, it achieved Lladró auction prices of $600-$625. These Gres pieces would be stunning as table centerpieces topped with fruit, flower heads, or gourds. (Photo courtesy of Lladró USA, Inc.)

"Girl's Head" (#2041) is another Gres that can serve as a centerpiece, with the bowl located in the top of the girl's head. Issued in 1971 and retired in 1975 at a last retail price of $55, its secondary market value today would be $375-$400. (Photo courtesy of Lladró USA, Inc.)

Miscellaneous Utilitarian Items

Lladró made many other models of practical items, including cups and saucers, chalices, spoons, bells, various kinds and shapes of covered boxes, paperweights, and bookends.

"Heart Box, Decorated" (#5266M, also produced in bisque as "Heart Box, White" [#5266.3]) was issued in 1984 and retired in 1990 at a last retail price of $55. It will cost you quite a lot more than that today, at a price range of $200-$220. The fact that not many people associate non-figural items with Lladró would tend to contribute to their relative scarcity. (Photo courtesy of Lladró USA, Inc.)

Most of these were more decorative than utilitarian: you would not have wanted to eat with a Lladró porcelain spoon or drink coffee from one of the Capricho cups or wine from its matte chalices. Rumor has it, however, that Lladró has even developed an entire line of dinnerware—although I have been unable to confirm its availability, nor have I seen pictures of it to be able to describe it here.

"Chalice—Decorated" (#5263M) is so named to distinguish it from the white version (#5263.3, which was produced in both glazed and matte forms, although the decorated version was produced only in matte). Issued in 1984 and retired in 1990, its secondary market value is $200-$250. (Photo courtesy of Lladró USA, Inc.)

Among its most famous and best-received contributions to the world of utility were its two chess sets, which could be purchased with or without boards. One of these sets is still active for your strategizing pleasure.

"Medieval Chess Set" (#6333) was first released in 1996 and is still active on the retail market. Each chess piece is made, of course, of Lladró porcelain, and each is quite substantial in size at 6.25 inches. The retail price for the chess pieces alone is $2120, but you can get the board, too, for just $145 more. (An older Lladró chess set [#4833] was retired in 1985, and that one is only slightly more pricey than the current retail for #6333.) (Photo courtesy of Lladró USA, Inc.)

Notes to Chapter 3

[1]Except where rarity is specifically indicated, decimal numbers in this chapter should be taken to indicate variations in size and color rather than rarity.

Utilitarian Wares Identification and Price Guide

Vases

#1115   Floral Jug white chalice-shaped vase with embossed, very stylized blue flowers (Ret. 1979)...................... $300-$350

#1115.3   White Floral Jug same as #115 but in bisque (Ret. 1978) .... $275-$325

#1138   Rooster Vase wide body tapering to slim neck, decorated with roosters, time-limited edition issued in 1971 and retired in 1972.... $1900-$2000

#1621   Pheasants and Mums Vase limited edition of 300, issued 1989, last sold 1998..... $3300-$3500

#4690   Yellow Dragon Vase decorated with Chinese dragon, 9.75" tall] (Ret. 1981) .... $500-$550

#5566   Nautilus Vase form of Chambered Nautilus shell, 5" tall (Ret. 1990) .... $225-$250

#5567   Double Nautilus Vase two nautilus shell forms joined (Ret. 1990)............. $275-$325

#5633   Water Dreamer Vase girl's face emerging from a cabbage-like shape (Ret. 1990)....... $350-$450

#5634   Water Baby Vase baby's face emerging from cabbage-like shape (Ret. 1990) .... $350-$450

#5635   Lladró Vase three-dimensional triangular shape with opening at top, 4.25" tall (Ret. 1990)$125-$165

#5636   Lladró Vase Deco design, square opening with two inverted triangle shapes at either side (Ret. 1990)...................... $150-$175

#6389   The Bouquet 8" narrow bud vase with embossed decoration around circumference about a third of way down the body (Ret. 1998)...................... $100-$125

Lamps

Prices quoted here assume mint condition of base and working condition of lamp. While most of the lamps Lladró made were geometric and non-figural, their shapes and sizes are difficult to differentiate from other items similar to them. (Anticipating a question, let me just say that the shades sold with these lamps were fairly generic and about as durable as such items ever are; therefore, the lamp bases usually appear on the secondary market without shades. Collectors need not fear purchasing the shadeless lamps on the secondary market and/or replacing the original shades with something more to their liking.) The following list is heavily weighted to the figural lamps because they are the easiest to describe verbally.

#1607   Nymph Lamp two young girls arranging garlands around a pole or trunk (Open)..... $1795

#1616   Carousel Lamp loose carousel form with painted detail (Ret. 1991) .... $1500-$2000

#1622   Birds and Peonies vase-shaped base with painted motif as per title, limited edition of 300 last sold in 1998 .... $3750-$3800

#2011   Horse Head (Ret. 1982) .... $450-$500

#2111   Elephant stylized Indian elephant in regalia forms base (Ret. 1985) .... $1000-$1200

#4526   Colombina ballerina in tutu and dance pose with legs crossed and torso bent to side, extremely delicate and graceful] (Ret. 1985) ...... $550-$600

#4544   Chinese Angel (Ret. 1970) .... $450-$500

#4545   Black Angel (Ret. 1975) .... $450-$500

#4573   Ducks Group three ducks, same models as figurines by same name (Ret. 1972) .... $475-$575

#4578   New Shepherdess seated as figurine of same name (Ret. 1976) .... $600-$700

#4579   New Shepherd seated as figurine of same name (Ret. 1976) .... $600-$700

#4702   Horse Head (Ret. 1972) .... $650-$700

#4727   Shepherd with Kid young shepherd carrying goat kid draped around neck (Ret. 1975) $450-$500

#4746   Octagonal Jar, Pink (Ret. 1973)........ $350-$375

#4748   Octagonal Jar, Blue (Ret. 1972)........ $350-$375

#4749   Octagonal Jar, Green (Ret. 1973)....... $350-$375

#6508   Pierrot's Proposal base features Pierrot down on one knee before long-skirted Colombina (Open) $1450

Clocks

#1781G   Allegory of Time clock draped by two women in flowing clothes, with scarves meeting in an arch above the clock, limited edition of 5000 last sold in 1998..... $1300-$1500

#5655.3G Diamond Clock (Open) $100

#5992G   Time for Love clock with bow on top flanked by little boy offering flower and shy little girl (Open) $760

#6601G   Clock white domed case accented with purple lattice on top and decorated with two flowers (Open) $190

Candleholders and Candelabra

#5226   Male Candelabra nude male figure with garland reclining between two cups of the holder (Ret. 1985) . . . . $900-$1200

#5227   Female Candelabra nude female figure with garland reclining between two cups of the holder (Ret. 1985) . . . . $900-$1200

#5949   Angel with Lyre Candleholder (Ret. 1997)$375-$400

#5950   Angel with Tambourine Candleholder (Ret. 1997) . . . . $375-$400

Christmas Plates

#7006   Christmas Caroling Navidad 1971 on rim $150-$225

#7008   Christmas Carolers Navidad 1972 . . . . . . $125-$200

#7010   Boy and Girl at Christmas Navidad 1973 $125-$175

#7012   Christmas Carolers Navidad 1974 . . . . . . $125-$175

#7014   Christmas Cherubs Navidad 1975 . . . . . $125-$150

#7016   Christ Child Navidad 1976 . . . . $125-$150

#7022   Nativity Navidad 1977 . . . . $125-$150

#7106   Christmas Caroling Child Navidad 1978 . $100-$125

#7108   Christmas Snow Dance Navidad 1979 . . $100-$125

Mother's Day Plates

The reader will note that the serial numbering on the annual mother's day plates issued in the decade of the 1970s is, for some reason known only to the makers, out of sequence for the first and last plates.

#7025   Mother's Day Plate Día de la Madre 1971 on rim . . . . $200-$225

#7007   Birds and Chicks Día de la Madre 1972 . $125-$175

#7009   Mother and Children Día de la Madre 1973 . . . . $125-$150

#7011   Nursing Mother Día de la Madre 1974 . . $125-$150

#7013   Mother and Child Día de la Madre 1975 . $100-$125

#7015   Tender Vigil Día de la Madre 1976 . . . . . $100-$125

#7021   Mother and Daughter Día de la Madre 1977 . . . . $100-$125

#7105   New Arrival Día de la Madre 1978 . . . . . $100-$125

#7107   Off to School Día de la Madre 1979 . . . . $100-$110

#7023   Mother's Day Plate Día de la Madre 1980 . $100-$110

Miniature Plates

Diameters on plates listed here are 4", though they may vary by as much as a quarter inch either way depending upon degree of kiln shrinkage.

#5998   Looking Out (Ret. 1998) . . . . $45-$55

#5999   Swinging (Ret. 1998) . . . . $45-$55

#6000   Duck (Ret. 1998) . . . . $45-$55

#6158   Friends (Ret. 1998) . . . . $40-$50

#6159   Apple Picking (Ret. 1998) . . . . $40-$50

#6160   Turtledove (Ret. 1998) . . . . $40-$50

#6161   Flamingo (Ret. 1998) . . . . $40-$50

#6162   Resting (Ret. 1998) . . . . $40-$50

Bowls and Centerpieces

#1111   Little Mermaid Bowl figural of mermaid with hands folded over head and "bowl" in the back of her tail (Ret. 1972) . . . . $450-$475

#4693   Decorative Pheasant stylized figural of pheasant with crested comb; bowl on back of wings (Ret. 1973) . . . . $475-$500

#4695   Mandarin Duck (Ret. 1975) . . . . $350-$450

#4738M   Star Two-level Fruit Bowl star-fish shaped bowls accented with seahorses, blue and yellow colors (Ret. 1972) . . . . $850-$900

#4738.3   M Star Two-level Fruit Bowl same as #4738 but in white with blue accents (Ret. 1972)$775-$800

Miscellaneous Functional Pieces

#2010   Horse's Head Bookends matching pair, uniform color in head and manes (Ret. 1981) . . . . $300-$400

#4626   Velazquez Bookend single bookend (Ret. 1975) . . . . $875-$950

#4627   Columbus Bookend single bookend of seated Columbus with charts in lap (Ret. 1975)$950-$1100

#4661   Horse Head Bookend single bookend, mane darker than rest of horse's head (Ret. 1972) . . . . $200-$250

#4833   Chess Set and Board (Ret. 1985) . . . . $2400-$2500

#4833.3   Chess Set, Pieces Only (Ret. 1985) . . . $2300-$2400

#5263.3   Chalice bisque grape and vine relief (Ret. 1988) . . . . $175-$225

#5267   Oval Box, decorated (Ret. 1990) . . . . . . $125-$150

#5267.3   Oval Box, white (Ret. 1988) . . . . $150-$200

#6138   Globe Paperweight contemporary continent masses (Ret. 1996) . . . . $100-$125

#7551M   16th Century Globe Paperweight (Open) $105

A LLADRÓ CHRISTMAS GALLERY

Nativity Figures

Detail of the three kings from the Belén Nativity. Left to right: "King Gaspar" offering a toy truck (#4674, retailing in glaze at $95), "King Balthasar" with teddy bear (#4675, retailing at $95), and "King Melchior" bearing a wrapped present (#4676, retailing at $95). (Photo by William B. Bradley, Jr., from the author's own collection.)

The three main characters in sculptor Juan Huerta's Belén Nativity: Mary (#4671, retail price $75), "Saint Joseph" (#4672, retail price $90), and "Baby Jesus" ensconced on pillow (#4670, retail price $55). (Photo by William B. Bradley, Jr., from the author's own collection.)

Detail of the three shepherds from the Belén Nativity. Left to right: "Shepherdess with Basket" (#4678, retail $90), "Shepherd with Lamb" (#4676, at $110 the most expensive figure in the set) and "Shepherdess with Rooster" (#4677, retailing at $90). The little "Shepherdess with Rooster" (#4677) in this picture is actually one of the elusive matte figures. The going secondary market price for the matte version is $150-$175. (Photo by William B. Bradley, Jr., from the author's own collection.)

Detail of face on "Cow." Furió is noted for his realism of detail, and it's all here, from the eyes to the ears to the nose—to that bony crest of tufted hair between the horns. (Photo by the author, from her personal collection.)

"Cow" (#1380G) sculpted by Salvador Furió as part of his large Nativity set, still active. The modeling is so exquisite in this animal that it can easily stand alone as a display piece. Retail price on the cow: $210. (Photo by the author, from her personal collection.)

Ornaments

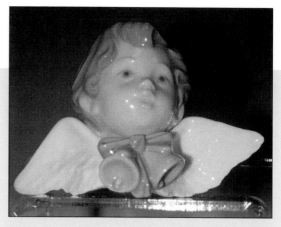

"Three Kings" ornaments, sold as a set (#5729), a time-limited edition from 1990 and the work of sculptor F. Polope. Originally issued at $87.50, the set is worth $125-$150 today. A little secret: If you were to take this set of miniature ornaments and add to them sets #5657 ("Holy Family" consisting of Mary, Joseph, and the Baby Jesus), #5809 ("Holy Shepherds"), and #6095 ("Nativity Trio" consisting of an angel, a calf, and a donkey), you'd have yourself an entire miniature Nativity scene! (Photo by William B. Bradley, Jr., from the author's own collection.)

"Seraph with Bells" (#6342G), ornament issued in 1996 and retired in 1997. Value today: $85-$95. (Photo by the author, courtesy of Carolyn Pearson and Reed's Antiques and Collectibles of Wells, ME.)

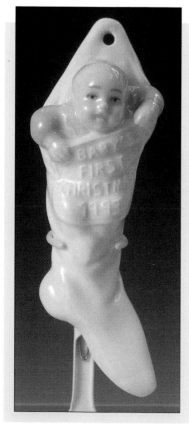

"Baby's First Christmas 1993" (#6037G). Issued at $57, even a dated ornament such as this today commands a price at least equivalent to its last retail and can go as high as $100. (Photo by William B. Bradley, Jr., from the author's own collection.)

"King Melchior" (#6391G), one of Lladró's Christmas ornaments, issued in 1996 and retired in 1997. This happy-faced monarch is accompanied by companion pieces (missing when this photo was taken): King Gaspar (#6380G) and "King Balthasar" (#6309G, issued in 1998 and retired in 1999). Their value today would be in the range of $85-$95 each. (Photo by the author, courtesy of Carolyn Pearson and Reed's Antiques and Collectibles of Wells, ME.)

Bells

A medley of Christmas Bells. Left to Right: 1990 (#5641, valued at $65-$95), 1991 (#5803, valued at $45-$75), 1996 (#6297, valued at $50-$75), 1992 (#5913, $45-$75) and 1994 (#6139, $50-$85). As you can see from the ranges, prices are quite unstable on these items. (Photo by William B. Bradley, Jr., from the author's own collection.)

1987 Christmas Bell (#5458M), first in a series of nine annual bells embossed with various Christmas scenes and with their respective year of issue. As the first in the series, this one is quite desirable, and it is not unusual for it to fetch prices of $75-$100. (Photo by William B. Bradley, Jr., from the author's own collection.)

1989 Christmas Bell (#5616M), for some reason the most sought after and expensive of the series of nine on the secondary market, at an average range of $125-$150. (As a point of comparison, the range for the rest of these bells is $35-$95.) (Photo by William B. Bradley, Jr., from the author's own collection.)

Christmas Balls

Christmas Balls, two of a series of ten started in 1988. Left to right: 1989 (#5656M) worth $75-$95 today and 1991 (#5829) worth $55-$75. We have pictured them with the date at front for identification purposes, but their other faces are more interesting: birds on three of the four panels of the 1989 ball and carolers and the Holy Family on two of the three panels on the 1991 ball. The 1989 ball is quite a lot the larger of the two. Beginning in 1990, these were downsized, as they are quite heavy; only the toughest tree limbs could accommodate that 1989 ornament. (Photo by William B. Bradley, Jr., from the author's own collection.)

Tree Toppers

"Heavenly Harpist" (#5831G), first in a series of "Angel Symphony" tree-toppers sculpted by Francisco Catalá and issued in the 1990s, beginning with this one in 1991. Her appreciation range of $250-$300 reflects her preeminence as the first in the series. (Photo by the author, from her personal collection.)

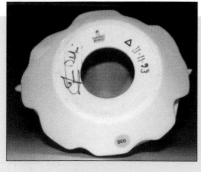

Photo of the base of a tree-topper angel showing that the hole in the base really is wide enough to accommodate a treetop at Christmas! Luckily, the tree-toppers all stand on their own just like any other Lladró figurine, which is how most collectors prefer to display them. The signature and dating are Jose Lladró's. (Photo by the author, from her personal collection.)

"Rejoice" (#6321G), issued in 1996 as the last and most expensive of the tree topper angels for that decade. Her retail price that year was already $220; even so, she commands $240-$250 on today's secondary market. By this time, Francisco Catalá may have tired of the series, for this model was created by Lladró's Department of Decoration and Design, composed largely of anonymous and very talented women. (Photo by the author, from her personal collection.)

"Angelic Cymbalist" (#5876G), another of the "Angel Symphony" limited edition tree toppers. Issue date 1992. Current value: $225-$250. (Photo by the author, from her personal collection.)

Christmas-Themed Figurines

"Dear Santa" (#6166G), issued in 1995 and retired in 1999. Estimated value today: $275-$300. (Photo by the author, courtesy of Virginia Herzog and Knotty Pine Antique Market in W. Swanzy, NH.)

"Santa Claus with Toys" (#4905G) was issued in 1974 and retired in 1978, along with its companion piece #4904, featuring the same Santa with the sack empty—for a sort of "before and after" display. Santa Claus with empty sack can occasionally be found on the secondary market for prices in the $1100-$1300 range, but I don't know anyone who has #4905 for sale. Lladró's Santa Claus figurines are popular and often hugely expensive on the secondary market, perhaps in part because that vivid red of the suit is so unusual a color on a Lladró. (Photo courtesy of Lladró USA, Inc.)

"Angel Tree Topper Angel, Pink" (#5831G), second in a series of three tree toppers, all sculpted by Francisco Catalá and distinguished by the color of their outer robes (in this case, pink). Value today: $150-$200. (Photo by the author, from her personal collection.)

92

A Lladró Christmas Wish List

Nativity Sets

Although some of the figures for the Nativity sets are pictured in the book with price and identification captions, I have chosen to depart from my usual procedure of omitting pictured items from the Nativity price and identification lists because I think it is useful to see the various forms of Nativity sets together with their variant versions for price comparison purposes.

#1386G Saint Joseph [standing, hands coming together in prayer] (Active) $385

#1386.3 Saint Joseph [white] (Ret. 1985) . . . . . . $400-$425

#1387G Virgin Mary [seated, hands crossed over chest] (Active) $385

#1387.3 Virgin Mary [white] (Ret. 1985) . . . . $400-$425

#1388G Baby Jesus [finger raised] (Active) $140

#1388.3 Baby Jesus [white] (Ret. 1985) . . . . $150-$175

#1389G Donkey (Active) $215

#1389.3 Donkey [white] (Ret. 1985) . . . . $250-$275

#1390G Cow (Active) $215

#1390.3 Ox [white] (Ret. 1985) . . . . $250-$275

#1423G King Melchior [kneeling, fur collar] (Active) . . . $440

#1423.3 King Melchior [white] (Ret. 1985) . . . . . $450-$475

#1424G King Balthasar [standing] (Active) $585

#1424.3 King Balthasar [white] (Ret. 1985) . . . . . $600-$650

#1425G King Gaspar [kneeling] (Active) $475

#1425.3 King Gaspar [white] (Ret. 1985) . . . . $550-$575

#4670G Baby Jesus (Active) $55

#4670M Baby Jesus (Ret. 1991) . . . . $75-$95

#4671G Virgin Mary (Active) $75

#4671M Virgin Mary (Ret. 1991) . . . . $100-$110

#4672G Saint Joseph (Active) $90

#4672M Saint Joseph (Ret. 1991) . . . . $135-$150

#4673G King Melchior [holding wrapped present] (Active) $95

#4673M King Melchior (Ret. 1991) . . . . $135-$150

#4674G King Gaspar [holding toy truck] (Active) $95

#4765M King Gaspar (Ret. 1991) . . . . $135-$150

#4675G King Balthasar [holding teddy bear] (Active) . . . $95

#4675M King Balthasar (Ret. 1991) . . . . $135-$150

#4676G Shepherd with Lamb (Active) $110

#4676M Shepherd with Lamb (Ret. 1991) . . . . . . $145-$175

#4677G Shepherdess with Rooster (Active) $90

#4677M Shepherdess with Rooster (Ret. 1991) . . . $135-$150

#4678G Shepherdess with Basket (Active) $90

#4678M Shepherdess with Basket (Ret. 1991) . . . . $135-$150

#4679G Donkey (Active) $100

#4679M Donkey (Ret. 1991) . . . . $135-$150

#4680G Calf (Active) $90

#4680M Calf (Ret. 1991) . . . . $135-$150

#5476G Saint Joseph [down on one knee, holding staff] (Active) $270

#2275 Saint Joseph [Gres version] (Active) $270

#5477G Mary [kneeling, blue, trim-embossed robe] (Active) $165

#2276 Mary [Gres version] (Active) $175

#5478G Baby Jesus (Active) $75

#2277 Baby Jesus [Gres version] (Active) $85

#5479G King Melchior [kneeling, dark hair and beard] (Active) $265

#2278 King Melchior [Gres version] (Active) $290

#5480G King Gaspar [kneeling, gray hair and beard] (Active) $265

#2279 King Gaspar [Gres version] (Active) $290

#5481G King Balthasar [standing] (Active) $265

#2280 King Balthasar [Gres version] (Active) $290

#5482G Ox (Active) $175

#2281 Ox [Gres version] (Active) $185

#5483G Donkey (Active) $175

#2282 Donkey [Gres version] (Active) $185

#5484G Lost Lamb [kneeling shepherd girl holding lamb protectively in one arm] (Active) $140

#2283 Lost Lamb [Gres version] (Active) $140

#5485G Shepherd Boy [standing shepherd with lamb on shoulders, ewe standing behind him] (Active) $205

#2284 Shepherd Boy [Gres version] (Active) $285

#5744G Bull and Donkey [double figure] (Ret. 1991) . . . . $300-$350

#5745G Baby Jesus [manger raised on crossed logs] (Ret. 1996) . . . . $210-$225

#5746G Saint Joseph [standing, elbow on
raised knee] (Open)*. $375

#5747G Mary [standing, hands on knees]
(Ret. 1996) . . . . $315-$335

#5748G Shepherd Girl (Ret. 1996) . . . . $200-$225

#5749G Shepherd Boy (Ret. 1996) . . . . $250-$275

#5750G Little Lamb (Ret. 1996) . . . . $75-$95

* This Saint Joseph figurine was apparently left open as a freestanding figure after the retirement of the rest of the Nativity set.

Christmas Ornaments

#1604G Angels Ornaments [set of 3] (Ret. 1988) . $175-$250

#5657G Holy Family [set of 3 – Mary, Joseph,
Baby Jesus] (Ret. 1989) . . . . $120-$175

#5809G Holy Shepherds [set of 3 - 2 shepherds and
a lamb] (Ret. 1991) . . . . $125-$250

#5840G Our First Christmas [two love-birds in nest,
embossed "Our First Christmas Together,
1991"; also #5923 for 1992 and #6038 for
1993] (Ret. 1992) . . . . $60-$100

#5841G Snowman Ornament [in top hat] (Ret. 1993) $65-$70

#5938G Elf Ornament [elf with paint brush]
(Ret. 1993) . . . . $60-$65

#5939G Mrs. Claus Ornament [ringing a bell]
(Ret. 1993) . . . . $65-$70

#5940G Christmas Morning [set of 3 kids with
presents in hand] (Ret. 1992) . . . . $110-$125

#5969G Nativity Lamb [lamb suspended by
porcelain ribbon and bow] (Ret. 1993) . . . . $80-$85

#6095G Nativity Trio [set of 3: reclining angel,
donkey, calf] (Ret. 1993) . . . . $140-$175

#6262G Rocking Horse (Ret. 1997) . . . . $85-$90

#6263G Doll (in bonnet with large bow tied under
chin) (Ret. 1997) . . . . $75-$80

#6264G Train [toy train engine] (Ret. 1997) . . . . . . $85-$90

#6343G Little Aviator [child with helmet and
goggles in little plane] (Ret. 1997) . . . . $85-$90

#6344G Teddy Bear (Ret. 1997) . . . . $70-$75

#6345G Toy Soldier [saluting] (Ret. 1997) . . . . . . $105-$110

#6381G Little Roadster [old fashioned convertible]
(Ret. 1998) $90-95

#6386G Little Harlequin [seated position with hands
on hips, tri-cornered hat] (Ret. 1998) . . . . . $85-$90

#6388G Circus Star [elephant] (Ret. 1998) . . . . $80-$90

#6588G Baby's First Christmas [sleeping baby
snuggled inside a wreathe] (Ret. 1998) . . . . $60-$65

Tree Toppers

#5125G Joyful Offering [angel in two-layered skirt,
holding a braided garland] (Ret. 1995) . . $275-$300

#6132G Angel of the Stars [angel holding a star]
(Ret. 1995) . . . . $225-$250

#6586G Angelic Light [tree topper spire topped by
star and with Baby Jesus] (Ret. 1999) . . . $200-$220

#6587G Message of Peace [tree topper, dove with
elongated wings held up, bells at feet]
(Ret. 1998) . . . . $150-$175

#6643G Message of Love [time-limited 1999
tree topper, dove with wings folded up]
(Ret. 1999) . . . . $165-$185

#6747G A Celestial Christmas [time-limited 2000
tree topper, two cherubs around a star]
(Ret. 2000) . . . . $290-$315

#6792G Star of the Heavens [time limited 2001
tree topper, angel holding blue star with
adhered pink rose in center] (Ret. 2001) . $150-$175

Christmas Balls

First Series

#1603M 1988 Christmas Ball (Ret./LE) . . . . $80-$85

#5656M 1989 Christmas Ball (Ret./LE) . . . . $75-$80

#5730M 1990 Christmas Ball (Ret./LE) . . . . $70-$75

#5829M 1991 Christmas Ball (Ret./LE) . . . . $45-$65

#5914M 1992 Christmas Ball (Ret./LE) . . . . $60-$75

#6009M 1993 Christmas Ball (Ret./LE) . . . . $60-$75

#6105M 1994 Christmas Ball (Ret./LE) . . . . $75-$95

#6207M 1995 Christmas Ball (Ret./LE) . . . . $60-$75

#6298M 1996 Christmas Ball (Ret./LE) . . . . $60-$75

#6442M 1997 Christmas Ball (Ret./LE) . . . . $55-$65

Second Series

#6561M 1998 Christmas Ball (Ret./LE) . . . . $60-$65

#6637M 1999 Christmas Ball (Ret./LE) . . . . $60-$65

#6699M 2000 Christmas Ball (Ret./LE) . . . . $65-$70

Christmas Bells

First Series

#5458M 1987 Christmas Bell (Ret./LE) . . . . $95-$125

#5525M 1988 Christmas Bell (Ret./LE) . . . . $35-$45

#5616M 1989 Christmas Bell (Ret./LE) . . . . $125-$150

#5641M 1990 Christmas Bell (Ret./LE) . . . . $65-$85

#5803M 1991 Christmas Bell (Ret./LE) . . . . $45-$50

#5913M 1992 Christmas Bell (Ret./LE) . . . . $45-$75

#6010M 1993 Christmas Bell (Ret./LE) . . . . $45-$55

#6139M 1994 Christmas Bell (Ret./LE) . . . . $75-$95

#6207M 1995 Christmas Bell (Ret./LE) . . . . $60-$75

#6298M 1996 Christmas Bell (Ret./LE) . . . . $60-$75

Second Series

#6441M 1997 Christmas Bell (Ret./LE) . . . . $50-$55

#6560M 1998 Christmas Bell (Ret./LE) . . . . $50-$55

#6636M 1999 Christmas Bell (Ret./LE) . . . . $70-$75

#6700M 2000 Christmas Bell (Ret./LE) . . . . $50-$55

Christmas Figurines

#1239G Christmas Carols [three child carolers and a dog] (Ret. 1981 . . . . $750-$775

#1499G Holy Family [Joseph leaning on staff behind seated Mary with Baby Jesus on her lap] (Ret. 1998) . . . . $400-$425

#1813 Santa's Journey [Santa seated next to a globe of the earth, limited edition of 1000] (Ret. 1999) . . . . $1350-$1400

#2198 A King Is Born [Gres, tableau of Holy Family] (Open) $895

#4904G Santa Claus [toy bag empty] (Ret. 1978) $1150 $1200

#4905G Santa Claus [toy bag full] (Ret. 1978) . $1200-$1300

#5427G Saint Nicholas [the original saint in bishop's garb] (Ret. 1991) . . . . $750-$800

#5711G A Christmas Wish [child sitting on Santa's knee] (Ret. 1997) . . . . $500-$525

#5897G Trimming the Tree [girl and boy in stocking cap on stepstool decorating tree] (Open) $925

#5971G A Special Toy [seated Santa with right arm around standing boy and holding toy horse in left hand] (Ret. 1996) . . . . $875-$900

#5975G Up and Away! [Santa in sleigh pulled by two reindeer] (Ret. 1996) . . . . $3000-$3100

#6008G Joyful Event [grouping, Joseph, Mary, and infant surrounded by ox and donkey] (Active) . $825

#2293 Joyful Event [Gres version] (open) $690

#6128G Christmas Melodies [young couple singing carols] (Ret. 1997) . . . . $425-$450

#6149G Christmas Wishes [girl in Santa cap, lying on stomach, composing Santa letter] (Ret. 1998) . . . . $250-$275

#6261G Christmas Tree [decorated Christmas tree, 5" high] (Open) $80

#6500G Jolly Santa [Sainta carrying bag over shoulder and ringing a handbell] (Ret. 1998) . . . . $250-$300

#6532G A Christmas Song [caroler in coat playing a horn] {Ret. 2000) . . . . $200-$225

#6533G The Christmas Caroler [caroling child holding songbook] (Ret. 2000) . . . . $175-$200

#6534G The Spirit of Christmas [caroling child playing violin] (Ret. 2000) . . . . $200-$225

#6575G A Gift from Santa [Santa down on one knee, lifting wrapped present from bag] (Ret. 2000) . . . . $225-$250

#6657G Santa's List [standing Santa holding long list in left hand, quill in right] (Ret. 2000) . . $225-$250

#6667G Visions of Sugarplums [from the Night Before Christmas Collection, small child asleep in stuffed wing chair] (Ret. 2001) . $265-$275

#6668G Up the Chimney He Rose [from The Night Before Christmas Collection, fireplace hung with wreath and stockings] (Ret. 2001) . . $375-$395

#6669G A Stocking for Kitty [from The Night Before Christmas Collection, little girl holding stocking looking down at kitty at her feet] (Ret. 2001) . . . . $250-$275

#6670G Christmas Is Here [from The Night Before Christmas Collection, a decorated Christmas tree, 12.75" high] (Ret. 2001) . . . . $500-$525

#6671G Ringing in the Season [from The Night Before Christmas Collection, a little girl kneeling next to hassock with bell in hand and holding kitten in lap] (Ret. 2001) . . . $250-$275

#6672G I Love Christmas [from The Night Before Christmas Collection, little boy standing on hassock holding Christmas ball aloft] (Ret. 2001) . . . . $250-$275

#6674G Thank You, Santa! [two little children in nightgowns gazing down at toys] (Ret. 2001) . . . . $335-$350

#6675G Cookies for Santa [from The Night Before Christmas Collection, covered box in shape of round table decorated for Christmas] (Ret. 2001) . . . . $335-$350

#6714G A Christmas Duet [girl in Santa suit holding songbook and looking down at seated dog, also singing] (Open) $315

One of Lladró's many famous ballerina figurines, "Beth" (#1358G) was part of a series of six young women (#s1356-1361), each wearing the same style leotard and tutu and each in a different seated pose. Their values today would range from $225-$275 apiece. Issued in 1978, they were all retired in 1993. (Photo by the author from her private collection.)

Chapter 4

IDENTIFYING INDIVIDUAL ITEMS:
HOW DO I KNOW IT'S A LLADRÓ?

As previously mentioned, your best bet for identifying an individual figurine, if you do not have the original box and if the serial number is not incised into the base, is usually a company picture catalog. The most handy is one of the series of Lladró authorized reference guides, the titles of which tend to vary from edition to edition. The format for these is a series of small black and white captioned photos, not much larger than postage-stamped size, but usually large enough and clear enough for identification purposes. Caption information includes English-language names and serial numbers as well as dates of issue, dates of retirement, current and last retail prices, and a Lladró-only auction history on those relatively few figurines that can boast one.[1] (Only a small percentage of the Lladró retired corpus has ever been featured at an exclusive Lladró auction.)

Generic price guide lists consisting of serial numbers, titles, and suggested prices but no pictures are of little help in identifying individual items. The English titles are suggested by English-language distributors of Lladró and are often unhelpful; not only do they bear little or no relation to the original Spanish, but they are also usually nondescript. ("Girl with Lamb" is not a helpful moniker for collectors seeking to distinguish their particular figurine from any number of other Lladró figurines featuring girls with lambs!) Another problem is that Lladró is not at all consistent with its English language titles, which change frequently and without apparent reason, sometimes in major ways, sometimes in minor.

Because generic lists are frustrating for Lladró identification purposes, I have included in the price lists for this book a brief description of the pieces listed. In so doing, I have tried to focus on distinguishing characteristics of particular items, especially those that are part of a series of similar theme. Nevertheless, a picture with accompanying title and serial number really remains the most helpful tool in identifying your particular figurine.

If the item is not pictured in a Lladró catalogue, that does not mean the item is not genuine. In such a case, it can be helpful to send a clear picture to Lladró USA for identification assistance. This may take some time, as particularly unusual items may require identification assistance from the factory in Spain.[2]

Little girl in poncho with teddy bear, matte finish, unmarked. The "look" is close; it may be an early NAO, but it would be unusual for a piece not at least to be marked "Made in Spain." Without even that bit of information, no conclusions can be drawn about the origin of the piece. (Photo by the author, from her personal collection.)

Lladró Brand Names vs. Lladró Imitations

If imitation is the sincerest form of flattery, then Lladró has many flatterers! The company has been aggressive in protecting the integrity of its mark and the prerogatives of its designs. The reality is, however, that neither a counterfeit nor a competing product poses a genuine threat because Lladró is, quite simply, inimitable. Once collectors develop an "eye" for it, they are seldom fooled by imitators, not even by those few unscrupulous manufacturers using counterfeit marks.

Internet auction descriptions are especially prone to touting figurines as being "Lladró-like." Often, the items in question are not even made in Spain and bear about as much resemblance to Lladró as a bicycle does to a car. Other items, however, are confusing because they are marked "Made in Spain" and look at least vaguely enough like Lladró to make people unfamiliar with Lladró wonder which brand names are affiliated with it and which are not.

While this book focuses exclusively on the core collection, it is important, in the interest of accurate information for collectors, to note that the following product names are or have been Lladró product lines: Zaphir, NAO, and Golden Memories (no longer being produced). The following Spanish companies are not affiliated with Lladró, nor have they ever been: Nadal (not to be confused with Nadal Collectibles, a Lladró secondary market broker located in California), Porceval, Casades, Miquel Riqueña, Tengra, Inglés, and Rex. These are the Spanish companies whose porcelain figurines will most often be found on the international secondary market.

There are other lesser known companies as well, including Raimond, Dalia, Levante, Paleesi, Segarra, Castilla, Arbalt, Porregamo, Torralba, Mirmasu, and Jando—just a sampling of the many names of Spanish makers of porcelain figurines not affiliated in any way with Lladró. And, despite what you may read in Internet auction listings, none of them are "like Lladró!"

Seventy percent (70%) of Spain's total porcelain production comes from Lladró's own region of Valencia. Lladró itself holds fully thirty percent (30%) of that market, with all other Valencian companies carving up the remainder between them. Most of these companies are small, family-owned concerns with very limited production capacity.[3]

The irony of this burgeoning Spanish porcelain industry is that, prior to the 20th century, Spain would not have been particularly famous for its porcelain production. The names most often associated with antique Spanish porcelain are Alcora and Buen Retiro, which are found today mostly in museums.

Amid the plethora of contemporary Valencian porcelain companies, Nadal should be mentioned as a special case. The company's founder, Jose Asuncion Marques Nadal, made his first porcelain figurine as far back as 1915, more than a decade before Juan, the oldest of the three Lladró brothers, was even born. It is unlikely that any of the

other porcelain companies in the Valencian region are as old as Nadal. Moreover, its figurines bear a striking resemblance to Lladró and are the most artistically well executed of those of any Lladró competitor. A unique feature of Nadal porcelain figurines is their combination matte-glaze finish.

Little is known about Nadal outside Europe; apparently, it has never had an aggressive overseas marketing program. Before they established their own company, the three Lladró brothers worked for another porcelain company until a labor dispute caused them to strike out on their own. Only one written Lladró source mentions the name of this company, which it renders "Nalda."[4] I have been unable to confirm the existence of a Spanish porcelain company with this name, and it would indeed be a striking coincidence should there be two companies in the same region of Spain making similar products with such similar names. "Nalda" is, however, a fairly popular first name in Spain and is occasionally used as a surname as well, so it is at least possible that the written source in question has mistakenly transposed the letters of the name "Nadal" and that this was the company for which the brothers initially worked.

A Word About Lladró "Seconds"

Occasionally, one hears the claim that "Lladró does not sell seconds." Recently, the company itself has begun qualifying this claim by saying that it doesn't export seconds, selling them only at its factory store in Spain. Serious collectors are not likely to take comfort from this assurance, as we are living in a global economy, with frequent commerce between the United States and Spain. The fact that the company doesn't allow the sale of seconds outside its factory store simply means they will make their way onto the secondary market outside Spain via tourists' suitcases.

The collector's task of distinguishing second-quality from first-quality merchandise is further complicated by the opening of a Lladró outlet store in Williamsburg, Virginia. (While this is, as of this writing, the only outlet store for Lladró in the United States, there may be others internationally that are not known to me.) The company uses this Williamsburg location to move warehouse inventory on just-retired pieces to make room for newer production. Unlike other Lladró-sponsored sales venues, the Lladró outlet in Williamsburg prices at a discount.

For some reason not entirely clear even after store personnel have explained it to me, the outlet defaces the mark on each item it sells by scraping off the logo flower on these otherwise mint condition pieces, thus rendering them suspect to any serious collector. (Ostensibly, the practice is meant to keep buyers from trying to "return" outlet purchases to authorized retail dealers for full retail price. One wonders if requiring a sales slip to authenticate original purchase at that dealership might not work as well!) It is usually obvious upon close inspection that the logo has been scraped off.

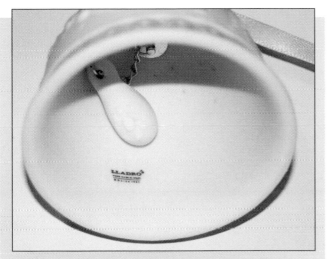

The logo has been scraped off this mark taken from the inside of a 1989 Christmas bell, indicating it as a "second" purchased at the factory or a formerly-mint piece from the Williamsburg outlet store. (Photo by the author.)

Aside from other condition factors, a piece with a defaced logo is arguably no longer "mint" if one considers the mark to be integral to the figurine. Because the company otherwise sets great store by the integrity of its mark, it will be difficult for at least some collectors to take an item bearing a defaced mark seriously. This is particularly the case when such wares are purchased at factory and outlet venues at substantial discounts off the last retail price.

The best advice I can give collectors on this issue is that, if you don't think you'll ever care about resale value, seconds and outlet pieces can be a relatively inexpensive way to acquire a piece you like and would otherwise be unable to find or afford. (It is, after all, still a genuine Lladró!) If, however, you think you or your heirs would ever be concerned about the resale value of your collection, you are best advised to avoid anything with a defaced mark, as the jury is still out on the impact such marks will have on long term value.

How Can I Tell
If It's a Real Lladró?

Those unfamiliar with Lladró often focus on color or glaze as distinctive aspects of it, but these are, in fact, the easiest elements to imitate. There are many figurines produced today with a high-gloss glaze, so I can't say that particular feature has ever been much help to me in distinguishing a Lladró from the universe of other glazed figures.

Likewise, many people assume the use of pastels is "Lladró-like," and they will make that comparison for everything from Scandinavian and German figurines to unmarked figurines of questionable origin. German and Scandinavian blues and grays can be differentiated from Lladró because they are usually deeper and crisper, more "icy" —as would be appropriate for such Nordic figures.

By contrast, the colors in Lladró look as if they'd been bleached by a warm Mediterranean sun. It is difficult for me to differentiate these colors further. Despite Lladró's much-touted color palette of over 5,000 subtle shades, it uses many of these very sparingly, and it seems to me there are only so many subtleties in shades of blue, gray or tan that can be discerned by any given collector.

"Girl with Piglets" (#4572G/M) is a good example of the pastoral themes that dominated the Lladró corpus in its early years. Issued in the late 1960s, the matte version was retired in 1991 and the glazed version not long after, in 1993. Secondary market range is $400-$475. This model also illustrates the kind of theme one might find in one of the Danish porcelains, but the colors of the Lladró will look sun-bleached in comparison to the crisp and icy colors of a Scandinavian figurine. (Photo courtesy of Lladró USA, Inc.)

Glazed figurines produced in the former East Germany may also use softer pastels, and amateurs will often confuse these with Lladró. However, figures from Germany that are marked with the country of origin but have no company name usually have another distinctive feature: the clothing on human figures will be painted under glaze in various colors, but faces will be completely white, relying on sculpting alone to define the facial features. The only time Lladró does completely white faces unaccented by color is when the entire figure is bisque.

A final detail helps to separate the German and Scandinavian figures from those produced in Spain. The former, including famous companies such as Rosenthal, Royal Copenhagen, and Bing & Grondahl, will glaze their figures completely, including the underside of the base. For the most part, Spanish figurines—including those of other Spanish companies mentioned in this chapter as well as those by Lladró—have unglazed undersides, even on glazed figurines. So, if you're wondering whether you have a Lladró and you're not sure about other identification factors, you should check the underside of the base: if it's glazed, then it's not a Lladró. If the underside of the base is unglazed, the figure is probably Spanish, though not necessarily—and, in fact, probably not—an "unmarked" Lladró. (This identification trick obviously doesn't work for matte figurines, where there will be no surface difference between the base of the figure and the figure itself. However, German and Scandinavian companies usually do not make matte figurines.)

There are other factors more important than color or glaze that help a discerning collector to distinguish a Lladró from its competitors on the secondary market, even without looking at the mark. These factors are generally related to technical and artistic quality. While some non-Lladró companies are better than others at imitating the Lladró style, none of them has so far been able to capture the artistic essence of a Lladró, and most don't even come close. Therefore, a Lladró is usually readily distinguishable from a "wannabe."

"Pas de Deux" (#6374G) measures 13" at its tallest point. This grouping, issued in 1997 and retired in 2000 at a last retail price of $725, illustrates well Lladró's mastery of artistic and technical challenge. I can't imagine a competitor trying to pull off a model like this. (Photo courtesy of Lladró USA, Inc.)

Left to right: Beagle Puppy and Beagle Puppy! The one on the right is the real Lladró "Beagle Puppy" #1071, the one on the left a copy. The copy is smaller than the genuine article and, if you turned it upside down, you'd see the bottom is not only unmarked but entirely glazed—a giveaway that it's not a Lladró. (Photo by William B. Bradley, Jr., from the author's own collection.)

Aesthetic and Technical Risk

The content and styles covered in the first chapters of this book underscore Lladró's commitment to artistic innovation. Part of innovation is technical risk-taking—not just in the development of different formulas for porcelain such as Gres, but also in the way that the figurines occupy space.

Although they have become bolder in recent years, most of Lladró's competitors will not take the artistic and technical risks that Lladró does in creating a figurine. After all, a chief advantage for a competitor would be its ability to undercut a famous rival in price. The more projecting parts there are on a figure and the more separate models it requires for its creation, the higher the cost of production and the greater the likelihood of breakage in the manufacturing process. For these reasons, Lladró competitors banking on a price advantage in the marketplace cannot hope to imitate the way that a Lladró occupies space, with its limbs and digits often projecting at risky and rakish angles.

Figures 1 and 2 on this page contrast two versions of a figurine treating an identical theme; the one on the right is a Lladró and the one on the left is one of Lladró's more competent competitors. These figures will be used in the sections that follow to illustrate factors that make Lladró distinctive. In making the comparisons, I have deliberately chosen a competitor figurine that is not bad on its own terms because I do not wish to gild the lily by contrasting Lladró with some of the worst work of its competitors.

In the Lladró model on the right of Figure 1, it would have been less risky for the manufacturing process had Lladró simply molded the girl's hair to the side of her head. There's no question, however, that those little jutting side ponytails make it a much more interesting figure—as does the gratuitous addition of the anxious, separately molded mother cat at her feet.

The other figurine, by contrast, appears conservatively tucked in on itself. Comparatively few separate molds would have been required to produce it. It takes no risks, either aesthetically or technically.

Faces Will Tell

There may be no other aspect of a Lladró figurine that is more definitive than its facial detailing. Lladró considers facial features to be such a signature aspect of its work that it reportedly has factory artisans whose sole job is face painting.[5]

Competitors of Lladró nearly all make the mistake of using jet-black paint to model eye features such as eyebrows and lids. Lladró never uses jet black in this manner; it uses pale browns, tans, or grays, very thinly drawn, which manage to suggest the presence of delicate facial hair without calling undue attention to it. The presence of thickly applied eye paint that coarsens the facial features is a dead giveaway that a figure, even though it be made in Spain, is not a Lladró.

Figure 1: Two models treating the same theme, one a Lladró and one a competitor. Left to right: competitor figurine from another Spanish company and Lladró's "Don't Forget Me!" (#5743G), first issued in 1991 and currently retailing at $160. The Lladró is distinguished by the technical risks it takes with individually molded parts and by the realistic draping of the girl's clothing. (Photo by William B. Bradley, Jr., from the author's own collection.)

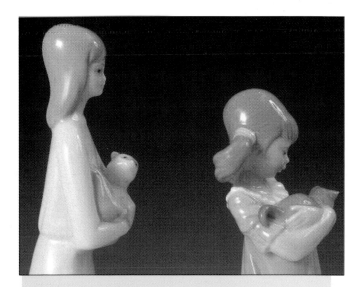

Figure 2: Detail of the Figure 1 items in profile. The facial features are carefully articulated on the Lladró; the competitor profile looks flat in comparison. (Photo by William B. Bradley, Jr., from the author's own collection.)

On animal figurines, the telltale characteristic will often be the muzzle. While very little is required by way of paint to create the illusion of whiskers on an animal's muzzle, Lladró competitors will often apply large spots of paint that manage to shout "WHISKERS!" rather than to suggest their presence. The mouth on a non-Lladró animal will often also be applied in a way that is more caricatured than realistic.

Figure 2 on page 101 shows the same Lladró and competitor figures from Figure 1, this time in profile. In the Lladró profile on the right of the photo, it can be seen that the little girl's cheeks, chin, nose, lips, and eye orbits are each and all well articulated. The facial profile of the other figure looks flat by comparison.

Close-up of facial detailing in the unmarked figure from the Mark Hayes collection that was pictured in Chapter 1. Faces usually tell, and this is arguably an unmarked Lladró. (Photo by William B. Bradley, Jr.)

Another example of Lladró's meticulous attention to detail is how it drapes garments on a human body. Referring to Figure 1 again, let's agree to put aside the superficial differences of color and style of nightdress. Note instead the many folds in the garment on the little Lladró figure, in which porcelain seems to suggest real cloth. Compare that to the relative absence of draping detail in the clothing on the other figure.

Once a collector masters these details of Lladró identification, that collector will never again too readily allege that such and such a company makes figurines that are "like Lladró." Again, the possible exception will be Nadal figurines, but these are usually quite distinctive in their own right (e.g. Nadal's combination glaze). They are also clearly marked with Nadal's own product stamp, which consists of the name in large block letters accompanied by a crown logo that would not be mistaken for Lladró's stamp.

Figures with "Made in Spain" Marks and No Company Name

Every once in awhile, a figure will appear on the secondary market with an impressed mark or blue backstamp that simply says "Made in Spain" with no company name. I have seen several of these items, and, in general, they much more closely resemble Lladró than do the products of most name competitors or the products of counterfeiters. Figure 3 (shown below) depicts one of these models, a dog group that could be either Irish wolfhounds or long-coated greyhounds. I purchased the figure in a local antique store after looking at it for weeks, unable to make up my mind whether it was an unmarked Lladró or not. (As previously noted, locating a genuine unmarked Lladró outside Spain is about as likely as winning the lottery!)

Figure 3: Dog Grouping, marked simply "Made in Spain," no company attribution. Very often, such unattributed pieces are among the closest things to Lladró that aren't; it is possible this one is the work of former Lladró artisans or artisans in training. (Photo by William B. Bradley, Jr.)

While the quality of these items marked simply "Made in Spain" is often surprisingly good, there will usually be something a little "off" about them—as if they'd been arrested in the process of full evolution into a Lladró. In this case, the faces of the dog figures are exquisitely drawn and detailed—right down to the teeth and tongues—but the modeling of curls in the body is somewhat coarsely rendered, and the porcelain has a hollow, metallic ring to it. Still, this and other Made in Spain/no-name figurines have enough affinity with Lladró that I suspect that at least some of them may be the work either of former Lladró artisans or of artisans in training at the Lladró workshop in Tavernes Blanques.

Counterfeits

As mentioned in Chapter 1, unscrupulous people have counterfeited the Lladró mark as a means of passing off shoddy goods on unsuspecting collectors and secondary market dealers. Fortunately, there are not many of these bogus marks out there because the real company is extraordinarily vigilant in prosecuting violators of its trademark and copyright. According to a notice on its Web site in July 2000, the company had just destroyed 5,000 pirated copies of twelve (12) of its designs. The copies were discovered at a warehouse in Spain but were traced back to a factory in China, against which Lladró has initiated legal proceedings. In 1994, Lladró also found and destroyed a cache of 3,000 pirated copies.

The numbers here may appear small, but when we consider that even if the average sale price of these items were only around $200 apiece, 5,000 copies would yield about a million dollars! Lladró did not specify which of its twelve designs were counterfeited in the most recent instance, but it is likely that forgers would leverage their risk by targeting the most popular and expensive items—i.e., those with the greatest return.

The circulation of at least some counterfeits means it is important to "know your Lladró" in style and quality as well as in mark. Paying attention to the distinguishing features of Lladró's work as described in this chapter should help insulate the collector against fraud. As in other pottery and porcelain fields affected by fakes and forgeries, it will usually be obvious upon close inspection that the piece "isn't right." In general, fakes are heavier, coarser, and not as well painted as the genuine articles.

The mark itself will usually be part of what's not right in a counterfeit Lladró; it may be made deliberately illegible or may have a fake logo. Careful inspection will usually "out" these irregularities. (It should also be said, however, that the Lladró logo itself doesn't always fire well in the kiln; sometimes it will come out "dangling" and only half there. Still, there will usually be enough of it present for an experienced collector to be able to confirm it as authentic.)

Side-by-side photos of the legitimate Lladró mark (L) and of the fake mark (R) from the counterfeit mermaid. Several features in the counterfeit stamp are "not right," including the color, that flourish on the o in Lladró where the trademark sign should be, and the blurred and almost illegible quality of the print. (Photo by William B. Bradley, Jr.)

Mermaids and clowns are among the most sought-after genuine Lladrós on the secondary market, so it is not surprising that scammers target them for "reproduction." Figure 4 shows a broken "Mermaid" figure marked with a counterfeit Lladró mark. The backstamp is black instead of the blue it is supposed to be, and the letters are blurred. There is an odd loop or flourish on the final o of the name, about where the trademark sign, missing in this fake, would appear in the real thing. All in all, the mark looks as if it were made from a poor photocopy of the real mark, but it is probably still plenty convincing enough to fool an amateur buyer.

Figure 4: A counterfeit mermaid. Without even looking at the mark, an experienced collector will note the sloppy paint job as well as the flesh-colored porcelain in the breaks. (Lladró uses white porcelain slip.) (Photo by William B. Bradley, Jr., courtesy of Janet Gale Hammer.)

"Dangling" mark. Every so often, a Lladró piece will come through production with the mark not fully stamped, which in no way impugns the authenticity of the piece. (Photo by William B. Bradley, Jr.)

103

It is a shame that we don't have the head to Figure 4, because I'm sure the quality of the face would also reveal the figure's bogus origins. Even without that clue, the damage to this figure reveals another telltale sign of a fake. With the exception of small decorative accents such as flowers, the earth-colored porcelain in Gres, and the colored porcelains used in the Goyesca series, Lladró uses white porcelain slip to form its models; the porcelain is then painted and fired. Therefore, breakage on a genuine Lladró will show white porcelain at the break. This fake shows that the flesh color has actually been integrated into the porcelain itself. Since flesh colors are difficult to paint, it is to a counterfeiter's advantage to integrate that particular color into the porcelain, thereby achieving an acceptable consistency; porcelain forgers are notoriously poor painters.

In this instance, a bad paint job is still evident. The coloring on the rock, including the painted-in foliage, is especially badly done, and the nipples on the mermaid's breasts consist of two amateur pink-painted dots. On the other hand, the scaling on the mermaid's lower body is surprisingly good; it appears to have been painted under glaze, while the foliage and the white on the tip of the mermaid's tail look as if they had been overpainted as an afterthought.

The real "Pearl Mermaid" (#1348G), issued in 1978 and retired in 1983 at a last retail price of $245. Its secondary market price of $1850-$1950 accounts for why this model would be attractive to counterfeiters. (Photo courtesy of Lladró USA, Inc.)

You would not find this particular model in the official Lladró books, and if company sources are often frustrating because they have not succeeded in cataloguing all the genuine pieces ever found by avid collectors, they also help protect amateurs against forgeries by raising the antenna of suspicion on items not pictured there. The closest genuine item to this counterfeit is a 1983 retirement called "Pearl Mermaid"

(#1348), which may be the most famous mermaid figure Lladró ever created. She fetched $2000 at one of the Lladró-only auctions and is offered at almost that price on the secondary market today. It is, therefore, not surprising that counterfeiters should try to capitalize on a similarity, however vague, to this piece.

Once again, if an item found on the secondary market is not in the company books, that doesn't necessarily mean it's not a genuine Lladró; nevertheless, if it isn't in the book, you should approach it with a healthy skepticism until you have verified its authenticity to your own satisfaction. Look the uncatalogued item over carefully, read it for telltale signs of authenticity or of forgery, and then trust your instincts; if it doesn't look "right," it probably isn't!

Notes for Chapter 4

[1] The best use made of these company guides is for figurine identification. Data inaccuracies can be found in caption information in all editions, and collectors are particularly cautioned not to take pricing data as definitive without verifying it with other reliable sources.

[2] In my experience, some of the more novice staff at Lladró USA are too readily inclined to dismiss as fakes any figurines that can't already be found in a published Lladró picture guide. While most of the vast work of cataloguing the core collection has been accomplished, a definitive cataloguing of every single item Lladró ever produced has not yet been achieved. Dr. Philip Reines ("The 2130 Brown Egyptian Cat; the Search for Authenticity—Successful at Last," *A Work of Art* 6:1 [Winter 1994/95]: 3-10) gives a fascinating account of his own nine year quest to have Lladró verify the authenticity of a very rare brown version of the Gres #2130 "Black Egyptian Cat" (also made in a white porcelain version, #5154). By dint of persistence, he was finally able to find staff at Lladró USA willing to link him with someone at the factory in Valencia, who was in turn able to confirm, in writing, that about forty (40) copies of the highly desired "Egyptian Cat" had been made in brown and that he was lucky enough to be the owner of one of them!

[3] Liane McAllister, "Valencia: Spanish Ceramics Show Growing Pains And Pluses," *Gifts and Decorative Accessories* 97:1 (January 1997).

[4] *Lladró; The Magic World of Porcelain* (Barcelona, Spain: Salvat Editores, SA, 1989): 24.

[5] "Brushing Up on Lladró," *Expressions* 3:2 (Summer 1987):16.

An Exhibit of Core Collection Figurines

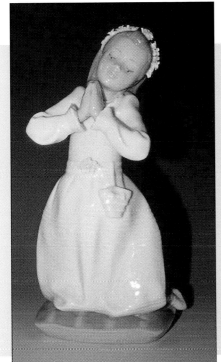

"Communion Prayer, Girl" (#6089G), issued in 1994, sculpted by J. Coderch. She is still active at a hefty retail of $225, a price accounted for not only by the flowerwork in the girl's hair and at her waistband, but also by the exquisite embossed decoration all over her dress and on the pillow on which she kneels. Note the tiny purse on her waistband! (Photo by the author, from her personal collection.)

"Skye Terrier" (#4643G) done by the great Lladró sculptor Salvador Furió. Issued in 1969 and retired in 1985, this little guy is pretty famous and much in demand. Value today: $400-$500. (Photo by the author, courtesy of John Sobr and The Vermont Antique Mall at Quechee Gorge, VT.)

"Rabbit's Food" (#4826G/M), issued 1972 and retired in 1993. Value range: $250-$300. The code on the base is F-22 JU. That tells me she was fired on the 22nd of July. But in what year? (Photo by William B. Bradley, Jr., from the author's own collection.)

"Girl with Umbrella and Ducks" (#4510G/M), a classical example of the early, elongated style of sculptor Fulgencio García (her feet are enormously long!). Issued in the mid- to late 1960s, it was retired in 1993 at a last retail of $245. Today, she is worth $300-$350. (Photo by the author, from her personal collection.)

105

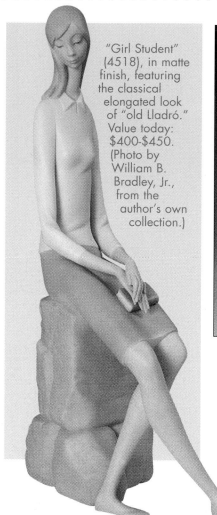

"Girl Student" (4518), in matte finish, featuring the classical elongated look of "old Lladró." Value today: $400-$450. (Photo by William B. Bradley, Jr., from the author's own collection.)

Four from the famous "Kids in Nightshirts" series. Left to right: "Girl Stretching" (#4872G, retired in 1999 and valued at $100-$125), "Girl Kissing" (#4873G, retired in 1997 and valued at $125-$135), "Boy Awakening" (#4870G, retired in 1999 and valued at $110-$125), and "Girl with Guitar" (#4871M, retired in 1991 and valued at $125-$135 for the matte; glazed version retired 2000 and worth $100-$110). (Photo by William B. Bradley, Jr., from the author's own collection.)

"A Time to Rest" (#5399G/M), issued in 1987 and retired in 1993 (matte in 1991). Note the mile marker. You'd have paid only $175 for him at the time of issue; he'll cost you at least twice that today: $350-$400. (Photo by the author, courtesy of Caren Reed and Reed's Antiques and Collectibles of Wells, ME.)

"Ceremonial Princess" (#6424G) had a very short retail run, from 1997 to 2000. Her retail price at that time was $240. By the time this book is printed, she'll be worth somewhere in the $250-$300 range. (Photo by William B. Bradley, Jr., from the author's own collection.)

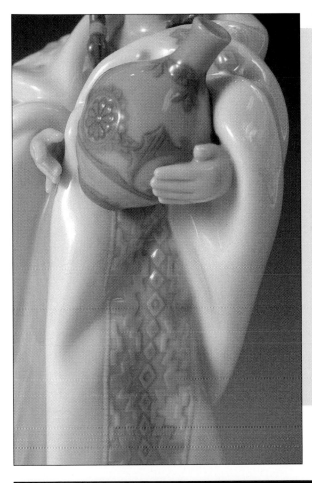

"Ceremonial Princess" showing embossed decorative detail, perhaps the most fetching aspect of this piece. (Photo by William B. Bradley, Jr., from the author's own collection.)

Glazed version of "Girl with Calf" (#4813G/M), issued in 1972 and retired in 1981. Achieved $650 at one of the exclusive Lladró auctions in the early 90s. (From the private collection of Francisca Madden of "La Dulcinea.")

Three of a series of four bunnies, with an issue date of 1992, among the last items from the hands of the great Lladró sculptor Fulgencio García, who died in 1994 at the age of 79. Left to right: "Preening Bunny" (#5906, retired in 1997), "Sitting Bunny" (#5907, retired in 1998), and "Sleeping Bunny" (#5904, retired in 1998). Not pictured: "Attentive Bunny" (#5905, retired in 1998). As the first retired, #5906 commands the highest prices on the secondary market at $95-$110. The others range in price from $90 to $95. They all came with Easter baskets such as that pictured, and huge boxes to accommodate the baskets. Unlike the rabbits, the baskets are of mediocre design and materials, and most collectors haven't bothered keeping them. Later models of the rabbits (#s 6097-6100) have flowerwork pasted all over them. (Photo by William B. Bradley, Jr., from the author's own collection.)

"Shepherd" (#4659G), sculpted by Vicente Martinez, in the classic elongated form that helped make Lladró famous. Issued in the mid- to late 1960s and retired in 1985. Value today: $300-$325. (Photo by William B. Bradley, Jr., from the author's own collection.)

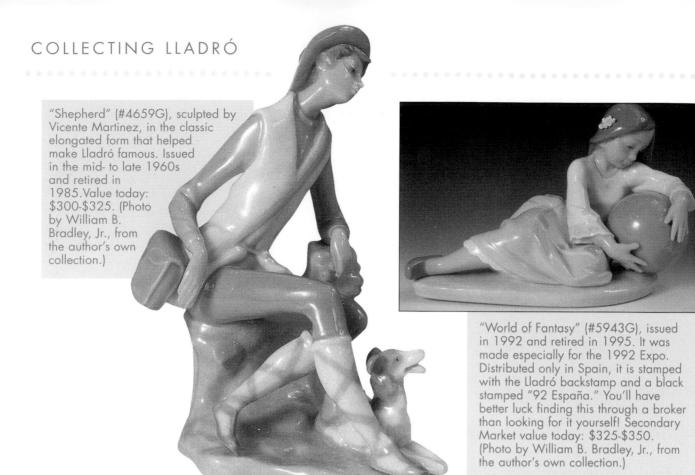

"World of Fantasy" (#5943G), issued in 1992 and retired in 1995. It was made especially for the 1992 Expo. Distributed only in Spain, it is stamped with the Lladró backstamp and a black stamped "92 España." You'll have better luck finding this through a broker than looking for it yourself! Secondary Market value today: $325-$350. (Photo by William B. Bradley, Jr., from the author's own collection.)

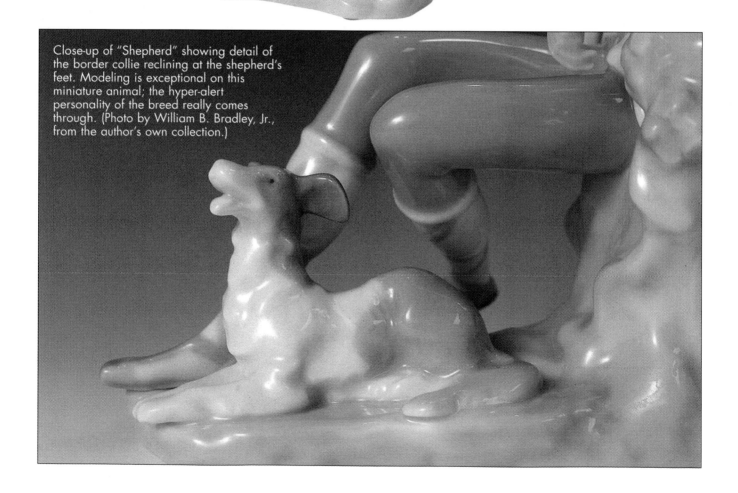

Close-up of "Shepherd" showing detail of the border collie reclining at the shepherd's feet. Modeling is exceptional on this miniature animal; the hyper-alert personality of the breed really comes through. (Photo by William B. Bradley, Jr., from the author's own collection.)

"Little Friends" (#6129G) had an unusually short retail run, from 1994 to 1998. The model itself is plenty appealing, and the cause of early retirement may well have been challenges in damage-free shipment due to the evident delicacy of the piece. Value range: $275-$350. (Photo by William B. Bradley, Jr., from the author's own collection.)

Detail from "Little Friends." (Photo by William B. Bradley, Jr., from the author's own collection.)

"Duck" (#1056G), issued in the mid- to late 1960s and retired in 1978—and long enough off the market we can be assured it really is retired! Sculptor was Julio Fernandez. Value today: $275-$325. Had you bought him at the issue price, you could have had him for a paltry $19 (yes, you read that right: nineteen)! (Photo by the author, from her personal collection.)

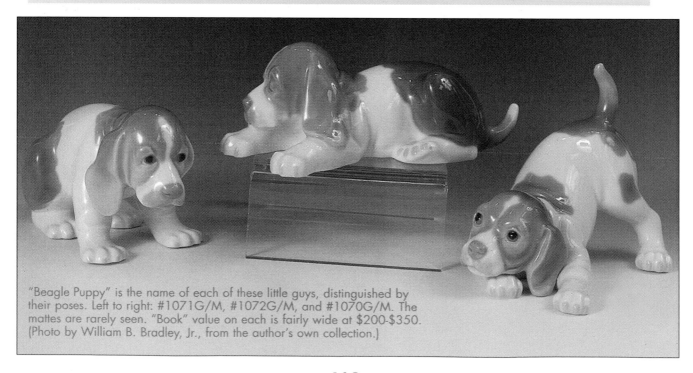

"Beagle Puppy" is the name of each of these little guys, distinguished by their poses. Left to right: #1071G/M, #1072G/M, and #1070G/M. The mattes are rarely seen. "Book" value on each is fairly wide at $200-$350. (Photo by William B. Bradley, Jr., from the author's own collection.)

"Fawn Surprise" with lid on to form exquisitely embossed egg. Displayed open or closed, these "egg surprises" make great Easter decorations! (Photo by William B. Bradley, Jr., from the author's own collection.)

"Fawn Surprise" (#6618G) features an egg whose top lifts to reveal a tiny fawn. Related items feature a "Kitty Surprise" (#280) and a "Puppy Surprise" (#6617G). All were issued in 1999 and retail for $280 apiece, a price determined in part by the flowerwork around the animals. (Photo by William B. Bradley, Jr., from the author's own collection.)

1995 Limited Edition Egg (#7548M, Horses), third in a series of five. Value today: $175-$200. Bas-relief on the rear side is a rustic log cabin. (Photo by William B. Bradley, Jr., from the author's own collection.)

1993 Limited Edition Egg (#6037M, Birds). As the first in a series of five, this egg fetches the biggest bucks. Its value today is in the $240-$300 range. At the $300 level, the piece has a 100% appreciation rate—in just seven years! (Photo by William B. Bradley, Jr., from the author's own collection.)

1994 Limited Edition Egg (#7532M, Swans), second in a series of five. Value today: $200-$250. (Photo by William B. Bradley, Jr., from the author's own collection.)

1996 Limited Edition Egg
(#7550M, Deer), fourth in a series
of five. Value today: $160-$175.
(Photo by William B. Bradley, Jr.,
from the author's own collection.)

1997 Limited Edition Egg (#7552M, Eagles), last in a series of five. Value today: $160-$175. (Photo by William B. Bradley, Jr., from the author's own collection.)

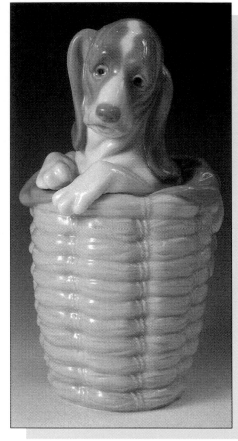

Sculptor Juan Huerta's "Dog in the Basket" (#1128G) features a basset hound ensconced in a laundry basket with a bedspread. Issued in 1971 at a first retail price of just $17.50 and retired in 1985 at a last retail of $92.50, he can fetch $400-$450 on today's secondary market. This one was a gift to me from dear friends, who know my collection is concentrated on animal figurines. It's one of my most treasured possessions. (Photo by William B. Bradley, Jr., from the author's own collection.)

"Sleepy Kitten" (#6567G) was issued in 1999 and retails at $250 despite its diminutive size. The cost is accounted for largely by the flowerwork. When pieces like this begin hitting the secondary market, they are difficult to find with the flowerwork in mint condition. (Photo by the author, from her personal collection.)

"Play with Me" (#5112), first issued in 1982 and just retired in 2000 at a last retail price of $80. Part of a series of cats (including "Feed Me!" #5113, still open at $80, and "Pet Me!" #5114 retired in 1999 at a last retail of $80). These have been among the most affordable items in the Lladró corpus. Ironically, it is just such items that are likely to be bid above their retail price at Internet auction. (Photo by William B. Bradley, Jr., from the author's own collection.)

"Cat and Mouse" (#5236G), first issued in 1984. This popular and diminutive piece retails for a modest $100. (Photo by William B. Bradley, Jr., from the author's own collection.)

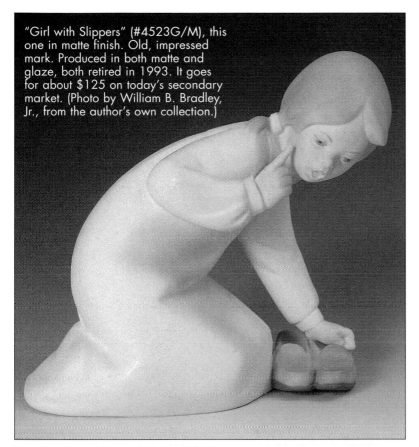

"Girl with Slippers" (#4523G/M), this one in matte finish. Old, impressed mark. Produced in both matte and glaze, both retired in 1993. It goes for about $125 on today's secondary market. (Photo by William B. Bradley, Jr., from the author's own collection.)

"Natural Wonder" (#6308G) had a very short retail run, from 1996 to 1999. Her hefty last retail, at $220 on such a small piece, is probably a function of the sculpted detail in the sarong and that small bit of flowerwork in her hair. (Photo by William B. Bradley, Jr., from the author's own collection.)

"Little Ducks Following Mother" (#1307G), miniature group sculpted by Juan Huerta, first issued in 1974 and currently retailing at $150. (Photo by William B. Bradley, Jr., from the author's own collection.)

"Chinese Angel" (#4536G/M) from Fulgencio García's famous group of child angels. His little bald head has endeared him to millions! All these child angels currently retail at $95. (Photo by William B. Bradley, Jr., from the author's own collection.)

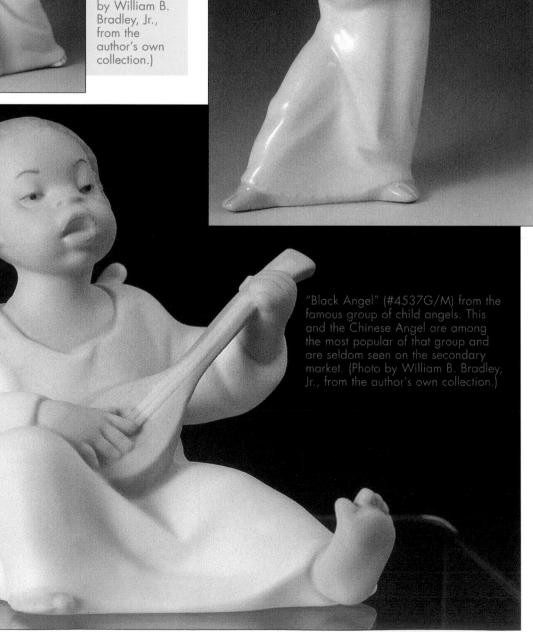

"Angel with Horn" (#4540G/M). The facial expressions on this little guy can vary from example to example, ranging from serene to downright mischievous! (Photo by William B. Bradley, Jr., from the author's own collection.)

"Black Angel" (#4537G/M) from the famous group of child angels. This and the Chinese Angel are among the most popular of that group and are seldom seen on the secondary market. (Photo by William B. Bradley, Jr., from the author's own collection.)

"Angel Praying" (#4538G/M). The most traditional of the group of six child angels. Well, someone has to uphold the standards of angelic decorum! (Photo by William B. Bradley, Jr., from the author's own collection.)

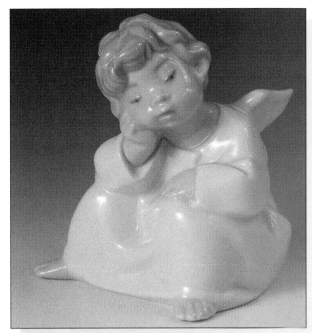

"Angel Thinking" (#4539G/M). Gotta love the chubby cheeks and quasi-sleepy expression on the face of this little guy. On some models, a paint variation features pale green or white paint spots applied evenly as decoration around the collar and hem of the angel's gown. (Photo by William B. Bradley, Jr., from the author's own collection.)

"Reclining Angel" (#4541G/M) from the group of child angels. I found this little guy in matte on the secondary market and was swept away by his nonchalance, his frank boredom with being good. I never cleaned him up. Somehow, the idea of a child angel with a dirty face is appealing! (Photo by William B. Bradley, Jr., from the author's own collection.)

Rear view of "Clean Up Time" shows the realism of a little girl struggling to complete her morning grooming while holding up her pajama bottoms. (Photo by William B. Bradley, Jr., from the author's own collection.)

"Clean Up Time" (#4838G/M), issued in 1973 and retired in 1993 (matte in 1993). Her last retail price was $170, but she would be worth $250-$300 today. Sculptor was Julio Fernandez. (Photo by William B. Bradley, Jr., from the author's own collection.)

"Polar Bear Miniature" (#5434G), a fine example of the work of miniaturist sculptor Antonio Ramos. Issued in 1987 and just retired in 2000 at a retail price of $115. Facial detailing is priceless. By the time this book is printed, the value of this figure will likely be in the range of $125-$150. (Photo by William B. Bradley, Jr., from the author's own collection.)

"Who's the Fairest?" (#5468G), issued in 1988 and retired in 2000 at a last retail of $205. The girl's face is painted in shades so pale that it appears as if the light from her hand mirror were reflecting back into her face. That is the kind of detail that places Lladró head and shoulders above its competition. Also made in a Gres version (#2313) issued in 1995 and retired in 1998 at a last retail of $230. (Photo by the author, from her personal collection.)

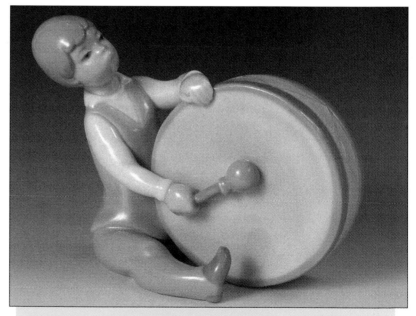

"Girl with Lamb" (#4584G/M) in the classic, elongated style. The sculptor is Alfredo Ruiz. Retired in 1993 (matte in 1991) at a last retail price of $170, she hasn't been particularly popular on the secondary market, where she often has trouble breaking through the $200 barrier. (Photo by the author, from her personal collection.)

"Boy with Drum" (#4616G), issued in the mid- to late 1960s and retired in 1979. This odd little guy with the strange body proportions was sculpted by Juan Huerta as part of a series of several child musicians. His value today is $350-$400, although he has achieved auction prices as high as $625. (Photo by William B. Bradley, Jr., from the author's own collection.)

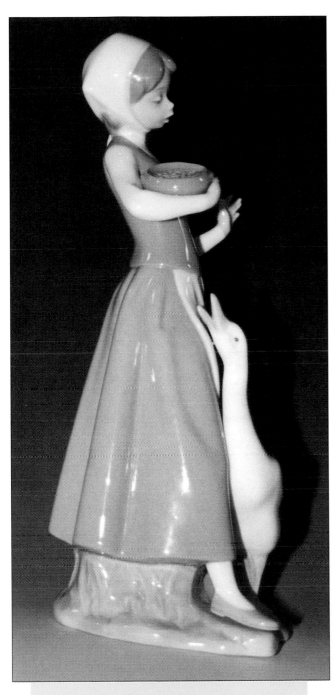

"Girl with Duck" (#1052G/M), more precisely translated from the Spanish as "Corn for the Goose." This particular example glazed. Issued in the mid- to late 1960s and retired as late as 1998 at a retail price of $210. Value today: $225-$235. (Photo by the author, from her personal collection.)

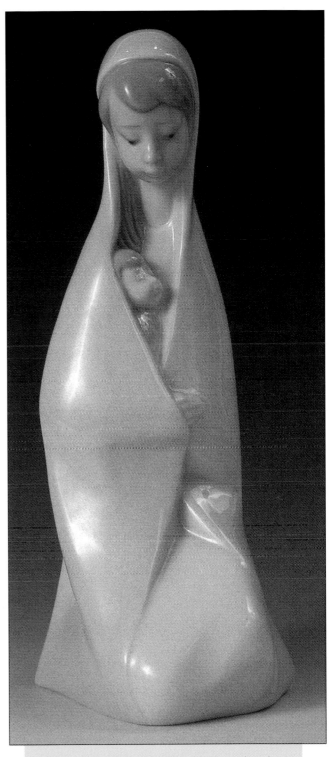

"Girl with Child" (#4636G/M) issued in the mid- to late 1960s and retired in 1979 at a last retail price of only $38.50. Even this relatively small, uncomplicated figure can achieve $275-$300 on today's secondary market. (Photo by William B. Bradley, Jr., from the author's own collection.)

"Good Bear" (#1205G) in brown, issued in 1972 and retired in 1989. Value today: $125-$135. This bear is part of a series of three (#1204-1206G) made from the same molds as the white polar bears (#1207-1209G). (Photo by the author, courtesy of June Seligman and The Vermont Antique Mall at Quechee Gorge in VT).

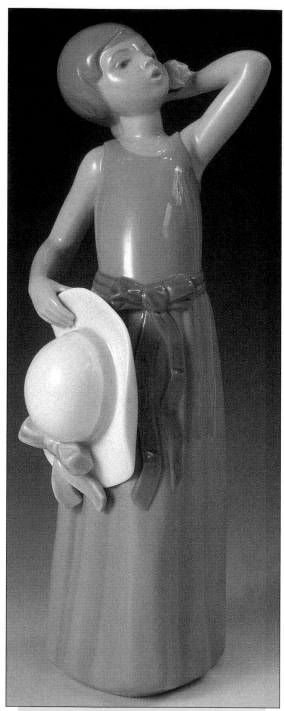

It is not unusual for Lladró to take interesting configurations of smaller elements from a grouping and spin them off as separate figurines. Left: "Duck Seller" (#1267G), issued in 1974 and retired in 1993. Value today: $275-$350. Right: "Ducklings" (#4895G), issued in 1974 and still retailing at $95. (Photo by William B. Bradley, Jr., from the author's own collection.)

"Prissy" (#5010G), arguably the most appealing of a series of girls in vividly-colored sleeveless dresses, each holding a broad-brimmed hat (#s 5006-5011G), sculpted by Francisco Catalá. Issued in 1978 and retired in 1997, "Prissy" fetches $250-$300 on the secondary market, while the range on the others, the last of which was retired in 1999, is $175-$200. (Photo by William B. Bradley, Jr., from the author's own collection.)

Facial detail in "Circus Sam." It takes real artists to make a personality shine through the clown makeup! (Photo by William B. Bradley, Jr., from the author's own collection.)

"Circus Sam" (#5472G), one of Lladró's ever-popular clown figures. Issued in 1988, he and his companion piece "Sad Sax" (#5471G) each retail for $205. (Photo by William B. Bradley, Jr., from the author's own collection.)

"Basset" (#1066G), issued in the mid- to late 1960s and retired in 1981. Value today is $550-$600; you'd have paid only $23.50 for him at issue time! The separately modeled tail and ears are an example of what makes Lladró great. (Photo by the author, courtesy of Phoebe Siemer and Champlain Valley Antique Center in South Burlington, VT.)

"Boy with Smoking Jacket" (#4900G/M), this one glazed. Issued in 1974 and retired in 1983, the boy appears to be standing in front of a humidor. Value today: $200-$300. (Photo by the author, courtesy of June Seligman and The Vermont Antique Mall at Quechee Gorge, VT.)

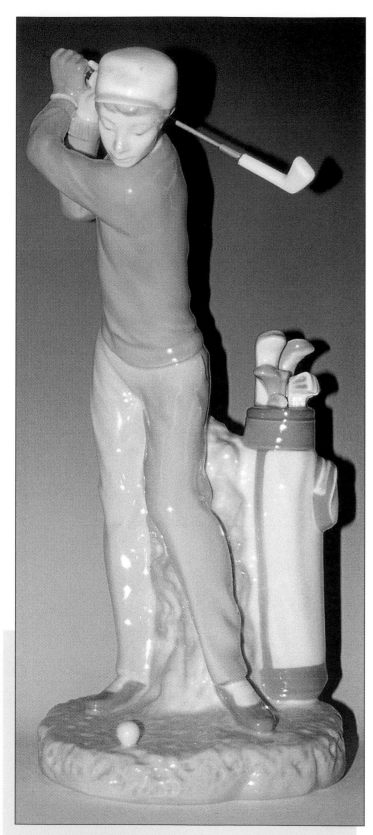

"Golfer" (#4824G), first issued in 1972 and retailing currently at $295. (Photo by the author, courtesy of Joe Uccello and Reed's Antiques and Collectibles of Wells, ME.)

"Medieval Soldier" (#6111G), issued in 1994 and retired in 1996. Part of a series of children in medieval costume (#s 6111-6115G). Value of the soldier today: $275-$300. (Photo by the author, courtesy of Frederica Edelman and Kennedy Brothers, Inc. in Vergennes, VT.)

"From This Day Forward" (#5887G), currently active, first issued in 1992 and retailing at $285. At 7-3/4" tall, it is small enough to be used as a wedding cake topper. (Photo by the author, courtesy of Stanley and Ethel Cortis and The Vermont Antique Mall at Quechee Gorge, VT.)

"Donkey in Love" AKA "Donkey with Daisy" (#4524G/M), an unusual excursion into caricature for sculptor Fulgencio García. The anecdotal secret of this piece is that each of the petals of the daisy is marked "Sí" or "No" as the animal plays a game of "She Loves Me, She Loves Me Not." The first petal plucked is adhered to the bottom of the donkey's hoof, and, because he started with "No," whichever way he goes around the circumference of the six-petal flower, he's bound to end up at "Sí." Smart donkey! (Photo by William B. Bradley, Jr., from the author's own collection.)

"Medieval Princess" (#6114G) from the series of children in medieval costume, several of whom are astride these odd little toy horses. Value today: $275-$300. (Photo by the author, courtesy of Frederica Edelman and Kennedy Brothers, Inc. of Vergennes, VT.)

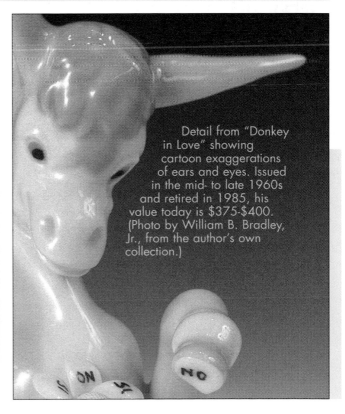

Detail from "Donkey in Love" showing cartoon exaggerations of ears and eyes. Issued in the mid- to late 1960s and retired in 1985, his value today is $375-$400. (Photo by William B. Bradley, Jr., from the author's own collection.)

A family of Lladró penguins, each called—you guessed it—"Penguin." Left to right: #5248G (5" high), #5249G (6" high), and #5247G (6.5" high). These are difficult to distinguish by anything other than relative height; after all, there are only so many ways a standing penguin can be posed! Issued in 1984 and retired in 1987-1988, these are valued at $200-$250 apiece. (Photo by William B. Bradley, Jr., from the author's own collection.)

Fulgencio García's "Ducks Group" (#4549G/M), issued in the mid- to late 1960s and retired in 1996. The anecdotal secret of the piece is a tiny snail on one of the rushes; ducks consider snails a great delicacy. Value today: $255-$275. The group is here arranged with the individual ducks spun off from it, once sold individually as #s 4551-4553G/M, but more recently sold as a set (#7909G) at a current retail of $144. (Photo by William B. Bradley, Jr., from the author's own collection.)

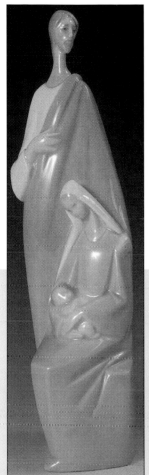

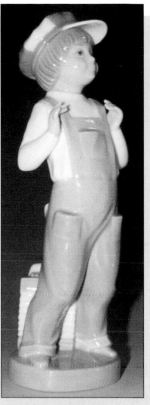

"Holy Family" (#4585G/M), issued in mid- to late 1960s and still retailing today at a modest $135. A small but elongated figure in the classic style of "old Lladró," which frequently included not just elongated torsos and limbs, but heads disproportionately small, giving the figures a delicate, ethereal quality. (Photo by William B. Bradley, Jr., from the author's own collection.)

Left to right, "Washing Up" (#5887G) and "Hippity Hop" (#5886G), part of a series of four rabbit figures that work as year-round décor but are also great as Easter accents. Not pictured: "That Tickles" (#5888C, featuring bunny on back looking at butterfly perched on rear foot) and "Snack Time" (#5889G, rabbit on hind legs holding carrot in front paws). Like many of the Lladró animal figures, these had a short retail run from 1992 to 1995. Value today: $125-$150 apiece. (Photo by William B. Bradley, Jr., from the author's own collection.)

"Boy from Madrid" (#4898G/M), this example glazed. Issued in 1974, the matte was retired in 1991 and the glazed in 1997. Value today: $175-$200. (Photo by the author, from her own collection.)

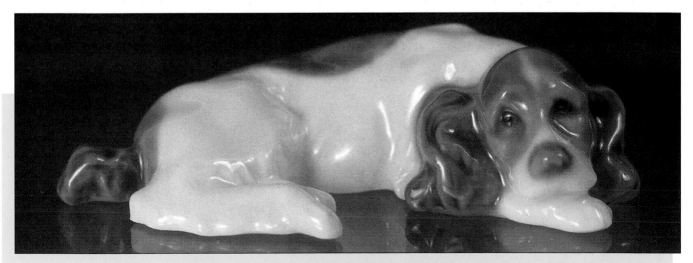

"Miniature Cocker Spaniel" (#5310G) was issued in 1985 and retired in 1993. Secondary market value: $125-$150. Another figure of the same name but with different markings and coloring is numbered 5309, issued and retired on the same dates, also valued at $125-$150. (Photo by William B. Bradley, Jr., from the author's own collection.)

"Kitty Confrontation" (#1442G), first issued in 1983 and still open at a retail price of $285. The price on this small grouping is in part a function of the exquisite flowerwork, but even if you took that away, you'd still have an irresistible piece! (Photo by William B. Bradley, Jr., from the author's own collection.)

Detail from "Kitty Confrontation" showing the showdown between kitten and frog. (Photo by William B. Bradley, Jr., from the author's own collection.)

"Girl with Milk Pail" (#4682G/M), this one in matte, sculpted by Vicente Martinez, is almost alive with anecdotal elements, from the two-legged stool propped on a tree stump to the duck copping a drink while the exasperated farm girl with arms akimbo looks on. Issued in 1971, it was retired in 1991 at a last retail price of $175. Value today: $275-$350. (Photo by the author, from her personal collection.)

"Male Siamese Dancer" (#5592G), issued in 1989 and retired in 1993. Value today: $525-$575. A companion piece (#5593G) features a female dancer, issued and retired the same years. Her value today: $450-$550. You don't have to be a company groupie to love a work like this. (Photo by the author, courtesy of Phoebe Siemer and Champlain Valley Antique Center, South Burlington, VT.)

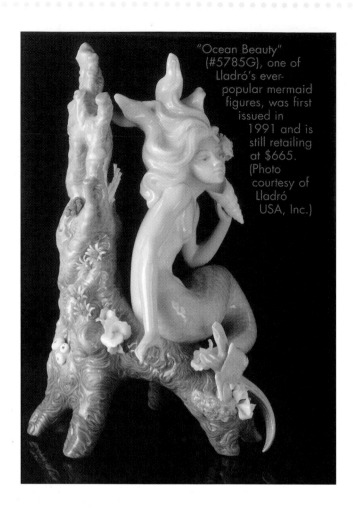

"Ocean Beauty" (#5785G), one of Lladró's ever-popular mermaid figures, was first issued in 1991 and is still retailing at $665. (Photo courtesy of Lladró USA, Inc.)

If Lladró has a "signature piece," it would have to be Salvador Furió's "Don Quixote" (#1030G/M), first issued in the mid- to late 1960s and so popular the glazed version is still retailing at $1450. The matte version, retired in 1991, would be worth slightly more, at around $1500-$1550. (Photo courtesy of Lladró USA, Inc.)

"Illusion" (#1413G) one of Lladró's enormously popular mermaid figurines, is still available on the retail market at $260. First issued in 1982. (Photo courtesy of Lladró USA, Inc.)

"Mirage" (#1415), last in a popular series of three Lladró mermaids issued in 1982 and currently retailing at $260. (Photo courtesy of Lladró USA, Inc.)

"Fantasy" (#1414G), second in a series of three popular mermaid models first issued in 1982, each of which still retails at $260. (Photo courtesy of Lladró USA, Inc.)

"Boy Meets Girl" (#1188G), issued in 1972 and retired in 1989. Value today: $400-$450. A young boy looks over the shoulder of a little girl so shy she is twisting her apron; he watches raptly as if he were trying to interpret the gesture. Where did such innocence go? (Photo by William B. Bradley, Jr., from the author's own collection.)

"Polar Bear Family" AKA "Bearly Love" (#1443G), issued in 1983 and retired in 1999, features a curious baby polar bear exploring the water in a hole in the ice while his equally curious but anxious parents look on. Value today: $165-$185. (Photo by William B. Bradley, Jr., from the author's own collection.)

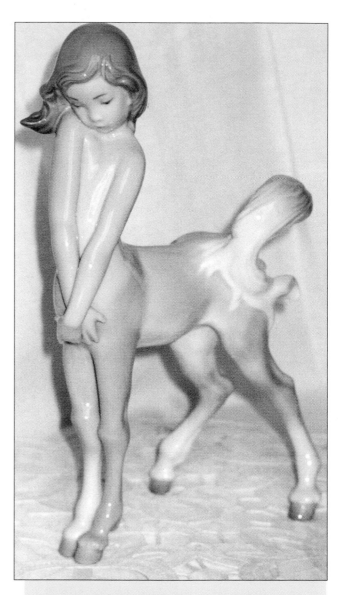

"Centaur Girl" (#1012G/M), along with its not-pictured companion piece "Centaur Boy" (#1011G/M, featuring a yawning young male centaur sitting back on his haunches with arms stretched), is one of the most famous older Lladrós . Value today for each of these two: $400-$450. (Photo courtesy of Francisca Madden of "La Dulcinea.")

"Daisy" AKA "Girl in Green Dress with Flowers" (#5118G), issued in 1982 and retired in 1985 at a last retail of $170. Sculpted by J. Puche, the "puffy" skirt form contrasts markedly with the thin, elongated form most commonly associated with Lladró. Puche did a series of four of these girls in big skirts (#s 5118-5121G), each of which have a secondary market value today of $600-$650. (Photo by the author, from her private collection.)

"Shepherdess with Goats" (#1001G/M) bears the first non-decimal serial number in the Lladró collection, but she is not necessarily older than the lowest numbers of the 4000 series, which were originally three-digit numbers under 1000. She was on the active market from the late 1960s through 1987. The secondary market price range is volatile at $550-$675 for the glazed version and $450-$750 for the matte. (Photo courtesy of Lladró USA, Inc.)

"Giraffe Group" (1005G) is small in scale, given its subject, topping out at a little over 6". This item is scarcely seen on the secondary market; it was only out for a year, from 1969 to 1970. It is not surprising, then, that it can command prices from $1700 to $1775. (Photo courtesy of Lladró USA, Inc.)

"Old Folks" (#1033G/M) was issued in the mid- to late 1960s and retired in 1985, one of those "banner years" in which many models were retired that would later become very significant on the secondary market. Secondary market price range for this item: $1100-$1475. (Photo courtesy of Lladró USA, Inc.)

"Boy with Book" (#1024G/M) is another example of the elongated style of older Lladró. Issued in 1969, he was retired in 1971. While you could have bought him then for a measly $47.50, you'd have to pay $500-$725 to get him today. (Photo courtesy of Lladró USA, Inc.)

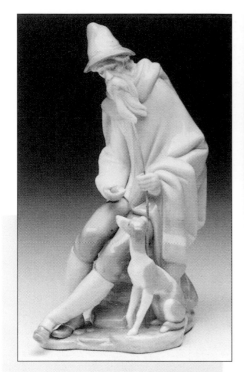

One of the most poignant models in the Lladró corpus, "Beggar" (#1094G/M) shares his bread with his dog. Issued in the late 1960s and retired in 1981 at a last retail price of $95. The secondary market demands princely sums of $650-$675 for him today, but even at that, he's a bargain. (Photo courtesy of Lladró USA, Inc.)

These 18" tall "Hunters" (#1048G/M), first issued in the late 1960s and retired in 1985, have become a Lladró classic. You could have bought these guys for $460 back in the mid-1980s, but they'll cost you dearly now, at a secondary market price range from $1400 to $1600. (Photo courtesy of Lladró USA, Inc.)

"Dog Playing Guitar" (#1152G) is part of a series of cartoon figures in a "hound dog band," each of which is almost grotesquely exaggerated. Issued in 1971 and retired in 1978, all these dog band pieces are famous among Lladró collectors and go for $550-$700 apiece on today's secondary market. (Photo courtesy of Lladró USA, Inc.)

"Girl with Hens" (#1103G/M), one of several Lladró models in traditional Dutch costume, first issued in 1971 and retired in 1981. Secondary market prices range from $375-$450. (Photo courtesy of Lladró USA, Inc.)

"Little Green-Grocer" (#1087G), issued in the late 1960s and retired in 1981 at a last retail price of a paltry $135. Prices on her today are in the $375 to $450 price range. (Photo courtesy of Lladró USA, Inc.)

"Friendship" (#1230G/M) is a classic treatment of youthful affection. First issued in 1972, it was on the retail market until 1991. Today, it can cost $450-$500 on the secondary market. (Photo courtesy of Lladró USA, Inc.)

"Flying Duck" (#1264G) issued in 1974 and retired in 1998. The modeling on the entire series of three ducks of which this is a part (#1263-1265) is extraordinary, from the webbing on the feet to the pinning on the feathers. Value: $110-$125. (Photo by William B. Bradley, Jr., from the author's own collection.)

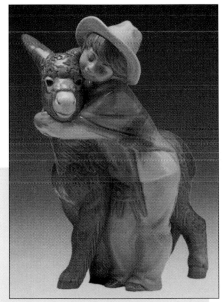

"Platero and Marcellino" (#1181G), issued in 1971 and retired in 1989, goes for $350-$450 on today's secondary market. The title is an allusion to a poem by Ramón Jiménez entitled "Platero y Yo [Platero and I]" about a little boy and his donkey, Platero. (Photo courtesy of Lladró USA, Inc.)

The elaborate open-issue "Lady at Dressing Table" (#1242G) was released in 1973 and retired in 1978. Should have bought her then, when you could have had her for $650 (even though it was a lot of money, especially back in the 1970s!) because she'll cost you $3250-$3650 today. (Photo courtesy of Lladró USA, Inc.)

"The Race" (#1249G), issued in 1974 and retired in 1988 could as well have been called "Rider in Trouble." On the retail market from 1974 to 1988, its last retail price was $1210. The elaborate nature of the grouping and its multiple elements account for its secondary market price of $2200-$2300 today. The sculptor for "The Race" was Julio Fernandez. The agitated geese appear to have been spun off as separate "ducks" for the series numbered 1263 to 1265 (two of which are also pictured here); these were issued the same year as #1249 but kept open another ten years longer. (Photo courtesy of Lladró USA, Inc.)

135

"Duck Jumping" (#1265), issued 1974 and retired 1998. Value: $110-$125. (Photo by the author, from her own collection.)

"Bird on Cactus" (#1303G) issued 1974, retired in 1983 at a last retail price of $350, trades on the secondary market for $800-$900. (Photo courtesy of Lladró USA, Inc.)

"Wrath of Don Quixote" (#1343G) is one of Lladró's most unforgettable creations, featuring the famous scene of the legendary idealist doing battle with the wineskin. First issued in 1977, it retired in 1990 at a last retail price of $490. Its secondary market value is $875-$1000. (Photo courtesy of Lladró USA, Inc.)

"Valencian Girl with Flowers" (#1304G) was first issued in 1974 and is still active on the retail market at $625. (Photo courtesy of Lladró USA, Inc.)

"Sad Chimney Sweep" (#1253G) is one of Lladró's most poignant models. Issued in 1974 and retired in 1983, this tall (17") model commands $1200-$1300 on today's secondary market. (Photo courtesy of Lladró USA, Inc.)

"Herons" (#1319G) is an extraordinarily graceful grouping first issued in 1976 and still retailing at $2625. (Its issue price in 1976 was $1500.) (Photo courtesy of Lladró USA, Inc.)

"The Astronomy Lesson" (#1355G) was available for two years, 1978 to 1979. Its last retail price was $575— a lot of bucks back in the late 1970s. Should you be able to find this on the secondary market, expect to pay four digit prices; I don't know anyone presently offering it for sale. (Photo courtesy of Lladró USA, Inc.)

One of the famous sculptor Salvador Furió's lesser-known models, "Chestnut Seller" (#1373G) is very hard to find, in part because she was only out for four years on the retail market (1978 to 1981). Last retail price on this early retiree was already $1,000. Secondary market prices since then have been under last retail at $750-$950; this undervaluing may be a function of limited collector familiarity with the piece. (Photo courtesy of Lladró USA, Inc.)

"Cathy and Her Doll" (#1380G) was issued in 1978 and retired in 1985. (It was one of three studies of girls in this pose, including also "Suzy and Her Doll" [#1378] and "Debbie and Her Doll" [#1379].) Lladró auction prices for this item ranged from $775 to $950, but the going secondary market price today is a little under that at $650-$750. (Photo courtesy of Lladró USA, Inc.)

"In the Gondola" (#1350G), a spectacular open issue retailing at the spectacular price of $3250. First issued in 1978. (Photo courtesy of Lladró USA, Inc.)

The last retail price on "Spring Birds" (#1368G) was $2500. Issued in 1978 and retired in 1990, this grouping runs $2500-$3000 on the secondary market—little to no appreciation over its steep retail price. The extraordinary flowerwork accounts for much of that price. (Photo courtesy of Lladró USA, Inc.)

"Reverie" (#1398G), one of a series of four studies sculpted by Salvador Debón that included #1395, also pictured here. (Photo courtesy of Lladró USA, Inc.)

Salvador Debon's "Full of Mischief" (#1395G) was one of four studies he did (#1395-1398) of little girls in traditional Valencian costume seated on an elaborate chair. All were issued in 1982 and retired in 1997. Secondary market trends on these are in the $900 to $1100 range. (Photo courtesy of Lladró USA, Inc.)

"Mariko" (#1421G) is one of several figures of women in traditional Japanese dress produced by Lladró sculptor Salvador Debón. Issued in 1992 and retired in 1995, her last retail price was $1575. She may cost you upwards of $2000 today. (Photo courtesy of Lladró USA, Inc.)

"Valencian Children" (#1489G) was first issued in 1986 and is still retailing at $1225—considerably above its first retail price of $700. Note the decorative trappings on the pony; such detail is part of what makes Lladró great. (Photo courtesy of Lladró USA, Inc.)

"Springtime in Japan" (#1445G), one of Salvador Debón's more elaborate groupings of Japanese women in traditional costume, was first issued in 1983 and is still retailing at $1800. (Photo courtesy of Lladró USA, Inc.)

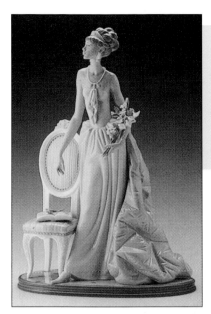

"A Lady of Taste" (#1495G) is one of Lladró's ever popular elegant ladies. If you bought her at the issue price of $575 in 1986, congratulate yourself because she retails for $1025 today. (Photo courtesy of Lladró USA, Inc.)

"Mayumi" (#1449G) has great sculpting lines. She is part of a series of figures of Japanese women sculpted by Salvador Debón (#1447-1451, two of which are still retailing: "Michiko" [#1447] at $495 and "Teruko" [#1451] at $550). The secondary market trend for Mayumi, who was retired in 1997 at a last retail price of $525, is $600-$625. (Photo courtesy of Lladró USA, Inc.)

"Here Comes the Bride" (#1446G/M) may well be Lladró's most popular bridal model ever. The glazed version was on the retail market from 1983 through 1997, at which time its last retail price was $997. The matte version, however, fell into that 1991 en masse retirement of matte figures. Secondary market prices for either are in the $1100-$1200 range. The sculptor for this model was J. Puche. (Photo courtesy of Lladró USA, Inc.)

"Flowers of the Season" (#1454G) is one of Lladró's most famous creations. First issued in 1983 at a retail price of $1460, its retail price today is $2550—a retail appreciation rate of about 75%. The sculptor for this model was J. Puche, but creation of the parasol and flowerwork would have been largely the responsibility of Lladró's phenomenal decoration and design staff. In this case, the flowerwork is absolutely integral to the theme, and the flowers portrayed include multiple varieties. (Photo courtesy of Lladró USA, Inc.)

"Kiyoko" (#1450G) is another of the retired items in Salvador Debón's studies of traditional Japanese women. Issued in 1983, she went off the market in 1998 at a last retail price of $550. Secondary market trend is $575-$625. (Photo courtesy of Lladró USA, Inc.)

"Female Equestrian" (#4516G/M) was first issued in the mid- to late 1960s, but the glazed version is still going strong on the retail market at $760. The matte version was retired in 1991 and has since been offered on the secondary market at prices closer to $800. (Photo courtesy of Lladró USA, Inc.)

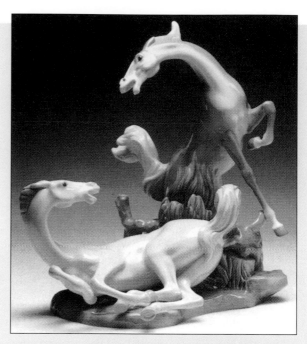

"Two Horses" (#4597G/M), whose original model was sculpted by Fulgencio García, features an elongated and highly stylized presentation which adds to the dynamism of the piece. Issued in the late 1960s and retired in 1990. Prices of $1350-$1450 are not unusual in the secondary market. (Photo courtesy of Lladró USA, Inc.)

"Little Girl with Goat" (#4812G) was issued in 1972 and retired in 1988. Typical secondary market prices in the $450-$500 range. (Photo courtesy of Lladró USA, Inc.)

While such scenes as "Deer Hunt" (#4521G) are more typical of the work of sculptor Salvador Furió, this one is attributed to Fulgencio García. Issued in the mid- to late 1960s, it was already retired by 1970 and there are no secondary market records available on it. (Photo courtesy of Lladró USA, Inc.)

"Not So Fast" (#1533G/M) is a classic: small girl is hauled along by large German Shepherd on leash. The matte version of this item was one of those retired in the en masse matte retirements of 1991. The glazed version was retired in 1996. This one is a secondary market "sleeper" at $300-$325, not much above the $285 last retail price for the glazed version. There is also a Gres version (#2303), retired in 1996 and valued on the secondary market at $450-$475. (Photo courtesy of Lladró USA, Inc.)

"Watchful Gazelle" (#4532G) was issued in the mid- to late 1960s and retired in 1970. Identified by Vicente Lladró in a 1996 issue of Expressions magazine (12:4) as one of his own favorite figurines, it is rarely seen on the secondary market, and there are no Lladró auction records for it. Given the extraordinary delicacy of the legs and ears, a mint example would be a fantastic secondary market find. (Photo courtesy of Lladró USA, Inc.)

"Embroiderer" (#4865G) was open for twenty years, from 1974 through 1994. That hasn't stopped her secondary market value from rising to the $725-$775 level, a nice appreciation over her last retail price of $645. (Photo courtesy of Lladró USA, Inc.)

"Ballerina" (#4559G) is a classic beauty in Lladró's older, elongated style. Issued in the mid- to late 1960s, she was retired in 1993 at a last retail price of $440. She could cost $500-$550 on the secondary market. (Photo courtesy of Lladró USA, Inc.)

"Grand Dame" (#1568G), one of several Lladró "Deco ladies." Issued in 1987, she was just retired in 2000 at a last retail price of $495. (Photo courtesy of Lladró USA, Inc.)

"Death of the Swan" (#4855.3M) was issued in 1983 and retired in 1987 at a last retail price of $130. Secondary market value on the bisque version is $250-$275. The figure was also made in a regular glazed form as (#4855G), issued in 1973 and retired in 2000 at a last retail price of $330. (Photo courtesy of Lladró USA, Inc.)

Sculptor Juan Huerta's "Hebrew Student" (#4684G/M) is one of the most popular older Lladrós. Issued in 1970, he was retired in 1985. His prices can range from $600-$950 although he was a real "sleeper" at a February 1999 Lladró-only Internet auction sponsored by Sea Ranch Gifts, gaveling down at only about half his value. (Photo courtesy of Lladró USA, Inc.)

"Café de Paris" (#1511G), a delightful and elaborate grouping first issued in 1987, was retired in 1995 at a last retail price of $2950. Given that last price, the secondary market has not allowed it to rise much above it, at $3000-$3200. (Photo courtesy of Lladró USA, Inc.)

"Bucks" (#4964G) is an example of a model that has been misnamed in English, as one of the "bucks" is clearly a "doe." (The Spanish title for this piece is "Pareja de Gamos," which literally translates as "Pair of Fallow Deer"; as in most deer species, only the male of this Eurasian species sports the antler rack.) This model was available on the retail market from 1977 through 1988, at which time its last retail price was $1000. Expect to pay two to three times that much—if you can even find it on the secondary market without damage to those delicate antlers and ears. (Photo courtesy of Lladró USA, Inc.)

"The Gossips" (#4984G), a whimsical treatment of an age-old theme, was open from 1978 through 1985. It can garner prices in the $900-$1000 range today. The sculptor was J. Roig. (Photo courtesy of Lladró USA, Inc.)

Sculptor Salvador Furió's "Sharpening Cutlery" (#5204G) had a quite short retail run from 1984 through 1988. Secondary market range is $925-$975. (Photo courtesy of Lladró USA, Inc.)

"The Fireman" (#5976G), an action figure if I ever saw one, ought to have appreciated above its last retail price when it went off the market in 1997. It hasn't gone beyond $500, which is not much over its last retail price. (Photo courtesy of Lladró USA, Inc.)

"Little Skipper" (#5936G) was issued in 1993 and retired in 1996 at a last retail of $320. Secondary market range is $350-$400. (Photo courtesy of Lladró USA, Inc.)

"Reading the Torah" (#6208G) was issued in 1995 and retired in 2000 at a last retail price of $535. (Photo courtesy of Lladró USA, Inc.)

Sculptor Francisco Catalá's "Watching the Pigs" (#4892G) was only available at retail from 1974 to 1978. Check out that hat! If you can find him on the secondary market, don't expect to buy him cheaply. He could run you anywhere from $1200-$1300. (Photo courtesy of Lladró USA, Inc.)

"Sheriff Puppet" (#4969G) was issued in 1977 and retired in 1985. This little dude has plenty of cross-collectible appeal for people involved in law enforcement or who collect memorabilia of the American West. Secondary market prices range from $650 to $800. This was one of several "puppet" or "doll" figurines produced by Lladró; I have seen them languish on the generic secondary market, in part because their form is not typical of Lladró and is unlikely to be recognized as such by any but veteran collectors. (Photo courtesy of Lladró USA, Inc.)

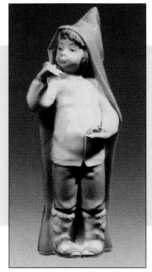

"Boy with Snails" (#4896G) was issued in 1974 and retired in 1979. Today's secondary market prices range from $400 to $500 although he reached a high of $600 at one of the Lladró auctions. Note the turned-in feet, an example of the disarmingly lifelike detail for which Lladró is justly famous. (Photo courtesy of Lladró USA, Inc.)

"Don Quixote and Sancho Panza" (#4998G) was issued in 1978 and retired in 1993. Even though its last retail price even then was a weighty $1275, it will run $2900-$3000 on today's market. Lladró auction prices have ranged from a low of $2625 to a high of $3300. (Photo courtesy of Lladró USA, Inc.)

"Gypsy Woman" (#4919G) might seem a somewhat unusual theme for Lladró were it not that its sculptor, Salvador Debón, made models representing a variety of racial and ethnic groups. "Gypsy Woman" was issued in 1974 and retired in 1981. It can command prices of $1400-$1800 on today's secondary market. (Photo courtesy of Lladró USA, Inc.)

"Dutch Couple with Tulips" (#5124G) had a very limited retail run from 1982 through 1985—a good example of how an open-issue model becomes a time-limited edition by default. Secondary market prices on this today are in the $900-$925 range, prices driven by both the relative scarcity and the flowerwork. (Photo courtesy of Lladró USA, Inc.)

"Act II" (#5035G) is another fabulous example of dynamism—a sense of movement—in a Lladró figurine. First issued in 1979, this remains a strong retail seller at $425. (Photo courtesy of Lladró USA, Inc.)

"Lilly Soccer Player" (#5134G) is an example of one of Lladró's "puppets," doll-like figures whose style bears so little resemblance to the rest of the collection that they often go begging on the generic secondary market for lack of recognition. In places where her identity is known, however, she can pull in $500-$600, and she even managed to fetch $900 in a case of Lladró auction fever. She and her brother "Billy" were on the retail market for a short time, 1982 to 1983. (Photo courtesy of Lladró USA, Inc.)

"Halloween" (#5067G) appears to partake of the "Snow White" myth as the witch offers the little girl an apple. Issued in 1980 and retired in 1983, it can reach prices of $1400-$1500 on today's secondary market. (Photo courtesy of Lladró USA, Inc.)

So poignant it is almost heartbreaking to look at, sculptor Salvador Furió's "Little Flower Seller" (#5082G) was open from 1980 through 1985 only. Retailing at $820 even then, this wonderful tableau will cost you much more now; just put a 2 in front of the 8 and that should about do it! Lladró auction range on this is $2350-$2850. (Photo courtesy of Lladró USA, Inc.)

"Billy Soccer Player" (#5135G), companion piece to "Lilly," issued in 1982 and retired the year after. Secondary market value $500-$600. These "puppet" figures are an acquired taste; I have repeatedly passed one up that is available on the secondary market in my area and at a very reasonable price, just because I couldn't imagine having to look at it on my mantel every day. Other collectors, however, find them, as Billy himself might say, "Awesome!" (Photo courtesy of Lladró USA, Inc.)

"Egyptian Cat, White" (#5145G) was issued in 1982 and retired in 1985. A black version in Gres (#2130) is also available (shown on page 165). Both of these 13" tall cats are scarce on the secondary market and may be undervalued at the current range of $450-$650 apiece. (Photo courtesy of Lladró USA, Inc.)

Trust Lladró to think of every imaginable subject for its animal models. "Miniature Bison Attacking" (#5313G) was part of a series of Lladró animal miniatures made between the years 1985 and 1990. Its last retail price was only $75, but miniatures tend to be especially popular in every collectibles field, as reflected in this one's secondary market range of $150-$225, which is typical for the series. (Photo courtesy of Lladró USA, Inc.)

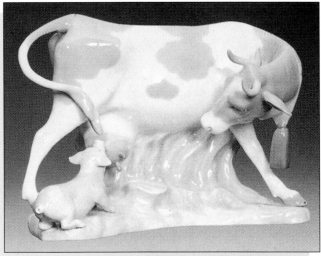

My vote for the most whimsical Lladró ever created goes to "Cow and Pig" (#4640 G/M). Sculpted by Vicente Martinez, it features a pig copping a drink from a belled milking cow. Issued in the late 1960s, it was retired in 1981 and will go for $650-$750 on today's secondary market. (Photo courtesy of Lladró USA, Inc.)

All is not hearts and flowers in Lladró. "Racing Motorcyclist" (#5270G) was issued in 1985 and retired a scant three years later in 1988. While it was able to reach $1050 at one of the Lladró auctions, its more usual trend on today's secondary market is $775-$850. (Photo courtesy of Lladró USA, Inc.)

"Ice Cream Vendor" (#5325G) would have to be most kids' idea of an ideal profession. On the retail market from 1985 to 1995, its last retail price was $650. The trend on the secondary market is now closer to $750. (Photo courtesy of Lladró USA, Inc.)

"Wine Taster" (#5239G) is one of Lladró's more unusual items in its series of models for various professions and careers. Issued in 1984, it currently retails at $445. And yes, that is a tiny glass in his hand! (Photo courtesy of Lladró USA, Inc.)

The detailing on this model of "Woman with Cow and Calf" (#4953G) is extraordinary even for a Lladró. Available on the retail market only from 1977 to 1979, its last retail price was already $460. I know of no one offering this figure for sale, but if you ever find it, expect prices in four figures—say, oh, somewhere in the $1500 to $1800 range. (Photo courtesy of Lladró USA, Inc.)

"Hindu Children" (#5352G) was first issued in 1986 and retails for $445. The Gres model of this figure (#2298) was issued in 1995 and retired in 2000 at a last retail price of $450. (Photo courtesy of Lladró USA, Inc.)

"Practice Makes Perfect" (#5462G) is a figure anyone ever forced to take piano lessons as a kid can relate to. Issued in 1988, it was retired in 1998 at a last retail of $545. Secondary market trends for this figure are upward at $600-$675. (Photo courtesy of Lladró USA, Inc.)

"Sewing Circle" (#5360G) issued in 1986 and retired in 1990 is an affectionate treatment of a subject to which Lladró has returned again and again for its several figurines of nuns in these winged coronet-type veils usually associated with the Sisters of Charity. The sculptor for this grouping was Salvador Furió. Last retail price on this was already up to $850, but that hasn't deterred the secondary market from letting it rise to the $1200-$1400 range today. (Photo courtesy of Lladró USA, Inc.)

"Hawaiian Beauty" (#1512G) was only on the primary market for four years, from 1987 through 1990. Her last retail price was $700. Her secondary market trend today is $850-$1200, a range wide enough to reflect a certain lack of consensus in the market. (Photo courtesy of Lladró USA, Inc.)

"Puppy Dog Tails (#5539G) is, of course, a group of boys with dogs, first issued in 1989. This tableau of multiple elements retails at $1700. (Photo courtesy of Lladró USA, Inc.)

"Spring Dance" (#5663G) issued in 1990 and retired in 2000 at a last retail price of a modest $210. (Photo courtesy of Lladró USA, Inc.)

This wonderful grouping, "Desert Tour" (#5402G), was first issued in 1987 and retired a mere three years later in 1990. Its last retail price was already pretty far up there at $1150, which may account for why the Lladró auction range has been under that at $850-$1050. The secondary market has allowed for prices in the range of $1150 to $1475 since that time. (Photo courtesy of Lladró USA, Inc.)

"Don't Look Down! (#5698G) was first issued in 1990 and currently retails at $410. (Photo courtesy of Lladró USA, Inc.)

"Making House Calls" (#6317G)— don't I wish! You can tell by the clothing that the activity in question really is a thing of the past. Issued in 1996 and retired in 1998, this 14" figurine is bargain-priced on the secondary market at $275-$300—not a lot above its last retail of $260. (Photo courtesy of Lladró USA, Inc.)

Doesn't "The Rabbi" (#6209G) look the very archetype of serene wisdom? He was only on the retail market for two years, from 1995 through the end of 1997, making him, in effect, a "limited edition." This model is appreciating nicely over its last retail price of $250; be prepared to pay $300-$325 today. (Photo courtesy of Lladró USA, Inc.)

"Fishing with Gramps" (#5215G) was first issued in 1984 and still retails at $905. The little boy's excitement is almost palpable. This popular figurine has been duplicated by Lladró "wannabes," so be sure to look for the Lladró mark; if the mark isn't there, it's not a Lladró, as this item was produced too late in the company's history to ever have gone without a backstamp. The genuine model was also produced in Gres and is still open at $1025. (Photo courtesy of Lladró USA, Inc.)

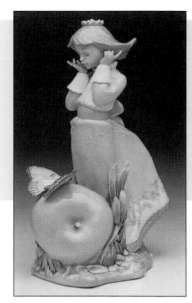

The very clever "Land of the Giants" (#5716G) was only on the retail market from 1990 through 1994. Its last retail at that time was $315, and its secondary market trend is already $425-$450. (Photo courtesy of Lladró USA, Inc.)

"Elegant Promenade" (#5802G) is a real crowd-pleaser, featuring not only an elegant lady, but two dogs—a combination of some of Lladró's most popular elements. This relatively tall figure at over 15" was first issued at $775 and currently retails at $825. (Photo courtesy of Lladró USA, Inc.)

"Alice in Wonderland" (#5740G) was first issued in 1991 and retired in 1998 at a last retail price of $440. Her value today would be $450-$550. (Photo courtesy of Lladró USA, Inc.)

"Caribbean Kiss" (#6144G) was first issued in 1994 and was active through 1999. Its last retail price was $340, and the secondary market trend is upward at $350-$375. (Photo courtesy of Lladró USA, Inc.)

"Seeds of Laughter" (#5764G) is a particularly humorous version of Lladró's very popular clown figurines. (Check out that totally incongruous water can balanced on his butt!) This had an unaccountably short retail life, from 1991 through 1995, when it could still be purchased at $525. This is a figurine vulnerable enough to damage that I wouldn't risk buying it at auction, so I'd probably have to pay a broker in the neighborhood of $675-$875 to get him today. (Photo courtesy of Lladró USA, Inc.)

"Preparing for the Sabbath" (#6183G) is one of Lladró's several figurines devoted to Judaic themes. Issued in 1995, this model was retired in 1999. The secondary market value is $425-$450. (Photo courtesy of Lladró USA, Inc.)

It doesn't get much more elaborate in a single-element model than "Feathered Fantasy" (#5851G). This tallish (11.5") figurine was expensive on the retail market at $1200 when it was issued in 1992. By the time it retired at the end of 1996, it had only added $50 more to its retail price, but the market doesn't seem to bear much more than that, and I have only seen one available through a broker for $1300. (Photo courtesy of Lladró USA, Inc.)

"Floral Admiration" (#5853G), issued in 1992 and retired in 1994, seems to have been a precursor of the mythical and fantastic figures that would come to dominate Lladró's new issues by the turn of the millennium. Going out at a last retail of $725, it has been popular enough on the secondary market to achieve prices in the $825-$875 range. (Photo courtesy of Lladró USA, Inc.)

"Shot on Goal" (#5879G), sculpted by Fulgencio García, has fabulous, almost aerodynamic lines. Out for four years only, from 1992 through 1996, it was retailing then at $1150. Secondary market prices in the range of $1250-$1275 have been the order of the day since then. A Gres version of this model was retired in 1998 and its value on the secondary market is $1000-$1100. (Photo courtesy of Lladró USA, Inc.)

"Mischievous Mouse" (#5881G) was part of a series of three also including a little girl in a mouse costume with a large beach ball and a kitty. All were issued in 1992, but "Restful Mouse" (#5882G) and "Loving Mouse" (#5883G) went off the retail market in 1996, while "Mischievous Mouse" soldiered on through 1998. Secondary market prices for all three are in the $350-$400 range. (Photo courtesy of Lladró USA, Inc.)

"Balloon Seller" (#5141G) was open from 1982 to 1996, at a last retail of $250. Her secondary market trend is $275-$300. (Photo courtesy of Lladró USA, Inc.)

A tall figurine at 18.5", "Lamplighter" (#5205G) was first issued in 1984 and is still popular on the retail market at $435. The sculptor was Salvador Furió. (Photo courtesy of Lladró USA, Inc.)

Issued in 1993, "Before the Dance" (#5972G/M) is the most elaborate ballet grouping ever produced by the Lladró company. The glazed version still retails at $3550, while the matte version, retired in 1999, may run you a couple or three hundred more if you can even find it on the secondary market. (Photo courtesy of Lladró USA, Inc.)

151

"Springtime Friends" (#6140G) was first issued in 1994, and its retail price has been constant since issue at $485. (Photo courtesy of Lladró USA, Inc.)

One of Lladró's numerous treatments of the Cinderella myth, "The Glass Slipper" (#5957G) was issued in 1993 and retails at $475. (Photo courtesy of Lladró USA, Inc.)

"Spring Joy" (#6106) was issued in 1994 and still retails at its issue price of $795. (Photo courtesy of Lladró USA, Inc.)

"Seesaw Friends" (#6169G) was issued in 1995 and retired in 2000 at a last retail of $795. (Photo courtesy of Lladró USA, Inc.)

"Litter of Fun" (5364G) is certainly that, and just the sort of thing a real little girl would do. Issued in 1986, it didn't retire until 2000, at a last retail price of $465. (Photo courtesy of Lladró USA, Inc.)

"Bath Time" (#6411G) is just about typical for toddler-sized bathers—always half in and half out. Lladró artists' powers of observation for the behaviors of actual children are part of what makes their child figurines so popular. Issued in 1997, this one retails at a modest $195. (Photo courtesy of Lladró USA, Inc.)

"Pumpkin Ride" (#6244G) was first issued in 1996 and was off the market by the end of 1999, at a last retail price of $695. If price was deterring buyers then, they can look forward to paying $750-$800 for it on today's secondary market. (Photo courtesy of Lladró USA, Inc.)

"Trick or Treat" (#6227G) is another example of Lladró's talent for whimsy, as the sheeted boy carries the jack-o-lantern and his trusty canine sidekick takes charge of the goody bag. This item should have been popular on the retail market, but may have gotten lost in a retail catalog as large as Lladró's at any given time. Whatever the reason, this model was only out two years, 1995-1997—which, given the popularity of the theme, just about guarantees a solid value appreciation. Priced at $250 when it went off the retail market, it'll run $300-$365 today. (Photo courtesy of Lladró USA, Inc.)

"Nature's Beauty" (#6252) is one of Lladró's three-quarter figures, issued in 1996 and retired in 1999 at a last issue price of $770. Its secondary market range today would be $800-$850. (Photo courtesy of Lladró USA, Inc.)

Those who reside in tropical climates probably recognize "How Skillful" (#6517G) from local tourist attractions featuring performing cockatoos and parrots. Issued in 1998, its current retail price of $395 is not a little influenced by the lovely flowerwork. (Photo courtesy of Lladró USA, Inc.)

Quite tall at just under 16", "Dreams of Aladdin" (#6285G) was issued in 1996 and retired in 1999. Its retail price throughout that time was $1440. On the secondary market, it runs $1600-$1675. (Photo courtesy of Lladró USA, Inc.)

"Elegance on Ice" (#6653G), Lladró's first and only model of a figure skater, was a year 2000 issue at a retail price of $365. (Photo courtesy of Lladró USA, Inc.)

"Thoughts" (#1272) was issued in 1974 and retired in 1998 at a last retail price of $3490. Its secondary market range today is $3550-$3700. (Photo courtesy of Lladró USA, Inc.)

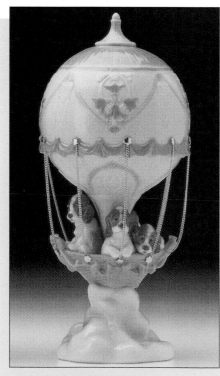

"Up and Away" (#6524G) is one of a series of hot air balloon models released in 1998. The one with flowers in the basket ("Flying High", #6523G) was retired in 2000 at a last retail price of $635. Apparently, consumers considered "Up and Away" a better bargain at $560—not to mention "Through the Clouds" (#6522), which features kittens in the basket and retails even better at $450. (Photo courtesy of Lladró USA, Inc.)

"The Goddess and the Unicorn" (#6007) was released in 1993 and is still active on the retail market at its issue price of $1675. (Photo courtesy of Lladró USA, Inc.)

"Clown's Head" (#5129) was recently retired in year 2000, many years after its first issue date in 1982. Its last retail price was $475. Collectors should be advised that this model has been widely copied; most of these "wannabes" are unmarked. (Photo courtesy of Lladró USA, Inc.)

"Romeo and Juliet" (#4750G/M) was issued in 1971. Although the glazed version is still open and retailing at $1250, the matte version was retired in 1989 and could cost $1300-$1500 on the secondary market. (Photo courtesy of Lladró USA, Inc.)

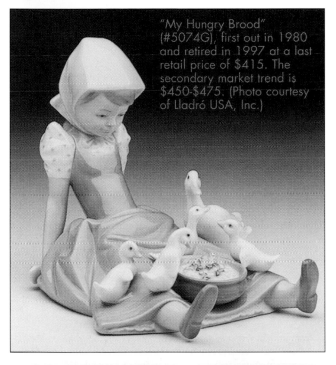

"My Hungry Brood" (#5074G), first out in 1980 and retired in 1997 at a last retail price of $415. The secondary market trend is $450-$475. (Photo courtesy of Lladró USA, Inc.)

"Hi There!" (#5672G) was on the retail market from 1990 through 1996, when it last retailed at $520. Its secondary market value today is $550-$575. (Photo courtesy of Lladró USA, Inc.)

"Backstage Preparation" (#5817G/M) was on the open market from 1991 through 1994. Produced in both finishes, its price range on the secondary market is $550-$650, with the upper end of the range going to the matte version. (Photo courtesy of Lladró USA, Inc.)

"Pottery Seller" (#5079G), issued in 1980, retired 1985. Secondary market price range is $650-$750. (Photo courtesy of Lladró USA, Inc.)

"Coquetry" (#4995G), one of Lladró's many models of elegant ladies in period costume, was available only in 1978 and 1979. Her secondary market price today would be $800-$850. (Photo courtesy of Lladró USA, Inc.)

155

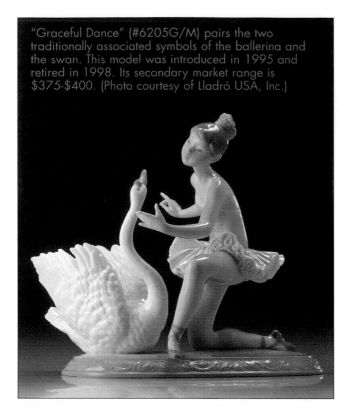

"Graceful Dance" (#6205G/M) pairs the two traditionally associated symbols of the ballerina and the swan. This model was introduced in 1995 and retired in 1998. Its secondary market range is $375-$400. (Photo courtesy of Lladró USA, Inc.)

Left: "Angel with Garland" (#6133G) was issued in 1994 and retired in 1999. Secondary market price range is $400-$450. Right: "Angel of Peace" (#6131G), also issued in 1994 but still active at #370 retail. (Photo courtesy of Lladró USA, Inc.)

"Under My Spell" (#6170G) was issued in 1995 and retired in 1999 at a last retail price of $200. Its secondary market price is not yet much above that. The Gres version of this model (#2352) retired in 1998 and is worth $225-$250 on the secondary market. (Photo courtesy of Lladró USA, Inc.)

"Magical Moment" (#6171G) is a companion piece to #6170 and was issued and retired in the same years and at the same last retail price. For some reason, many of Lladró's issues of the mid- to late 1990s were only available on the retail market for a short time. (Photo courtesy of Lladró USA, Inc.)

Sculpted by Salvador Debón, "Swans Take Flight" (#5912G) is a very large model at 22.75" tall. Issued in 1992, it currently retails for $2950. Imagine this on an occasional table in your living room—or as the centerpiece on your mahogany dining table! (Photo courtesy of Lladró USA, Inc.)

"Graceful Ballet" (#6240G/M) makes the heart soar just to look at it. I was very surprised when this went off the retail market after a brief run from 1995 through 1998. Her last retail was $815, but her secondary market price is already trending in the $900-$925 range. Sculptor for this model was J. Coderch, a relative latecomer to the Lladró workshops. (Photo courtesy of Lladró USA, Inc.)

"Minstrel" (#4927G) was available on the retail market from 1974 to 1980. Secondary market price range: $1450-$1475. (Photo courtesy of Lladró USA, Inc.)

"At the Ball" (#5398G) is one of Lladró's many models of romantic couples. This one was available on the retail market in the years 1986 through 1991. Last retailing at $620, it has been appreciating modestly on the secondary market since then at a range of $650-$750. (Photo courtesy of Lladró USA, Inc.)

"Anniversary Waltz" (#1372G) was first issued in 1978 and is still active on the retail market at $570. (Photo courtesy of Lladró USA, Inc.)

"Little Troubadour" (#1314G) was issued in 1974 and retired in 1979 at a last retail price of $435—which would have made him very expensive back in the 1970s. I know of no one offering this piece for sale on the secondary market. (Photo courtesy of Lladró USA, Inc.)

Heads up all you Thanksgiving revelers in the U.S.! "Pilgrim Couple" (#5734G) is a great decorative piece for the holiday—perhaps displayed with one or more figurines of the Native Americans, who, after all, made it possible for the pilgrims to survive that first winter. This figurine was on the retail market from 1990 through 1993 only and will be hard to find now. Its last retail price was $525, and it would be worth $550-$600 today. (Photo courtesy of Lladró USA, Inc.)

"Woodcutter" (#4656G) was issued in the late 1960s and retired in 1978. His going secondary market value is $600-$785. (Photo courtesy of Lladró USA, Inc.)

The voluptuous "Nude with Rose" (#2079) is tall at 18" even though the model is kneeling. Issued in 1978 and retired in 1979, I don't know of anyone who has her currently available for sale, so she will be hard to find and don't be surprised to see a price tag of $1500 or more if you do. (Photo courtesy of Lladró USA, Inc.)

"On the Town" (#1452G) was on the retail market from 1983 through 1993, when it last retailed at $440. Secondary market price range: $500-$600. (Photo courtesy of Lladró USA, Inc.)

"Valencian Boy" (#1400G) was issued in 1982 and retired in 1988. Its secondary market price range today is $500-$560. (Photo courtesy of Lladró USA, Inc.)

"Happy Travelers" (#4652G) was issued in the late 1960s and retired in 1978. Its secondary market price range is broad at $650-$1000. (Photo courtesy of Lladró USA, Inc.)

"Blue Moon" (#1435) was a fantasy figure from the 1980s (1983-1988). She achieved a highest auction price of $600, but secondary market prices since have ranged more modestly at $350-$500. (Photo courtesy of Lladró USA, Inc.)

"At the Circus" (#5052G) was issued in 1979 and retired in 1985. The Lladró auction price range is $1000 to $1500, with subsequent secondary market prices trending at $1200-$1250. (Photo courtesy of Lladró USA, Inc.)

This seated "Afghan" (#1069G) was first issued in the mid- to late 1960s and retired in 1985. Secondary market prices have trended nicely with its Lladró auction range of $525-$650, nudging toward the higher end of that range. A later standing version of the dog (#1282G) was issued in 1974 and retired in 1985. Its trend on the secondary market is somewhat lower at $500-$550. (Photo courtesy of Lladró USA, Inc.)

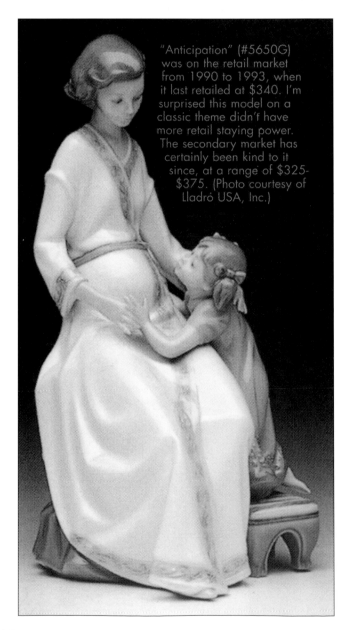

"Anticipation" (#5650G) was on the retail market from 1990 to 1993, when it last retailed at $340. I'm surprised this model on a classic theme didn't have more retail staying power. The secondary market has certainly been kind to it since, at a range of $325-$375. (Photo courtesy of Lladró USA, Inc.)

"Dutch Mother" (#5083G) was more recently also known as "Lullaby and Goodnight" in the English titles' somewhat irritating penchant for change over time. This model was available on the retail market from 1980 to 1983 and trades on the secondary market in a range of $1100-$1150. (Photo courtesy of Lladró USA, Inc.)

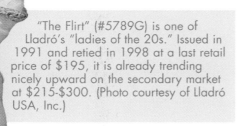

"The Flirt" (#5789G) is one of Lladró's "ladies of the 20s." Issued in 1991 and retied in 1998 at a last retail price of $195, it is already trending nicely upward on the secondary market at $215-$300. (Photo courtesy of Lladró USA, Inc.)

"Twilight Years" (#5677G) is one of two romantic Lladró models (the other being #1033 G/M) featuring aging couples, an inclusion for which the company is to be much commended. Number 5677 was available on the retail market from 1990 through 1997, when it last retailed at $420. Its secondary market range since then has been $550 to $675. It was also produced in a Gres version (#2302) retired in 1997 and valued at $425-$450. (Photo courtesy of Lladró USA, Inc.)

"Bathing Beauty" (#5615G) was on the retail market from 1989-1991. Secondary market price range: $350-$450. (Photo courtesy of Lladró USA, Inc.)

"Flowers for Sale" (#5537G) was first issued in 1989 and is a very recent retirement in year 2000, last retailing at $1550. The decorative elements on this would have been quite time-consuming to make, featuring not only all those flowers but a parasol as well. (Photo courtesy of Lladró USA, Inc.)

Issued from 1989 and retired in 1991, "Startled" (#5614G) is a nice example of Lladró's imaginative whimsy, featuring a girl being terrorized by a starfish. Check out that old-fashioned bathing suit! Secondary market range: $375-$425. (Photo courtesy of Lladró USA, Inc.)

"Trino at the Beach" (#5666G) retailed from 1990 through 1995 at a last retail price of $460. This charming piece trends on the secondary market in a range of $500 to $550. (Photo courtesy of Lladró USA, Inc.)

"Botanic" (#1351G) was made in the style that is distinctively that of the sculptor Salvador Furió. Available on the retail market from 1979-1980, this botanist is scarce on the secondary market at a price range of $1400-$1500. (Photo courtesy of Lladró USA, Inc.)

"Scottish Lass" (#1315G) was available on the market from 1974 through 1979. It is a tall figure at 15.5" and its size accounts in part for its substantial last retail price of $800. Her price range on the secondary market is $2500-$2800. (Photo courtesy of Lladró USA, Inc.)

"Southern Charm" (#5700G) was on the retail market from 1990 through 1997. Its last retail price was $1025, and it has been going up on the secondary market ever since, at a range from just over retail to $1225. (Photo courtesy of Lladró USA, Inc.)

"Peaceful Moment" (#6179G) is one of Lladró's ever-popular mother-child figurines. Issued in 1995, it currently retails at $385. (Photo courtesy of Lladró USA, Inc.)

"Goya Lady" (#5125G) was issued in 1982 and retired in 1990 at a last retail price of $175. Its secondary market price range is $300-$350. (Photo courtesy of Lladró USA, Inc.)

"Dutch Girl" (#1399G/M) issued in 1982 and retired in 1988 was a rare example of a general issue figurine whose secondary market prices (in this case, $650-$850) have failed to achieve the level of its last retail price ($935). There seems to be a price ceiling, even for Lladrós, above which the market simply will not venture. Having said that, if you buy her right on the secondary market, you could still have yourself a bargain, as Lladró's figurines of people in traditional Dutch costume are otherwise popular. (Photo courtesy of Lladró USA, Inc.)

Issued in 1972 and retired in 1979, "Fisherman" (#4802G) is valued on the secondary market in a wide range: $550-$825. (Photo courtesy of Lladró USA, Inc.)

"Walk with Father" (#5751) retailed from 1991 through 1994. Last retail price was $410, and the secondary market range is $400-$500. (Photo courtesy of Lladró USA, Inc.)

Despite its short retail life from 1978 to 1979, "Hunter with Dog" (#5002G/M) has done well on the secondary market: $1250-$1300. (Photo courtesy of Lladró USA, Inc.)

"Flower for My Lady (#1513G) is a representative Lladró romantic tableau that was on the retail market from 1987 through 1990. It went out at a last retail price of #1375, the expense being driven by the multiple elements. It achieved a high Lladró auction price of $2000, but the range elsewhere on the secondary market has been $1400-$1750. (Photo courtesy of Lladró USA, Inc.)

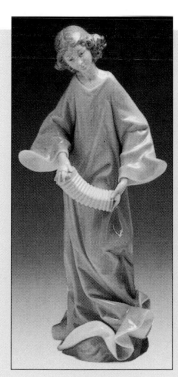

"Angel with Accordion" (#1323G) was issued in 1976 and retired in 1985. Its secondary market price range is $400-$450. Lladró's angels are always popular, and the company has made enough of them that an entire section of the *Authorized Collection Reference Guide* is devoted to this theme. (Photo courtesy of Lladró USA, Inc.)

"Bust with Black Veil" (#1538M) is one of three models of a girl's head wrapped in a porcelain-dipped lace veil. The facial modeling is exquisite on these examples of items produced not by an individual sculptor but by Lladró's incredible and largely anonymous "Department of Decoration and Design." This example retails at $1390. The same figure in a white veil is numbered 1538.3M and retails at $1050. A smaller version in white veil, "Small Bust with Veil" is numbered 1539M and retails at $490. (Photo courtesy of Lladró USA, Inc.)

Gres Finish Figurines

"Nuns" (#2075) in a Gres finish. Issued in 1977 and retired in 2000, their value today is $250-$275. Sculptor of these elegant lines was Fulgencio García. (Photo by the author, courtesy of Robert Graves and Kennedy Brothers, Inc. in Vergennes, VT.)

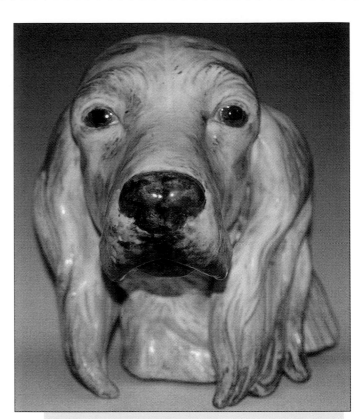

Front view of setter's head. (Photo by the author, courtesy of Carolyn Pearson and Reed's Antiques and Collectibles in Wells, ME.)

"Setter's Head" (#2045), a beautiful example of the decoratively versatile Gres finish. Issued in 1971 and retired in 1981. Value today: $550-$675. Sculptor: Juan Huerta. (Photo by the author, courtesy of Carolyn Pearson and Reed's Antiques and Collectibles in Wells, ME.)

"Egyptian Cat, Black" (#2130), the Gres version of the one in white, was issued in 1983 and retired in 1985 along with its white counterpart. A very rare brown version is also known. (Photo courtesy of Lladró USA, Inc.)

"Intermission" (#2370) features a Gres ballerina. First issued in 1997, she retails for $690. She is quite tall at 14".(Photo courtesy of Lladró USA, Inc.)

"Monkey Love" (#2066) is a Gres bust issued in 1977 and retired by the end of 1979. It goes for $650-$700 on the secondary market. (Photo courtesy of Lladró USA, Inc.)

The Gres bust "Little Girl" (#2024) was issued in 1971 and retired in 1985. Her secondary market range is $450-$650. (Photo courtesy of Lladró USA, Inc.)

"Eskimo Riders" (#2270) in Gres was issued in 1994 and retails for $280. It has a counterpart of the same name in the regular porcelain formula (#5353G/M) that retails at $270. It would be fun to have one of all three finishes: matte, glazed, and Gres! (Photo courtesy of Lladró USA, Inc.)

"Devoted Friends" (#2199) is an exceptionally endearing Gres bust issued in 1990 and retired in 1995. Its last retail price was already $895, so it's not surprising that it goes for $950-$965 on the secondary market. (Photo courtesy of Lladró USA, Inc.)

"Dancer" (#2123) is a good example of how the Gres porcelain formula can be used to good advantage in depicting ethnic and oversize figures (this one measuring just under two feet tall). It was on the retail market from 1980 to 1985 at a last retail price of $790. Today's value would be in the range of $1200 to $1500. (Photo courtesy of Lladró USA, Inc.)

"The Shepherdess" (#2330) in Gres is one of the rare pastoral figures issued in recent years. She was on the market from 1996 through 1999, at which time her last retail price was $410. Her secondary market trend is upward at $425-$450. (Photo courtesy of Lladró USA, Inc.)

"Autumn Shepherdess" (#2133) is the companion piece to #2132 and was available on the retail market during the same period. I can't really account for the fact that its last retail price was only about half of #2132 ($285 vs. $450). The secondary market range on #2133 is ill defined at $425-$1250. (By the way, there is no "Winter" or "Summer Shepherdess.") (Photo courtesy of Lladró USA, Inc.)

"Spring Shepherdess" (#2132) is a Gres 3/4 model available on the retail market from 1983 to 1985. Its secondary market range is $1250-$1500. (Photo courtesy of Lladró USA, Inc.)

Measuring almost two feet tall, this Gres "Mother Feeding Baby" (#2126) features a theme as old as human time. It was on the retail market from 1981 to 1985, at a last retail price of $1300. The price on today's secondary market would be in the $2000 to $2250 range. (Photo courtesy of Lladró USA, Inc.)

"Knowledge" (#2015) is a Gres that was on the retail market from 1970-1985. It is one of Lladró's tallest figures at 35". Its secondary market value today is $2500-$2750. (Photo courtesy of Lladró USA, Inc.)

The Gres bust of "Lola" (#2078) was available on the retail market from 1978 to 1981. Its secondary market value is $650-$850. (Photo courtesy of Lladró USA, Inc.)

"The Sultan" (#2339) is a Gres Lladró issued in 1996 and retailing at $480. (Photo courtesy of Lladró USA, Inc.)

The Gres "Mother's Pride" (#2189) was issued in 1990 and retired in 1999 at a last retail of $375. Its secondary market trend is upward at $400-$425. (Photo courtesy of Lladró USA, Inc.)

"Heavenly Strings" (#2194) is one of several Gres angels. Out for only four years on the retail market (1990-1993), its value today would be $250-$275 over a last retail price of $195. (Photo courtesy of Lladró USA, Inc.)

"Woman with Mandolin" (#2107) is a half-figure issued in 1978 and retired in 1981. Its secondary market value would be $1700-$1850. Lladró made a number of half and three-quarter figures. This one is a Gres. (Photo courtesy of Lladró USA, Inc.)

Selected Core Collection Figurines with Value Ranges

There are a couple of things about this price list that set it apart from most others. First, it gives price ranges rather than suggesting established values—unless the item is still open and has a specific retail price. Ranges underscore the reality that price guides are just that: guides. The wider the range indicated, the more "volatile" (i.e., unstable, pending consensus) the item is on the secondary market.

Second, the list contains not just titles, but descriptive information about the items. This is important to collectors when they are trying to identify a figurine from among several possible titles. I have therefore omitted from the list any of the more generic items to which it is difficult to attach specific descriptions (e.g. multiples of girls with flowers, ladies with parasols, and ballerinas in various poses, not to mention several groupings of cranes and various doves).

As mentioned before, the Lladró core collection is huge, at approximately 4,000 figures. It follows that the list included here will be far from comprehensive. In compiling the list, I have included Gres versions of glazed figurines with their glazed counterparts rather than listing them separately under the 2000 series. The Gres items separately listed under the 2000 numbers were made in Gres only.

> *In the interest of providing as many values as possible in the book, this list does not include items already pictured, as captions already give information on identity and value.*

#1006G Pan with Cymbals [small satyr seated on column and holding cymbals] (Ret. 1975) . . $500-$650

#1007G Pan with Pipes [small satyr seated on column and playing pan flute] (Ret. 1975) . $500-$650

#1008G Satyr Group [pan with cymbals seated on column, pan with pan flute seated on ground] (Ret. 1975) . . . . $800-$1000

#1010G/M Girl with Lamb [girl with side pony tails nuzzling lamb in arms] (M-Ret. 1989, G-Ret. 1993) . . . . $200-$300

#1021G Horse's Group [three horses, one down, one nipping at another's flank] (Open) $2465

#1022M Horse's Group, White (Open) $2150

#1031G/M Sancho Panza [sitting on stool, legs out before him, hat on knee] (Ret. 1989) . . . $500-$600

#1038G Girl with Turkeys [girl with basket on arm, pair of turkeys at feet] (Ret. 1978) . $450-$550

#1039G/M Violinist and Girl [tall man in cap with violin under arm behind girl seated on ground with flowers] (Ret. 1991) . . . . $850-$1000

#1040G/M Girl with Letter [elongated figure holding letter and standing in front of jar] (Ret. 1978) . $400-$450

#1041G/M Hen [pecking at ground] (Ret. 1975) . . $325-$350

#1042G/M Hen [alert, head raised] (Ret. 1975) . . . $250-$350

#1043G/M Cock [alert rooster, bushier tail than hens] (Ret. 1975) . . . . $300-$350

#1064G Deer [small, reclining] (Ret. 1986) . . . . . $325-$425

#1081G/M Girl with Brush [girl in pajamas, seated on hassock, holding mirror and brushing hair] (Ret. 1985) . . . . $300-$325

#1062G Bull with Head Down [spotted coloring] (Ret. 1975) . . . . $1100-$1250

#1063G Bull with Head Up [solid coloring] (Ret. 1975) . . . . $925-$1100

#1065G Fox and Cub [mother fox reclining, folded around baby, head of which is visible] (Ret. 1985) . . . . $400-$450

#1068G Great Dane [spotted, reclining] (Ret. 1989) . . . . $500-$600

#1083G/M Girl with Doll [girl in pajamas, seated on hassock, doll in one arm, other hand lifting imaginary teacup] (Ret. 1985) . . . . $225-$325

#1084G/M Girl with Mother's Shoe [girl in pajamas seated on hassock, mother's shoe on foot supported by small pillow] (Ret. 1985) . $275-$325

#1088G/M Girl with Flowers [seated girl with ribbon in hair, chin on hands, basket of flowers in lap, dog at feet] (Ret. 1989) . . . . $650-$750

#1091G Girl and Gazelle [young woman feeding baby gazelle as mother gazelle looks on] (Ret. 1975) . . . . $1500-$2000

#1121G Pups in a Box [four dogs in a packing crate] (Ret. 1971) . . . . $1200-$1800

#1149G Dog's Head [head of hound dog] (Ret.1981) . . . . $400-$450

#1150G Elephants Walking [bull elephant, cow and calf behind, walking up incline] (Open). . $795

#2297 Elephants [Gres version of 1150] (Open) $875

#1151G Two Elephants [mother with small baby [trailing, both with trunks extended] (Ret. 1999) . . . . $450-$475

#1163G   Soldier with Saber [child in uniform, saber held up against shoulder; white jacket w/blue piping, blue pants] (Ret. 1978) . . . . $375-$400

#1164G   Soldier with Gun [blue jacket with gold piping, white pants. rifle standing at side] (Ret. 1978) . . . . $375-$400

#1165G   Soldier with Flag [flag formed from gun barrel held at side, blue jacket, white pants] (Ret. 1978) . . . . $475-$500

#1166G   Soldier with Cornet [boy soldier blowing horn, blue jacket, white pants] (Ret. 1978) . $475-$500

#1167G   Soldier with Drum [blue jacket, white pants] (Ret. 1978) . . . . $475-$500

#1187G/M Little Girl with Cat [girl in long skirt with cat rubbing around legs] (Ret. 1989) . . . $325-$400

#1210G   Blowfish [puffed to fullest; very rare] . . $625-$675

#1224G   Eagle Owl [hunched owl with wings spread] (Ret. 1978) . . . . $400-$450

#1229G   Young Harlequin [child harlequin sitting asleep on formal chair, kitten in lap] (Ret. 1999) . . . . $575-$675

#1245G   The Cart [girl pulling wagon carrying doll and dog] (Ret. 1981) . . . . $500-$650

#1251G   Pony Ride [girl and smaller boy riding pony] (Ret. 1979) . . . . $1200-$1400

#1257G   Mother with Pups [standing poodle, nursing pups] (Ret. 1981) . . . . $650-$700

#1274G   Lovers in the Park [couple seated on park bench, 1890s costumes, he holding closed umbrella and hat and offering flower, she holding closed parasol] (Ret. 1993) . . $1365-$1400

#1274M   Lovers in the Park [matte version] (Ret. 1991) . . . . $1365-$1400

#1283G   Little Gardener [little boy in straw hat and overalls pushing wheelbarrow full of flowers] (Open) $785

#1289G   Good Puppy [attentive, seated puppy with long ears, 3" in height] (Ret. 1985) $225-$250

#1300G   Bird and Butterfly [bird with wings spread looking at butterfly perched on one of two flowers] (Ret. 1985) . . . . $800-$950

#1302G   Blue Creeper [grayish bird perched above lush, pink peony-like flower] (Ret. 1985) . $650-$675

#1345G   Sacristan [elderly sacristan in vestments holding lamp on pole] (Ret. 1979) . . $2100-$2300

#1354G   Girl Watering [girl in Dutch cap watering flowers with watering can] (Ret. 1988) . $650-$700

#1367G   Playful Dogs [two poodles with tipped-over basket] (Ret. 1982) . . . . . . $750-$800

#1383G   A Rickshaw Ride [man pulling rickshaw for Japanese girl with parasol] (Open) $2150

#1420G   Born Free [three horses running] (Open) . . . $3285

#1426M   Male Tennis Player [in tennis whites and poised to serve] (Ret. 1988) . . . . $300-$400

#1427M   Female Tennis Player [foot forward, left hand back for balance, racket lowered in right hand to return ball] (Ret. 1988) . . $400-$450

#1439G   How Do You Do? [mother duck and three ducklings eye snail perched on flowers] (Open) . $295

#1453G   Golfing Couple [man and woman holding clubs casually up] (Open) $545

#1469G   Girl on Carousel Horse [girl seated sidesaddle] (Ret. 2000) . . . . $945-$975

#1470G   Boy on Carousel Horse [boy in sailor suit and cap riding with one hand outstretched] (Ret. 2000) . . . . $945-$975

#1501G/M Rag Doll [doll seated with legs dangling over shelf] (Ret. 1991) . . . . $300-$350

#1502G/M Forgotten [doll lying on stomach on shelf, one hand hanging down] (Ret. 1991) . . $300-$375

#1507G/M Boy and His Bunny [kneeling boy in bunny suit holding bunny] . . . . $250-$300

#1508G/M In the Meadow [kneeling child in bunny suit holding armful of flowers] (Ret. 1991). $275-$300

#1509G/M Spring Flowers [boy in bunny suit seated on ground and holding a bouquet of flowers] (Ret. 1991) . . . . $275-$325

#1528G   I Love You Truly [large figurine of bride and groom dancing] (Open) $595

#1534G   Little Sister [older child seated on floor next to kneeling little sister whose head is resting on arms next to sleeping kitten in lap] (Open) . $240

#2261   Little Sister [Gres version] (Open) $280

#1610G   Flight to Egypt [Joseph leading donkey bearing Mary with Christ Child in arms, clothing billowing] (Ret. 2000) . . . . . $1150-$1200

#2000   Monkeys [Gres, mother monkey with infant] (Ret. 1975) . . . . $500-$600

#2001   Cat [Siamese cat crouching low to ground] (Ret. 1975) . . . . $600-$625

#2040   Fawn Head [very large Gres sculpture of fawn's head] (Ret. 1985) . . . . $450-$550

#2044   Horse Head [very large Gres sculpture of horse's head] (Ret. 1975) . . . . $500-$600

#2052   Magistrates [Gres, two Jewish lawyers in ancient garb] (Ret, 1981) . . . . $950-$1200

#2055   Harlequin [Gres three-quarter figure of harlequin with right hand touching hip] (Ret. 1978) . . . . $1400-$1500

#2058   Thai Couple [Gres male and female dancers in traditional costume and dance pose] (Open) . $1885

#2067   Dogs Bust [Gres, heads of two young dogs with collars] (Ret. 1979) . . . . $800-$900

#2070   A New Hairdo [Gres figure of standing woman behind seated woman whose hair she is arranging] (Open) $1525

#2077   The Rain in Spain [Gres figure of two children in rain gear walking under umbrella] (Ret. 1990) . . . . $475-$550

#2084   Don Quixote Dreaming [Gres, Don Quixote sitting on stack of books, chin resting on right hand, left hand on knee] (Ret. 1985) . . . . $1800-$2100

#2087   Big Partridge [Gres, 9" tall] (Ret. 1981) . $375-$400

#2088   Small Partridge [Gres, 5" tall] (Ret. 1981) . $225-$300

#2121   Harpooner [Gres figurine of sailor standing in prow of boat and holding a harpoon] (Ret. 1988) . . . . $1100-$1200

#2127   Indian Chief [Gres bust of Native American in war bonnet] (Ret. 1988) . . . $600-$750

#2148   Head of Congolese Woman [Gres] . . . . . $500-$700

#2150   A Tribute to Peace [Gres female nude, half-figure, garland in hair, holding white dove] (Open) $1000

#2153   Chinese Boy [Gres, boy in Chinese straw hat lugging two large clay pots] (Ret. 1990). $250-$275

#2157   Eskimo Girl with Cold Feet [seated Eskimo child in parka and rubbing feet] (Open) $300

#2158   Pensive Eskimo Girl [seated Eskimo girl in parka, chin in hands] (Open) $220

#2178   Harvest Helpers [Gres, little girl in peasant dress leaning on pitchfork, looking down at two ducks looking up at her] (Open) $285

#2195   Heavenly Sounds [seated Gres angel playing mandolin] (Ret. 1993) . . . . $250-$300

#2204   Farmyard Grace [Franciscan monk in apron feeding small animals at feet] (Ret. 1993) . $300-$325

#2216   Laundry Day [little girl in hat and apron washing clothes in small wash tub on stump while looking down at mother duck and duckling] (Open) $400

#2228   Snowy Sunday [Gres, two children in winter clothing seated on bench under snow-covered umbrella] (Open) $625

#2302   Twilight Years [Gres, elderly couple walking arm in arm, he leaning on cane, she carrying closed umbrella] (Ret. 1997) . . . . $425-$450

#2326   Physician [Gres, standing doctor in whites] (Ret. 1997) . . . . $375-$400

#2336   Young Water Girl [Gres, girl down on one knee, tipping clay water jug] (Open) $315

#2369   Early Awakening [Gres, female nude wearing open robe and carrying water pitcher casually at side] (Open) $595

#2370   Intermission [Gres, ballerina seated on floor] (Open) $690

#2375   Emperor [Gres, seated Japanese emperor in wide robes and tall headgear] (Ret. 2000). $775-$800

#2376   Empress [Gres, Japanese empress resting back on knees on large pillow] (Ret. 2000) $750-$775

#2379   Arctic Explorer [Gres, man with walking staff, Husky dog beside him] (Ret. 2000). $550-$575

#2380   A Comforting Friend [girl sitting, chin in hand, white bear in lap] (Open) $330

#2384   What About Me? [Gres, standing woman in cap and wearing apron with stylized vines on border holding lamb while blatting ewe looks up] (Open) $790

#2386   Low Tide [Gres, woman in kerchief and apron standing on rocks, holding long oar up beside her] (Ret. 2000) . . . . $575-$600

#2388   Ready to Go [Gres, little girl in mother's hat, coat, and scarf carrying suitcase and hat box] (Open) $350

#2389   Time to Go [Gres, little boy in Dad's hat and coat carrying suitcases] (Open) $330

#2397   Little Chief [Native American boy in blanket and war bonnet seated cross-legged and cross-armed] (Open) $325

#2398   Conversing with Nature [Native American girl in head-band and feather, wrapped in blanket and reclining with arms around water jar, watching small bird perched on her knee] (Open) $370

#2401   Little Shepherd [Gres, boy wrapped in large blanket, wearing beret, holding shepherd's staff, small dog reclining at feet] (Open) $275

#2402   Africa [Gres, semi-nude woman in white veil, holding water jar down by left side, reaching up with right hand to steady jar carried on head] (Open) $700

#3554   Stormy Sea [full-figured Gres, helmsman at ship's wheel] (Open) $1600

#4502G   Marketing Day [woman in white apron and shawl, market basket on arm, cloth bundle on head] (Ret. 1985) . . . . . $375-$400

#4503G   Seated Harlequin [elongated reclining harlequin holding guitar] (Ret. 1975) . . . $400-$550

#4514G   Diana [elongated figure of woman in kerchief standing in front of gazelle-like deer craning its neck around her] (Ret. 1981) . $750-$850

#4517G   Boy Student [tall, elongated figure leaning against pile of rocks, reading from book held in right hand] (Ret. 1978) . . . . $475-$500

#4570G   Girl with Goat [elongated figure of seated shepherdess next to standing goat] (Ret. 1978) . . . . $650-$700

#4571G   Resting [shepherd sitting on rock, leaning on right arm, ewe and lamb on knees at his feet] (Ret. 1981) . . . . $400-$475

#4587G   Rooster [rooster with colored plumage, posturing, body to ground, tail in air—8" high] (Ret. 1979) . . . . $375-$450

#4588G   White Cockerel [same as 4587, in white] (Ret. 1979) . . . . $300-$325

#4589G   Small Rooster [same as 4588 but smaller—7" high] (Ret. 1981) . . . . $275-$300

#4594G   Lady with Greyhound [lady in long dress and hat held on by scarf, holding closed umbrella and standing with greyhound dog] (Ret. 1981) . . . . $700-$850

#4611G/M   Nuns [two white-habited nuns with hands in sleeves, winged veils] (Open) $155

#4617G Group of Musicians [seated boy with base drum and standing boy with horn] (Ret. 1979) . . . . $500-$550

#4618G Clown [long clown with enormous shoes lying on stomach, ball at feet] (Open) $415

#4621G/M Sea Captain [man in skipper's hat and sailor pants, standing with pipe in mouth] (Ret. 1993) . . . . $300-$350

#4622G/M Old Man with Violin [man in long coat and hat, violin under arm] (Ret. 1982) . $650-$750

#4641G Pekinese Sitting (Ret. 1985) . . . . $300-$450

#4650G/M Girl with Calla Lilies [standing girl in veil holding armful of calla lilies] (G-Ret. 1998, M-Ret.1991) . . . . $175-$200

#4653G/M Orchestra Conductor [conductor behind podium, right arm extended forward] (Ret. 1979) . . . . $850-$950

#4655G Horse Group [two horses running] (Ret. 2000) . . . . $775-$800

#4660G/M Shepherdess with Dove [reclining shepherdess, dove next to her on branch] (Ret.1993) . . . . $250-$300

#4677G Birds [two wren-like birds, no surrounding foliage] (Ret. 1985) . . . . . . $200-$250

#4731G German Shepherd with Pup [reclining in dog basket] (Ret. 1975) . . $950-$1000

#4755G Boy with Dog [reclining boy leaning against rock, dog resting paws on leg] (Ret. 1978) . . . . $400-$450

#4756G Girl with Goat [reclining girl next to reclining goat] (Ret. 1978) . . . . $400-$500

#4762G/M Dentist [wearing dentist's smock with tools in front pocket, right hand raised at right angle] (Ret. 1978) . . . . $500-$550

#4772G/M Rabbit Eating [brown and white, hunkered next to fallen branch with leaves] (Ret. 1998) . . . . $150-$165

#4773G/M Rabbit Eating, Gray [gray and white] (Ret. 1998) . . . . $150-$165

#4780G Boy with Goat [tall boy, arms raised in surprise, finds himself astraddle a goat] (Ret. 1978) . . . . $500-$650

#4798G/M Female Tennis Player [leaning against wall, ankles crossed, racket under left arm] (Ret. 1981) . . . . $350-$450

#4800G Gypsy with Brother [little girl carrying baby brother on back; baby has finger in mouth] (Ret. 1979) . . . . $425-$550

#4807G Geisha [in kimono, seated in front of arch of greenery] (Ret. 1993) . . . . $475-$600

#4808G/M Wedding [groom holding top hat, looking at bride holding flowers; often used as cake topper] (Open) $190

#4809G/M Fisher Boy [boy in hat and hip-waders, pole in one hand, creel in other] $160

#4811G/M Dutch Boy [boy in Dutch clothing and cap, pail in each hand] (Ret. 1988) . . . . $350-$400

#4814G Little Girl with Turkey [standing, with long hair, holding tom turkey with fanned tail] (Ret. 1981) . . . . $450-$475

#4827G Caressing a Little Calf [kneeling girl caressing reclining calf] (Ret. 1981) . . . . $550-$600

#4831G Romance [standing ballerina leaning arm across shoulders of seated harlequin with mandolin on lap] (Ret. 1981) . . . . $1350-$1500

#4837G/M Girl with Lamb [little girl in long skirt and apron, lamb under one arm, basket over other] (Ret. 1991) . . . . $250-$350

#4840G Oriental Girl [kneeling Japanese girl in traditional dress, arranging pot of flowers on low table] (Ret. 1997) . . . . $550-$600

#4852G Woman Golfer [girl in short skirt and knee-socks, club and ball at ready for putt] (Open) $280

#4861G Horse [Percheron horse grooming rear hoof] (Ret. 1978) . . . . $500-$550

#4862G Horse [Percheron horse with left front foot raised] (Ret. 1978) . . . . $500-$575

#4863G Horse [Percheron horse down on front knees] (Ret, 1978) . . . . $400-$550

#4867G See-Saw [boy with arms up on high end of see-saw, held down by girl at other end as puppy looks on] (Ret. 1996) . . . . $425-$450

#4888G The Kiss [girl hugging seated fireman in full gear] (Ret. 1983) . . . . $700-$775

#4894G Boy Tennis Player [seated, towel around shoulders, racket under right arm] (Ret. 1980) . . . . $425-$500

#4902G Moping Dog [gangly seated dog with rounded back and hanging head] (Ret. 1979) . . . . $325-$350

#4914G Lady with Shawl [lady in long dress and wind-blown scarf holding open parasol and walking afghan on leash] (Ret. 1998) . . . $740-$800

#4922G Sea Breeze [wind blown girl facing left] (Open) . $375

#4922.3 Wind Blown Girl [Sea Breeze in white] (Ret. 1985) . . . . $275-$300

#2309 Wind Blown Girl [Gres version] (Ret. 1998) . . . . $350-$375

#4965G Little Red Riding Hood [looking down at crouching wolf] (Ret. 1983) . . . . $500-$575

#4966G Tennis Player Puppet [caricature tennis player in visored cap, ball in one hand, racket under other arm] (Ret. 1985) . . . $600-$650

#4967G Soccer Player Puppet [caricature in porkpie hat, ball under arm] (Ret. 1985) . $525-$575

#4970G Skier Puppet [caricature shooshing downhill, poles out behind him] (Ret. 1983) . . . . $600-$650

#4971G Hunter Puppet [caricature in visored hat holding rifle, reclining dog wrapped around feet] (Ret. 1985) . . . . $675-$800

#4972G/M Girl with Lilies, Sitting [seated girl in veil, holding calla lilies] (Ret. G-1997, M-1991) $250-$275

#4982G Naughty Dog [puppy pulling down girl's skirt] (Ret. 1995) . . . . $275-$350

#5029G The Flower Peddler [boy on pedal-powered cart full of flowers] (Ret. 1985) . $1350-$1500

#5031G Girl with Flowers in Tow [girl riding three-wheel bicycle pulling basketful of flowers] (Ret. 1985) . . . . $1700-$1800

#5032G Little Friskies [little girl seated on floor holding kitten away from Dalmatian puppy] (Ret. 1997) . . . . $275-$300

#2266 Little Friskies [Gres version] . . . . $275-$300

#5033G Avoiding the Goose [girl protecting little brother from reach of goose] (Ret. 1993) . $350-$375

#5034G Goose Trying to Eat [seated girl trying to keep basket in lap out of reach of craning goose] (Ret. 1996) . . . . $350-$375

#2312 Goose Trying to Eat [Gres version] (Ret. 1997) . . . . $350-$375

#5036G Jockey and Lady [jockey on horse standing next to lady in long dress and hat who holds closed parasol down beside her] (Ret. 2000) . . . . $2400-$2550

#5037G Sleigh Ride [very large figure of two children on sled hitched to dog] (Ret. 1996) . . . . $1400-$1500

#2349 Sleigh Ride [Gres version] (Ret. 1998) . $1550-$1600

#5044G Girl with Toy Wagon [little girl in bonnet and long dress pulling tiny cart with seated doll] (Ret. 1997) . . . . $275-$325

#5046G Organ Grinder [old man with white beard, long coat, and hat, carrying monkey on shoulder, man cranking organ hung around neck] (Ret. 1981) . $1650-$1750

#5049G At the Pond [boy and girl feeding two swans] (Ret. 1981) . . . . $650-$750

#5057G Clown with Violin [clown with head down holding violin behind back] (Ret. 1985) . . . . $800-$850

#5058G Clown with Concertina [clown seated, head in hands, concertina on ground behind feet] (Ret. 1985) . . . . $600-$625

#5059G Clown with Saxophone [seated clown in pointed hat, holding saxophone and looking down at Dalmatian puppy] (Ret. 1985) . . . $700-$725

#5070G Napping [little boy asleep in big armchair, feet dangling] (Ret. 1983) . . . $650-$800

#5078G Teasing the Dog [little girl in bonnet holding ball on string just out of reach of dog up on hind legs] (Ret. 1985) . . . . $500-$600

#5085G Angelic Harmony [seated girl angel caressing puppy in arms while standing girl angel looks on] (Ret. 1997) . . . . $600-$650

#5089G The Jockey [jockey on horse jumping a hedge] (Ret. 1985) . . . . $900-$1200

#5110G Looking for a Clue [bloodhound with nose to ground] (Ret. 1985) . . . . $625-$650

#5111G Baffled [seated bloodhound looking confused] (Ret. 1985) . . . . $550-$600

#5116G Young Matador [child matador in full costume, holding cape against body with right hand, left hand raised] (Ret. 1985) . . . . $325-$500

#5123G My Precious Bundle [Chinese peasant girl in traditional costume and broad-brimmed hat carrying baby on back] (Ret. 1998) . . . . . $275-$300

#5132G Miguel de Cervantes [writer in ruffled collar, seated in chair, cape draped over lap and arm, quill held in right hand] (Ret. 1988) . $1200-$1600

#5137G Billy Baseball Player [in uniform at bat] (Ret. 1983) . . . . $700-$750

#5138G Billy Golfer [golf club back for a swing] (Ret. 1983) . . . . $800-$1000

#5147G "I" Is for Ivy [girl holding dot atop the vowel I] (Ret. 1985) . . . . $550-$600

#5148G "O" Is for Olivia [girl sitting inside vowel O, chin in hands] (Ret. 1985) . . . $450-$575

#5149G "U" Is for Ursula [girl standing inside the vowel U] (Ret. 1985) . . . . $525-$550

#5161G Old Fashioned Motorist [man on motorcycle, woman in sidecar] (Ret. 1985) . . . . $2800-$3000

#5166G/M Sea Fever [seated boy holding sailboat in lap beside dog on rock] (Ret. 1993) . . $325-$350

#5167G Jesus [Christ in long white robes, hands and arms open at sides] (Open) $265

#5170G Moses [tablets in right arm, left arm raised skyward] (Ret. 2000) . . . . $425-$450

#5172G Fish Aplenty [Chinese woman in traditional costume and wide-brimmed hat holding baskets of fish suspended from pole across shoulders] (Ret. 1994) . . . . $425-$450

#5178G Stubborn Donkey [boy pulling bridle of donkey sitting down on job while small dog looks on; saddle bags carry water jars] (Ret. 1993) . . . . $500-$525

#5197G Female Physician [standing lady doctor] (Open) . $275

#5214G The Architect [in suit and hardhat leaning over blueprints] (Ret. 1990) . . . . $450-$550

#5228G Playful Piglets [reclining mother pig with two piglets] (Ret. 1998) . . . . $185-$225

#5232G Playful Kittens [little girl with mop set upon by 3 kittens] (Open) $300

#2268 Playful Kittens [Gres version] $300

#5277G Pierrot with Puppy [little clown seated on floor, puppy lying in lap] (Open) $160

#5278G Pierrot with Puppy and Ball (open) $160

#5279G Pierrot with Concertina [playing for little dog perched on a die] (Open) $160

#5282G Over the Threshold [groom carrying bride] (Open) $290

#5288G Mallard Duck [swimming male] (Ret. 1994) . . . . $550-$600

#5298G Girl Sitting Under Trellis [girl in hat and long skirt framed in round trellis with flowering vine] (Ret.1988) . . . . $750-$800

#5299G/M Mother with Child and Lamb [standing mother, daughter, lamb] (Ret. 1988) . . . $400-$500

#5303G Playing with the Ducks [kneeling girl and seated boy feeding ducks at pond] (Ret. 1990) . . . . 600-$800

#5305G Visit with Granny [toddler sitting on piano bench next to grandmother in shawl] (Ret. 1993) . . . . $600-$625

#5307G Miniature Kitten (Ret. 1993) . . . . $100-$150

#5311G Miniature Puppies [set of 3, one reclining, two begging] (Ret. 1990) . . . . $200-$225

#5312G Miniature Bison, Resting [recumbent, head resting on legs] (Ret. 1990) . . . . . . $150-$165

#5314G Miniature Deer [reclining) (Ret. 1990) . . $150-$175

#5315G Miniature Dromedary [reclining camel] (Ret. 1990) . . . . $150-$175

#5316G Miniature Giraffe [reclining] (Ret. 1990) $225-$400

#5317G Miniature Lamb [reclining, looking back over shoulder] (Ret. 1990) . . . . . . $180-$200

#5318G Miniature Seal Family [mother seal with two babies] (Ret. 1990) . . . . $250-$295

#5319G Wistful Centaur Girl [reclining centaur with flowers in hair and holding bouquet] (Ret. 1990) . . . . $375-$450

#5326G The Tailor [wearing suit and working on suited manikin] (Ret. 1988) . . . . . . $800-$1100

#5320G Demure Centaur Girl [reclining centaur with flower necklace, flowers in hair, hands behind back] (Ret. 1990) . . . . . . $350-$425

#5331G Gymnast with Ring [girl gymnast on stomach, working ring with left hand and foot] (Ret. 1988) . . . . $300-$425

#5332G Gymnast Balancing Ball [gymnast on floor, leaning on left elbow, right leg raised, ball balanced on right hand] (Ret. 1988) . . . . $300-$375

#5333G Gymnast Exercising with Ball [gymnast seated on floor, holding ball behind her] (Ret. 1988) . . . . $300-$350

#5334G Aerobics Pull-ups [girl in leotard, balancing on shoulders with legs and lower body raised in air] (Ret. 1988) . . $250-$300

#5335G Aerobics Floor Exerciser [girl in leotard, lying on stomach, upper body supported on forearms] (Ret. 1988) . . . . $250-$300

#5336G Aerobics Scissor Figure [girl in leotard, body to side, supported by right arm, legs scissored] (Ret. 1988) . . . . $200-$350

#5337G La Giaconda [Mona Lisa, bust] (Ret. 1988) . . . . 400-$600

#5348G On the Scent [small beagle with head and front paws down, tail in air] (Ret. 1990) . . $325-$375

#5350G On Guard [standing, alert beagle with collar] (Ret. 1990) . . . . $300-$325

#5351G Woe Is Me [seated beagle looking up, one paw raised] (Ret. 1990) . . . . $200-$250

#5356G Wolfhound [seated, 4" high, very long nose] (Ret. 1990) . . . . $200-$250

#5363G Still Life [girl in beret sitting before canvas on easel, paintbrush in hand] (Ret. 1997) . . . . $475-$500

#5377G Can Can [two female dancers swishing skirts, one with leg extended up and out] (Ret. 1990) . . . . $1200-$1400

#5390G Spanish Dancer [little girl in ruffled dress down on one knee, left hand on hip, right arm raised over head] (Ret. 1990) . . . . . . $450-$500

#5392G Balancing Act [seal on round dais balancing ball on tip of nose] (Ret. 1990) . $175-$200

#5403G The Drummer Boy [in uniform, white jacket with red piping, blue pants, white plume on helmet] (Ret. 1990) . . . . $400-$450

#5404G Cadet Captain [in uniform, saber against shoulder; white jacket with red piping, white plume in helmet] (Ret. 1990) . . . . $375-$400

#5405G The Flag Bearer [flag in barrel of rifle at side, white jacket with red piping, white helmet plume] (Ret. 1990) . . . . . . $400-$450

#5406G The Bugler [boy cadet blowing bugle, white jacket with red piping, white plume in helmet] (Ret. 1990) . . . . $375-$400

#5407G At Attention [cadet standing at attention, white jacket with red piping, white plume in hat] (Ret. 1990) . . . . $325-$350

#5415G Mexican Dancers [couple in Mexican dance costume, man wearing Mexican sombrero] (Open) $1195

#5428G/M Feeding the Pigeons [woman seated on park bench feeding pigeons] (Ret. 1990) . $650-$700

#5433G Kangaroo [mother kanga with joey in pouch] (Ret. 1990) . . . . $225-$300

#5435G Cougar [miniature cougar stalking] (Ret. 1990) . . . . $275-$300

#5436G Lion [miniature recumbent lion with mane] (Ret. 1990) . . . . $200-$250

#5437G Rhino [miniature] (Ret. 1990) . . . . $175-$200

#5438G Elephant [miniature] (Ret. 1990) . . . . . . $250-$275

#5448G/M Naptime [little girl asleep in rocking chair with doll in arm] (Open) $260

#2322 Naptime [Gres version] $275

#5455G Bashful Bather [little girl in pony tail bathing hound dog in wash basin] (open) $190

#2273 Bashful Bather [Gres version] (Open) $220

173

#5466G   Chit-chat [seated girl on phone, dog lying at feet] (Open) $210

#2310   Chit-Chat [Gres version] (Ret. 1998) . . . $275-$325

#5486G   Debutantes [Young girl in hat and long gown leaning over couch chatting with seated girl, hat on arm of sofa] (Ret. 1997) . $725-$750

#5497G   Dress Rehearsal [two ballerinas facing each other, attached at tutu] (Open) $420

#5502G   Meditation (Blue) [blue-habited nun with white winged veil kneeling at prie-dieu] (Open) $110

#5550G   Serene Moment (Blue) [standing blue-habited nun in white winged veil, holding vase with flower] (Ret. 1993) . . $250-$275

#5550.3   Serene Moment (White) (Ret. 1991) . . . $250-$275

#5501G   Time to Sew (Blue) [seated nun in blue habit and white winged veil, sewing in lap] (Open) . . $110

#5551G   Call to Prayer (Blue) [blue-habited nun in white winged veil ringing hand-bell] (Ret. 1993) . . . . $250-$275

#5551.3   Call to Prayer (White) (Ret. 1991) . . . . . $250-$350

#5552G   Morning Chores (Blue) [blue-habited nun in apron, holding bucket and broom] (Ret. 1993) . . . . $250-$275

#5552.3   Morning Chores (White) (Ret. 1991) . . . $250-$275

#5553G   Wild Goose Chase [little girl in long skirt, bent over trying to catch flapping white goose] (Ret. 1997) . . . . $300-$325

#5593G   Siamese Dancer [female Siamese dancer in traditional costume, left hand raised, left lowered] (Ret. 1993) . . . . $400-$550

#5595G   Joy in a Basket [girl with puppies in basket] (Ret.1997) . . . . $300-$350

#5665G   Hang On! [girl in parka hood seated behind boy on sled] (Ret. 1995) . . . . . . $325-$350

#5679G   In No Hurry [girl on tricycle at rest, puppy at feet] (Ret.1994) . . . . $650-$700

#5681G   On the Road [salesman in trench coat and hat, closed umbrella in one hand, sample case in other, suitcase behind him] (Ret. 1991) . . . . $450-$550

#5684G   Barnyard Reflections [elderly, seated monk with white beard leaning hands and chin on staff before him, surrounded by birds and farmyard animals] (Ret. 1993) . . . . . $650-$750

#5688G   Dog's Best Friend [little girl with flowers in hair covering dog with blanket] (Open) $310

#2287   Dog's Best Friend [Gres version] (Ret. 2000) . . . . $325-$350

#5697G   Over the Clouds [little pilot with helmet and goggles seated in toy airplane] (Open) . . . $310

#5703G   Behave! [boy pointing finger at puppy held on lap] (Ret.1994) . . . . $325-$350

#5705G   The Swan and the Princess [child riding on back of swan] (Ret. 1994) . . . . $450-$500

#5706G   We Can't Play [seated girl with arm in sling beside commiserating dog] (Ret. 1998) . . . $200-$275

#5711G   A Christmas Wish [child sitting on Santa's knee] (Ret. 1997) . . . . $450-$500

#5715G   Mommy, It's Cold! [mother seated in chair about to wrap child in large bath towel] (Ret. 1994) . . . . $450-$500

#5717G   Rock a' Bye Baby [small girl asleep in cradle with doll] (Ret. 1999) . . . . $350-$375

#5722G   Follow Me [miniature mother swan swimming with cygnets behind her] (Open) . . $160

#5724G   Angelic Voice [angel singing from open book] (Open) $145

#5726G   Sweep Away the Clouds [angel with broom] (Open) $145

#5731G   Carousel Charm [little girl astride carousel horse, holding on to her hat] (Ret. 1994) . . . . $2000-$2100

#5732G   Carousel Canter [boy wearing hat with pom-pom and holding satchel while riding carousel horse] (Ret. 1994) . . . $2000-$2100

#5733G   Horticulturist [man in old fashioned clothing, including lace cravat, kneeling to plant a tree] (Ret. 1993) . . . . $495-$550

#5739G   Lap Full of Love [seated girl in kerchief holding three kittens in long skirt] (Ret. 1995) . . . . $350-$365

#2320   Lap Full of Love [Gres version] . . . . . . $450-$500

#5753G   Hold Her Still! [boy milking goat held by girl] (Ret.1993) . . . . $700-$750

#5769G   Faithful Steed [little girl on rocking horse] (Ret. 1994) . . . . $350-$400

#5787G   Sophisticate [lady in 20s costume, standing straight, right hand on skirt] (Ret. 1998) . $225-$250

#5788G   Talk of the Town [lady in 20s costume, standing straight, left hand on skirt] (Ret. 1998) . . . . $225-$250

#5795G   Floral Getaway [girl on scooter with sidecar full of flowers] (Ret. 1993) . . . . . $750-$825

#5804G   Playing Tag [three naked toddlers running] (Ret. 1993) . . . . $250-$300

#5811G   Littlest Clown [child clown holding bunch of balloons] (Open) $240

#5814G/M   Curtain Call [ballerina bowing] (Ret. 1994) . . . . $550-$575

#5826G/M   Little Unicorn [reclining] (Ret. 1997) . . . $300-$400

#5843G   A Quiet Afternoon [elderly couple in old-fashioned garb sitting on park bench feeding pigeons; pigeon is perched on her hand] (Ret. 1995) . . . $1200-$1250

#5845G   Dressing the Baby [mother seated cross-legged on floor, naked infant in lap, reaching for clothing beside her] (Open) $295

#2289   Dressing the Baby [Gres version] (Ret. 1997) . . . . $350-$375

#5846G/M All Tuckered Out [little boy asleep in rocking chair toy horse on wheels beside chair] (Open) . \$260

#2321 All Tuckered Out [Gres version] (Open) \$275

#5852G Easter Bonnets [girl in hat with round hat box hanging from one arm, square box on ground beside her] (Ret. 1993) . . . . . \$400-\$450

#5862G Fragrant Bouquet [seated girl in broad-brimmed hat, arms full of flowers] (Open) . . . \$370

#2305 Fragrant Bouquet [Gres version] \$330

#5880G Playful Unicorn [white unicorn sitting on rear haunches] (Ret. 1998) . . . . \$350-\$365

#5896G The Loaves and Fishes [Christ standing looking up to heaven, eyes raised, basket of loaves and basket of fishes at his feet] (Ret. 1997) . . . . \$950-\$975

#5899G Just One More [father sitting on edge of child's bed reading a story] (Ret. 1997) . \$500-\$550

#5901G Surprise [clown lifting coat to reveal two puppies sitting at either side of him] (Ret. 2000) . . . . \$335-\$350

#2290 Surprise [Gres version] (Open) \$335

#5921G Take Your Medicine [little girl holding medicine bottle and trying to spoon contents into dog with bandage around head] (Ret. 1998) . . \$425-\$450

#5947G General Practitioner [standing doctor in white coat, folded stethoscope in left hand] (Ret. 1997) . . . . \$400-\$425

#5988G Taking Time [altar boy on floor, reclining back on elbows next to small dog] (Ret. 1998) . \$200-\$225

#2318 Taking Time [Gres version] (Ret. 1998) . \$225-\$235

#5991G Love Story [caped prince and lady on white horse] (Ret. 2000) . . . . \$2850-\$2900

#5993G/M Unicorn and Friend [unicorn looking back at bird perched on tail] (Ret. 1998) . . . . . \$390-\$425

#5997G One More Try [boy in winter clothing standing behind fallen girl on skis, lifting her by the arms] (Ret. 1996) . . . . \$750-\$775

#6004G Bar Mitzvah Day [boy in prayer shawl reading from Torah] (Open) \$430

#6028G Mazel Tov! [Jewish wedding couple, groom with foot on glass] (Open) \$395

#6029G Hebrew Scholar [standing boy in yarmulke looking down at books held at side] (Ret. 1996) . . . . \$275-\$300

#6032G On the Green [male golfer with club back over left shoulder at end of wing] (Open) \$645

#2315 On the Green [Gres version] (Ret. 2000) . \$575-\$600

#6034G Monkey Business [three monkeys, right with hand shading eyes, middle with hands behind ears, left with hands framing its chattering mouth] (Ret. 1994) . . . . \$850-\$875

#6090G Baseball Player [seated boy with hands and chin resting on end of vertical bat in front of him] (Ret. 1997) . . . . \$400-\$425

#6091G Basketball Player [seated boy in player's uniform, holding ball] (Ret. 1997) . . . . . \$350-\$375

#6101G Follow Us [boy wearing ski cap and long coat with dangling sleeves holds mother duck, ducklings follow] (Ret. 1997) . . . . \$225-\$250

#6107G Football Player [young boy in football uniform, down on one knee with football in front of him and helmet under arm] (Ret. 1997) . . . . \$350-\$375

#6108G Hockey Player [boy skated up and in uniform, down on one knee, holding stick] (Ret. 1998) . . . . \$350-\$375

#6137G Baseball Star [boy in cap and uniform sitting cross-legged, bat resting against leg, fingers in victory sign] (Ret. 1997) . . \$315-\$335

#6140G Springtime Friends [little girl in broad-brimmed hat seated on tree limb conversing with two squirrels] (Open) \$485

#6141G Kitty Cart (girl pushing cart full of kittens and flowers) (Open) \$795

#6172G Coming of Age [boy in suit and yarmulke ready to cut Bar Mitzvah cake] (Ret. 1998) . \$375-\$395

#6185G Team Player [little girl down on one knee, soccer ball on ground before her] (Ret. 1999) . . . . \$350-\$265

#6192G American Indian Boy [boy in headdress, arms folded across chest] (Ret. 1998) . . . \$250-\$265

#6207G Hanukkah Lights [little boy and dog leaning against table look longingly at small menorah] (Ret. 1999) . . . . \$425-\$450

#6210G Gentle Surprise [small beagle-type puppy looking back to find butterfly perched on tip of tail] (Open) \$125

#6212G Little Hunter [hound puppy with nose to ground, tail horizontal to body] (Ret. 2000) . . . . \$115-\$125

#6226G Snuggle Up [girl in shawl kneeling with puppy under either arm] (Ret. 2000) . . \$175-\$200

#6228G Special Gift [stork on rooftop carrying baby in blue blanket] (Open) \$265

#6229G Contented Companion [little girl with brush astride a reclining Saint Bernard] (Ret. 2000) . . . . \$200-\$225

#6233G Chef's Apprentice [boy chef in tall chef's hat and bow-tie, seated on floor getting ready to peel a sack of potatoes] (Ret. 1998) . . . \$300-\$325

#6234G The Great Chef [little boy with tall chef's hat carrying huge pot with cover] (Ret. 1998) . . . . \$225-\$235

#6242G/M Winged Companions [Pegasus on cloud looking at small bird on upturned hoof] (Ret. 1999) . . . . \$300-\$350

#6243G Sweet Symphony [girl in long dress and hat playing violin from music on stand] (Open) . . \$450

#6248G Regatta [racing sailboat tilting over waves] (Ret. 1996) . . . . \$700-\$725

#6256G   Making Rounds [standing uniformed nurse holding chart in left hand, gazing at thermometer held in right] (Open) $295

#6273G   Pharmacist [standing pharmacist in full white apron holding mortar and pestle] (Ret. 2000) . . . . $300-$325

#6286G/M Tennis Champion [on knees with arms, head, and racket raised in victory] (Ret. 1999) . . . . $350-$400

#6288G/M Taking Flight [white dove with wings open to take off] (Ret. 1999) . . . . $165-$175

#6291G/M Love Nest [pair of white doves, one in background with tail fanned and wings spread, one in foreground recumbent] (Ret. 1999) . . . . $275-$300

#6299G   Little Bear [toddler girl in high chair holding teddy bear in arms] (Ret. 1999) . . $300-$325

#6300G   Rubber Ducky [boy toddler in baseball cap sitting in high chair, rubber ducky on tray] (Ret. 2000) . . . . $300-$325

#6303G   Tuba Player [band uniform] (Ret. 1998) . $315-$335

#6304G   Bass Drummer [boy in band uniform leaning over bass drum, front of which says "Music Band"] (Ret. 1998) . . . . $400-$450

#6305G   Trumpet Player [in uniform] (Ret. 1998) . $275-$300

#6306G   Majorette [in uniform with baton] (Ret. 1998) . . . . $310-$350

#6318G   Little Distraction [boy with chin in hands sitting before a pile of books, top one open with bird perched on it] (Ret. 1999) . . . . $365-$375

#6319G   Beautiful Rhapsody [girl in long dress playing flute in front of music stand] (Open) . . $450

#6320G   Architect [suited man wearing hardhat, briefcase in right hand, rolled up floor plans in left] (Ret. 1999) . . . . $350-$375

#6332G   Concerto [Girl in broad-brimmed hat playing cello and reading from music stand] (Open) . . . $490

#6337G   Poodle [small reclining] (Ret. 2000) . . . . $150-$175

#6339G   Country Sounds [male Country-Western singer playing guitar] (Ret. 1999) . . . . . . $825-$850

#6340G   Sweet Country [girl Country-Western singer playing banjo] (Ret. 1998) . . . . . . $750-$800

#6348G   Little Veterinarian [girl in white dress and cap holding bog on lap and bandaging tail he holds in air] (Ret. 1999) . . . . $225-$250

#6363G   St. Joseph the Carpenter [Joseph seated on bench with arm around boy Jesus standing on bench] (Ret. 1999) . . . . . $1200-$1300

#6369G   Indian Maiden [kneeling Native American girl in traditional dress petting white dog] (Ret. 1999) $600

#6370G   Country Chores [woman in long skirt holding feeding basket, scattering seed to hen and chicks at feet] (Ret. 2000) . . . . $275-$300

#6376G/M Light and Life [tall girl in long, flowing dress carrying candle] (Ret. 2000) . . . . $220-$225

#6377G/M Unity [tall girl in long, flowing dress holding a wreath] (Ret. 1999) . . . . $230-$250

#6378G/M Beginning and End [tall girl in long, flowing dress, holding a star] (Ret. 1999) . $230-$250

#6379G/M Love [tall girl in long, flowing dress, holding a heart] (Ret. 2000) . . . . $220-$225

#6382G   New Arrival [stork on rooftop carrying baby in pink blanket] (Open) $265

#6397G   In Neptune's Waves [half-figure of Neptune holding triton in left hand and mermaid in right arm] (Ret. 1999) . $1030-$1050

#6398G   Morning Delivery [basset hound with newspaper in mouth] (Open) $160

#6404G/M Sister with Sax [white-habited nun with winged veil playing saxophone] (Ret. 1999) . . . . $200-$225

#6405G/M Sister Singing [white-habited nun singing into microphone] (Ret. 1999) . . $175-$200

#6406G/M Sister with Guitar [white-habited nun playing guitar] (Ret. 1999) . . . . $200-$225

#6407G/M Sister with Tambourine [white-habited nun playing tambourine] (Ret. 1999) . . . $200-$225

#6408G   Sweet Song [seated girl in long dress and broad-brimmed hat playing mandolin from music on stand] (Open) $480

#6417G   Unlikely Friends [small sleeping cat curled up under chin of sleeping bulldog] (Open) . . . $125

#6418G   So Beautiful! [woman in long skirt holds out hand on which is perched a butterfly] (Ret. 2000) . . . . $325-$335

#6419G   Arms Full of Love [little girl with puppy under each arm] (Open) $180

#6420G   My Favorite Slippers [little girl holding bunny slippers in front of her] (Ret. 1999) . . . . $150-$175

#6421G   Off to Bed [little girl in nightdress wearing bunny slippers] (Ret. 1999) . . . $150-$175

#6422G   My Chubby Kitty [little girl carrying cat draped across arms] (Open) $135

#6425G   Female Attorney [in open robe over dress, holding papers in right hand, carrying brief case with left] (Ret. 2000) . . . . $300-$325

#6426G   Male Attorney [standing in robe, brief case held against body with left hand] (Ret. 2000) . . . . $300-$325

#6430G   Pony Ride [two small children on decorated pony, followed by dog] (Ret. 2000) . . . . $825-$850

#6436G   The Dolphins [group of four] (Open) $1000

#6437G   Timid Torero [child toreador holding cape in mouth and arms] (Ret. 1999) . . $200-$220

#6438G   Young Toreador [child toreador in full costume, holding cape low in front of him] (Open) $240

#6440G   Time for Bed [small girl in long nightgown, pacifier around neck, candle in left hand, doll in right] (Ret. 1999) . . . . $175-$195

#6450G Dentist [seated white-coated dentist holding instruments] (Ret. 2000)...... $235-$250

#6452G Spring Recital [girl in broad-brimmed hat seated at harpsichord, basket of flowers on floor nearby] (Open)........... $710

#6455G Collie [seated and alert] (Ret. 2000).... $295-$325

#6459G Collie with Puppy [reclining mother, pup's front paws on back] (Ret. 2000).. $350-$375

#6469G Our Cozy Home [two Yorkshire terriers in ruffled basket/bed] (Open)............ $195

#6470G A Swimming Lesson [mother dolphin with baby] (Open)..................... $260

#6476G A Symbol of Pride [eagle with wings spread, one leg touching ground] (Open).... $730

#6479G Heavenly Slumber [baby asleep inside crescent moon] (Open).................. $185

#6483G It's Morning Already? [child in long nightdress and stocking cap, hands in sleeves] (Open)... $105

#6500G Jolly Santa [Santa standing with pack over back, ringing hand-bell] (Ret. 1998)... $250-$275

#6502G Please Come Home [two puppies standing in large, curtained window, pots of flowers in front of it] (Open)................... $750

#6519G Our Winter Home [2 little squirrels outside a snow-capped toadstool] (Ret. 1999).... $90-$95

#6522G Through the Clouds [hot air balloon in flight with kittens in basket] (Open)........ $450

#6523G Flying High [hot air balloon aloft with flowers in basket] (Ret. 2000)....... $635-$650

#6524G Up and Away [hot air balloon, puppies in basket] (Open)..................... $560

#6531G A New Life [reclining deer with fawn] (Ret. 2000).....................$515-$535

#6553G Grandparents' Joy [old man standing behind seated wife holding baby in lap while dog stands with front paws on woman's knee] (Ret. 2000)............ $700

#6540G Cozy Companions [boy and puppy asleep on bed] (Open)................. $185

#6541G Bedtime Buddies [sleeping girl and cat on bed] (Open)..................... $195

#6544G On Our Way [mother in suit, lapel flower, holding briefcase and standing behind little girl in blue coat holding books and school satchel](Open)..................... $340

#6556G Safe and Sound [1999 Event figurine, terrier dog holding child by nightshirt scruff] (Ret.) $200-$225

#6558G Great Dane [spotted, sitting] (Ret. 2000) $935-$975

#6563G A Day's Work [little farmer in hat astride toy tractor pulling cart of flowers, puppy trotting along] (Open)................. $615

#6564G Want a Lift? [little girl in toy bucket loader with two kittens in bucket, flowering box behind tractor] (Open)................. $515

#6569G Milky Way [first in Inspiration Millennium series of four figures, girl with stars flowing from her hair, holding star up in left hand; stars embossed on hem of gown] (Ret. 2000)..................... $750-$775

#6570G New Horizons [second in the Inspiration Millennium series, girl in billowing gown and shawl, doves forming arc above her head] (Ret. 2000).................. $575-$600

#6571G Rebirth [third in the Inspiration Millennium series, featuring woman with flower in raised hand looking down at baby nestled in a bower of flowering vines arcing above them] (Ret. 2000)............... $1270-$1350

#6573G Parading Donkey [prancing donkey with flowerwork at sides] (Ret. 2000).. $275-$300

#6591G Elegant Trio with Base [three swimming swans, wooden base] (Open)............ $675

#6593G My Bat Mitzvah [young girl in blue jacket and white skirt reading from scroll on dais] (Open). $345

#6599G Bosom Buddies [sleeping dog and cat snuggled together] (Open)............. $235

#6610G Faithful Companion [seated girl in 20s-style suit and hat, seated greyhound beside her] (Open).. $675

#6625G The Master Chef [white-clothed chef in tall chef's hat carrying plate with food] (Open)... $240

#6628G Adagio [seated winged cherub playing hand held harp] (Open)................ $160

#6629G Allegro [seated winged cherub with foot propped on opposite knee, playing mandolin] (Open)... $160

#6630G A Little Romance [little boy and girl in formal attire sitting either side of a small table, hands touching] (Open)............ $695

#6632G "A Birthday Kiss" [little girl in hat kneeling to kiss sitting Saint Bernard with birthday cake in front of him] (Open).............. $575

#6633G Sancho [Panza standing with sword pointing down held in right hand, chewed hat in left] (Open)........................... $255

#6635G My Pretty Puppy [small girl kneeling next to hassock atop which stands a small dog with bow in hair] (Open)................... $295

#6640G Little Explorer [boy in buckskin jacket and coonskin cap rowing small canoe, white dog aboard] (Ret. 2000)....... $430-$450

#6641G The Flamingos [pair standing white flamingos with pink and black beaks] (Open). $495

#6642G Little Stowaway [Spaniel pup wearing sailor's hat and riding in paper boat] (Open).. $155

#6665G Let's Fly Away [Spaniel pup with goggles atop head riding paper airplane atop cloud] (Open). $155

#6696G Father Time [holding staff with "Millennium" banner in right hand, hour glass in left; last figure in Inspiration Millennium series] (Ret. 2000)..................... $450-$475

#6742 Underwater Explorers [two angel fish swimming through coral reef] (Open)... $655-$90

"Bird in Nest" (#1299G), issued in 1974 and retired in 1985, sculpted by Vicente Martinez. Value today: $700-$750. Some secondary market dealers are nervous about carrying such delicate items. Probably not the sort of thing I'd want to risk buying at Internet auction. (Photo by the author, courtesy of Caren Reed and Reed's Antiques and Collectibles of Wells, ME.)

Chapter 5

SMART BUYING
ON THE RETAIL AND
SECONDARY MARKETS

Lladró's retail distribution is managed by the company through a network of sparsely-occurring authorized dealerships. From a collector's perspective, this has both advantages and disadvantages. For those who live in rural areas, as I do, it can be a nuisance to have to drive for several hours to reach the nearest authorized dealer. On the other hand, limited distribution also means that Lladró does not flood the market the way some collectibles do, and this bodes well for its future appreciation.

Retail pricing is also controlled by the company; Lladró would rather remainder core collection items to its outlet store in Williamsburg (about which there is more later in this chapter) than have them suffer the indignity of sales or discounts at authorized dealerships. Still, there are ways to buy smart on the retail market without breaking your bank. Here are some tricks of the trade.

1. Buy Early on the Retail Market

The best time to buy a desirable open issue piece is when it's still on the retail market—and as early in its retail run as possible. Chances are, you'll never be able to buy it that cheaply again on the secondary market. Can you imagine what it must have been like to have been in on the ground floor of some of those issues that came out in the late 1960s and early 1970s? How much of a thrill must it be today to be the proud owner of one of those little Dalmatian puppies that now go for hundreds of dollars, knowing that you paid $25 apiece for yours when they first came out? Or to have bought one of those little girls with the five vowel letters—say "A is for Amy" (#5145)—for $110 in 1982 (the year she came out) knowing that any number of buyers would line up to pay you $1400 or more for her today? The lesson is clear. If you love it, buy it early!

"'E' is for Ellen" (#5146G) was the second in the vowel series, and, like "Amy," she is hard to find. She can cost $1200-$1300 today. (Photo courtesy of Lladró USA, Inc.)

"'A' is for Amy" (#5145G), and she really is an ace when it comes to what people are willing to pay to have her. Part of a set of 5 "vowel" figurines that were only out for three years (1982-1985), "Amy" is the most difficult to find—and the most expensive on the secondary market, at prices of $1400 to $1500. (Photo courtesy of Lladró USA, Inc.)

2. Buy Recently Retired or About to Retire Items While Still on the Retail Market

Many authorized dealers have recently-retired items in their shop inventories. It's not that unusual to find at an authorized dealership leftovers that have been retired as many as two years previously. Secondary market brokers usually begin pricing these things upward as soon as they hit retirement; the prices at an authorized retail dealer, however, will usually remain at last retail. If you buy what you like, and are smart about focusing your purchases on those items already retired or shortly due to retire (the company usually makes such announcements fairly early in the retirement year), you can pick up some wonderful "bargains" at prices under their appreciated value.

Items retired after a short retail run can also be an especially good buy. Bear in mind that a figure issued one year and retired the next—for whatever reason—is a limited edition by default, and you won't have to pay limited edition prices to get it.

"Peruvian Group" (#4610G) was issued in the late 1960s and retired in 1970. It was not unusual for these early figurines to have short retail runs, making them "limited editions by default." This baby may cost you $1700-$1800 on the secondary market— if you can find it! (Photo courtesy of Lladró USA, Inc.)

"A Quiet Moment" (#6384G) was issued in 1997, and I'd thought I might buy her then. But those who snooze lose and, by the time I came to at the end of 1999, she'd gone off the market. She appealed to me because she reprises the elongated elegance of older Lladró. Last retailing at $275, I'll have to pay $300-$325 if I want her now— and the longer I wait, the more she'll appreciate. (Photo courtesy of Lladró USA, Inc.)

3. Complete Your Sets!

If you care about completing sets of items, don't wait. In 1991, Lladró retired most of its matte corpus, to this day leaving many collectors scrambling to complete matte sets, especially of the Bethlehem Nativity (#4670-4680) pictured on page 195. One of the things I did early on to cushion myself against the impact of an unanticipated retirement of the glazed version of this Nativity was to make sure that I had completed my set of eleven as early as I possibly could.

While all Lladró items are created with the ability to stand alone, many are parts of sets of three to six or more. The famous kids in nightshirts series (#4868-4874, several of which are pictured on page 106), the three polar bears (#s 1207-1209, two of which are shown on page 189), and the six child angels (#s 4536-4541, page 194) are cases that come immediately to mind. While most of these have been on the retail market for about thirty years, I wouldn't rely on the secondary market to fill in my gaps should these retire. Some of the child angels, for example, are harder to find than others; the little African American angel and the Chinese angel are less often seen on the secondary market than their more Caucasian-looking counterparts, and the two are much in demand.

180

4. Look for Retail "Sleepers"

After you've been collecting awhile, you'll start to have a "feel" for retail pricing and will be able to make some intelligent decisions about what seems hyperpriced as well as what seems undervalued. For one thing, flowerwork on any piece—even if it's only a flower in a girl's hair—commands a price premium. Take a careful look at an expensive figurine with a lot of flowerwork on it and ask yourself this question: What would the item be without the flowerwork? Sometimes, Lladró flowers seem to "carry" what might otherwise be a nondescript piece.

"Puppet Show" (#5736G) has to be one of Lladró's most endearing creations. Issued in 1991 and retired in 1996, it was a retail bargain at $295 for a multiple-element model, and it's still a sleeper on the secondary market at $325-$375. (Photo courtesy of Lladró USA, Inc.)

These two groups had overlapping retail lives. What this means is that the collector of the "decorated" rabbits was paying an extra $30-$60 just for the flowerwork on the later models. This is not to say that you may not still decide to pay a premium for the flowerwork if you value it that much. My point here is merely that you should recognize you're paying for the flowerwork.

"A Barrow of Blossoms" (#1419G), first issued in 1982, currently retails at $675. Her issue price was $350—which gives you an idea of how steeply Lladró appreciates even during its retail life. Lesson? If you like it, buy it early! (Photo courtesy of Lladró USA, Inc.)

One of the best examples of how flowerwork affects price is provided by an analysis of a series in which Lladró first issued a group of animal figures and then later issued the same models with flowers added to them. The series of white rabbits in various positions, #s 5904-5907 (see page 107), issued in 1992 and retired between 1997 and 1998, all retailed for $80 apiece. Two years later, in 1994, the company issued the same models with flowers pasted all over them. Of these flowered versions, two are retired: #6097 ("Sleeping Bunny with Flowers" in 1997 at a last retail of $110) and #6099 ("Preening Bunny with Flowers" (also in 1997, at a last retail of $140). The others are still retailing at prices of $110 for #6100 ("Sitting Bunny with Flowers") and $140 for #6098 ("Attentive Bunny with Flowers").

"Out for a Spin" (#5770G) had a short retail life, from 1991 through 1994. The market has seemed to regard its last retail price of $420 as being expensive enough; it reached only $400 at one of the Lladró auctions and has not broken through the $500 mark since. (Photo courtesy of Lladró USA, Inc.)

Now contrast an otherwise mediocre model with flowerwork to a figurine without flowerwork such as "Swan with Wings Spread" (#5231G, shown on page 187), issued in 1984. Its retail price just went up in 1999 from $135 to $145. This piece is large and elegant, and its feathering is lushly detailed. I call it a great bargain at its current retail price, and it has plenty of room to appreciate on the secondary market once it retires.

As porcelain gets more and more expensive to make, it gets more expensive to acquire. At the same time, there seems to be a price ceiling above which even Lladró will not appreciate on the secondary market. This means that the more expensive the piece is to buy on the retail market, the less room it has to appreciate in secondary market value. We are already beginning to see signs that modestly-sized pieces with lots of flowerwork or other extraneous features that add to retail cost are having difficulty breaking that last-retail-price barrier on the secondary market. Having said that, if you really like and want the item—if it gives you pleasure—buy it anyway. Being economically astute in your retail purchase decisions doesn't mean you shouldn't on occasion violate the tenets of practicality for the sake of artistic appeal. People who buy Lladró only out of financial considerations are market speculators, not collectors.

"Flock of Birds" (#1462) is such a modest, understated title for a work of astonishing technical and artistic brilliance. This is a great example of how Lladró artisans are always stretching the medium to see how far it will go. Issued in 1985 in an edition size of 1985, it is surprising that it is still retailing at $1750 after all these years. If there are any "Sleepers" in the world of high-end limited editions, surely this must be one of them. (Photo courtesy of Lladró USA, Inc.)

5. Beware the "Gray Market" in Retail Purchases

Lladró distributes its retail merchandise via a system of authorized dealerships, with the company itself determining the pricing structure for its own products. Aside from its efforts to move newly-retired items via its Williamsburg outlet, Lladró does not "discount" slow-moving items; it simply retires them. So whenever you are dealing with a retail establishment, whether online or in person, that offers a discount off the usual retail price, chances are you are dealing with what is called the "gray market" in Lladró.

The gray market is distinguished from the secondary market. The secondary market is an after-retail market and presents itself as such. The gray market, by contrast, "fronts" itself as a legitimate retail market. As the phrase implies, the "gray market" is not quite the "black market," but it's not entirely licit, either. From a consumer's perspective, the ethical ambiguity typically results from the gray market dealer not having the authorized contacts to make good on special orders or on purchase returns and in the dealer's failing to inform the customer of those limitations. In other words, the gray market has a certain element of deception inherent in it. Many consumers lured by the prospect of a price break may not even know they are dealing on the gray market; to them, any dealer in Lladró is as good as any other. They may find out the contrary only after complaining directly to the company about an unhappy purchase only to discover that the place where they bought the questionable item was not authorized by Lladró to sell its products.

The gray market in retail Lladró is real *caveat emptor* territory. Want a price break? Look for it on the secondary (after-retail) market. Typical secondary market venues are auctions and antique and consignment shops. You may still have to worry about condition and guarantees on the items you want to buy, but at least you'll know the item has been elsewhere before it came into your hands, and you'll expect to have to keep your guard up accordingly.

The bottom line is that a discount price for Lladró on the retail market should always be a red flag. If you have any doubt about the legitimacy of a retail dealer, you should ask for proof of authorized status. Also, ask up front about return policies, and be suspicious if there is any stonewalling. Any authorized dealer should be willing to stand behind the condition of the merchandise and to make good on legitimate returns. Finally, check on the dealer's ability to order current merchandise not in stock in the store. Remember that access to these pieces for a gray market dealer will be limited to his contacts outside the company. If you can't order the current issues you want through a particular dealer, then chances are that dealer is operating outside the authorized system.

The Genesis of a Secondary Market

The Lladró secondary market got its first boost with the exclusive Lladró auctions sponsored by Rostand Fine Jewelers in California and, later, by Thalheimer's Auction Gallery in Florida. Begun by Herb Rostand in 1989, these Lladró-only auctions managed to get in a good five years before giving up the ghost. Efforts later in the 1990s to resuscitate them in other venues and under other management have been unsuccessful.

Lladró auctions are difficult to sustain for two basic reasons. First, most Lladró collectors are loathe to part with their collections; death, financial need, or collection upgrade are usually the only things that can pry serious collectors loose from their Lladrós. Herb Rostand, in the Summer 1990 issue of *Expressions* magazine estimated that it takes about 200 good quality, retired figurines to make such an auction fly, and sponsors of both the East Coast and West Coast sites have testified this was always a difficult quota to reach.[1]

The second reason these auctions are difficult to sustain is that promoting and launching them is tremendously expensive, in both time and money. Most businesses that might otherwise be willing to step up

to the bat in sponsorship are not large enough to absorb the expenses incurred.

While the Lladró auctions were instrumental in establishing a secondary market baseline, auctions do not make an exact science of secondary market valuation. Prices often enough succumb to opposite extremes, either falling to the bargain basement or spiking auction fever.

Auction fever does seem to have played a key part in some gavel-down prices at Lladró auctions. It has been difficult to convince every owner of one of those modest little "Olympic Puppet" figurines (#4968) that theirs can't be expected to command the astronomical price of $3800 one fetched at the first-ever Lladró auction held as long ago as 1989. It's also been difficult to convince every owner of the first Lladró Society piece, "Little Pals," that theirs probably needn't command the more than $4,000 achieved as its highest Lladró auction price. Most of the more rational prices achieved by items sold at those auctions, however, have withstood the test of time.

Well, here he is, folks: that illustrious "Olympic Puppet" figurine (#4968G) who blew everyone away at the first-ever Lladró auction when he gaveled down at the astronomical price of $3800! (At a subsequent Lladró auction, by the way, the winning bidder took it at a far more modest $650.) Issued in 1977 and retired in 1983, his more typical secondary market price range is fairly broad at $800–$1200—prices which still seem inflated by that first-ever auction price. (Photo courtesy of Lladró USA, Inc.)

As instrumental as the Lladró auctions were in bringing about a U.S. secondary market, Lladró collecting is probably best pursued, at this point in the evolution of that market, in venues other than Lladró-only auctions. These venues include Lladró secondary market brokers, general auctions, Internet auctions, estate sales, consignment shops, and resale shops and malls for antiques and collectibles.

"Pharmacist" (#4844G/M), the earlier of two Lladró models of pharmacists (the later being #6273) is the most expensive of the several professional figurines produced by Lladró as prices are currently being realized on the secondary market. Issued in 1973 and retired in 1985, this earlier pharmacist model typically runs in four figures ($1200-$1500), with his highest-ever Lladró auction price topping out at an incredible $2150. I once saw a mint example in an antique shop for somewhere around $300, but didn't buy him because he didn't fit in thematically with the rest of my collection. (Photo courtesy of Lladró USA, Inc.)

Benefits of Brokered Transactions

There are advantages to buying Lladrós from a broker or dealer who handles Lladró mainly or exclusively. First, you have the broker's reputation standing behind the merchandise; reputable brokers do not knowingly represent defective merchandise. Lladró brokers or dealers who have a large inventory of retired figurines are also just about the only places where collectors can find, or hope to find, the oldest and most elusive retired pieces. Also, if the original box is important to you, you are more likely to find it with brokers who deal largely or exclusively in Lladró. Packing and shipping are also safe and reliable. There is no extra cost to the buyer for buying from a broker, as commissions are assessed to the seller.

Sculptor A. Ballester's spectacular early limited edition, "The Forest" (#1243G), was first issued in 1973, and by 1976, its edition size of 500 was fully subscribed. Its last retail price even then was $1500, and it will cost you dearly today. (At this writing, A Retired Collection had one available for $8,250! Good luck finding this baby in mint condition without the assistance of a broker.) (Photo courtesy of Lladró USA, Inc.)

The downside to dealing with a broker is that the prices are often at the value "cap" for what the item is worth at the time of secondary sale. Prices typically include not only a base value for the item, but also consignment costs (as brokers are usually representing other sellers). Some broker prices are more expensive than others, of course; in general, the broader and deeper the broker's access to hard-to-find inventory, the more expensive the service will be in order to cover that value added. Still, the price may be entirely worth it to collectors who have otherwise been trying unsuccessfully for years to find elusive retired pieces or who may be looking for rarities never previously

catalogued. Also, some pieces will continue to appreciate even after purchase from a broker. In January of 1997, I purchased "Koala Love" (#6451G, pictured on page 20) from "A Retired Collection" for $225; by 2000, the same brokerage was offering it at $300, a price consistent with trends elsewhere in the secondary market.

Note the lovely, flowing lines in "The Harpist" (#6312G), issued in 1996 and retired in 1999 at a retail price of $850. I have seen this one offered through a broker at $950. Given its extraordinary delicacy, I'd say your chances of finding it in mint condition elsewhere on the generic secondary market are not good. (Photo courtesy of Lladró USA, Inc.)

An example of a series that is very difficult to find without the assistance of a broker would be the "Painful Animals" (#s 5018-5023), consisting of several wild animals (polar bear, elephant, monkey, giraffe, lion, kangaroo) with bandages around various parts of their anatomy. Lladró's animal figurines, which are among its most popular on the secondary market, tend to have short retail runs, and this series, produced only from 1979 to 1981, is no exception. The series had an odd distribution pattern that seems to suggest a limited retail availability in the U.S. A broker can, therefore, be invaluable in locating the "painful animal" you're looking for to round out your own collection.

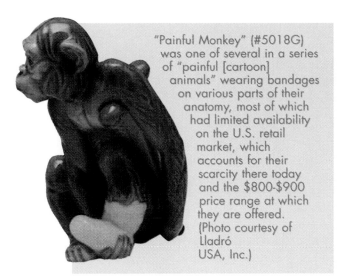

"Painful Monkey" (#5018G) was one of several in a series of "painful [cartoon] animals" wearing bandages on various parts of their anatomy, most of which had limited availability on the U.S. retail market, which accounts for their scarcity there today and the $800-$900 price range at which they are offered. (Photo courtesy of Lladró USA, Inc.)

Savvy Tips for the Generic Secondary Market

There are two types of Lladró merchandise to be found on the generic secondary market. First, and most often found, are the items that are still in production and have made their way prematurely to the secondary market. Second are the figurines in various stages of retirement from newly retired to long retired.

Collectors should be very careful about buying current-issue merchandise on the secondary market, as the price is often inflated above retail—even in bargain shoppers' virtual paradises such as eBay™. In order to avoid paying too much for current issue pieces on the secondary market, it is worth investing in the latest edition of *The Lladró Authorized Reference Guide* published by the company itself. This guide has the current prices on retail items as well as the last retail prices on retired ones.[2]

As an alternative source of current prices, several authorized Lladró retail dealers have Web sites that include stock lists with prices. You can find these simply by typing "Lladró" in the search field of your favorite search engine. Again, from the Lladró company's perspective, Lladró prices are standardized, and authorized dealers do not discount them.

If you do find a good retail piece on the secondary market, make sure you have a price incentive for purchasing it there. In other words, the only really good reason to buy retail Lladró from a secondary market source—thereby forgoing all the quality and packing assurances provided by the company in its retail distribution system—is to get a break on the price.

The second and best type of Lladró merchandise found on the secondary market is retired figurines, i.e., those that are no longer in production. In fact, by definition, the secondary market is the only place in which to find older, retired figurines. In Lladró's case, "retired" means the items are no longer being manufactured—and there are no plans to "reissue" them in things like "special anniversary reproductions," an annoying temptation to which many collectibles firms have succumbed but which Lladró has thus far resisted.

The relative advantages and disadvantages of buying from non-brokered secondary market venues—e.g., Internet auctions or antique shops that have an occasional Lladró only—are pretty much the inverse of those for brokered transactions. In these other venues, you will usually not get the quality assurances you would get with a broker and will have to rely more upon your own eyes to ensure the condition of the figurine. You will not get the selection you'd get from a brokerage. You will usually not get the original box (if that's important to you), and shipping processes may be less timely and reliable than those of an established broker. On the other hand, you can usually buy a limited pool of items much more cheaply on the generic secondary market than you can from a broker, and for collectors of limited means, this can be a decisive factor.

"Painful Elephant" (#5020G), another of the "painful animals" series, each of which garners $800-$900 on today's secondary market—when they can be found at all. Collectors who have several of these naturally want them all, and demand for them continues to outstrip secondary market supply. (Photo courtesy of Lladró USA, Inc.)

"Three Ducks" (#s 4551-4553) when originally sold in the mid- to late 1960s, but now sold as a set (#7909). It is not unusual to see these on the secondary market for $75-$125 apiece—highway robbery, when you consider you can buy the whole set for $144 retail! (Photo by the author, from her own collection.)

Many of these retired items are considered highly desirable by collectors and hence are seldom seen. That does not mean, however, that they are "rare"—a badly abused word among secondary market sellers, especially at Internet auction sites. Collectors should always maintain a healthy skepticism about the "r-word" on secondary market tags and descriptions.

Up to 1991, the company retired a specific group of figurines on a schedule of every other year on odd years; in 1992, it began retiring figurines every year. Within the chronology of retirement, there appear to have been certain "banner years" (e.g. 1985 and 1991) when large numbers of items, including many of the most desirable items of the corpus, were retired.

There are many reasons why figurines retire from production. One of the more practical reasons cited by the company itself is that its overall corpus has become so large that it has to forcibly retire, on a regular basis, some of its older items just to make room in company inventory for newer productions. However, there is usually more of a rhyme and reason to the process than the need to make room in storage. Other factors that influence retirement decisions include the item's durability in manufacture and/or shipping and the relative health of its retail sales. In other words, figures that break easily, in either manufacture or shipping, or that aren't selling well on the retail market become prime candidates for retirement.

The Capricho series (see Chapter 2) is an example of items that were so delicate and so prone to breakage that, in 1991, the company retired virtually the entire series. Conversely, the company has little incentive to retire durable items that enjoy consistently healthy retail sales—which accounts for the extremely long retail run of some popular items that have been open more than thirty years.

Perversely, the value of retired items on the secondary market is often inversely related to their retail difficulties. Mint examples of items susceptible to damage during their retail life or items that did not do well on the retail market tend to command hefty prices on the secondary market. In the first instance, there is simply less mint-condition product around. In the second instance, items are sometimes slow to catch on with collectors, and an early retirement because of flagging retail sales means there will be less of them available when the market finally discovers them.

A final caution is in order about the definition of a "retired" item. I have already mentioned Lladró's laudable resistance to the temptation to reissue later "anniversary" clones of retired figurines. From time to time and for reasons not known, however, the company has discontinued production of certain items with no fanfare and without actually retiring them. Typically, what happens is that they simply disappear from retail dealer price lists—meaning that retailers do not order them. However, because the company has not officially retired them, they can reappear in production and retail lists a year or two later.

Several examples could be cited. The famous "Sad Harlequin" (#4558) was apparently discontinued and reissued several times, after production hiatuses of varying lengths, before it was definitively retired in 1993.[3] The limited edition figures "Classic Spring" (#1465) and "Classic Fall" (#1466) disappeared for about three years from Lladró retail lists—long enough, again, for people to have assumed there had been an edition sell-out or retirement and long enough for them to have appeared at Lladró-only auctions, which made it a point to feature retired-only figurines. Both figurines showed auction activity in each of three successive years, 1990 through 1992, on both coasts. The items then reappeared on Lladró retail price lists for 1993 at prices consistent with their last retail prices rather than the higher auction prices they had by then achieved.[4]

Another equally strange case involved the two items "Graceful Swan" (#5230) and "Swan with Wings Spread" (#5231, mentioned earlier). Apparently, through another of those production continuity glitches, an assumption was made by collectors and secondary market dealers in the U.S. that both of these pieces had been retired by 1991, for both of these items appeared on the 1991 California auction list. "Graceful Swan" went out at the princely sum of $550, with "Swan with Wings Spread" not far behind it at $500. Not only that, but these items were long enough off the retail radar screen that they were featured again at the 1993 Florida auction. There, "Graceful Swan" was gaveled down to a price of $600 and "Swan with Wings Spread" to the truly astonishing price of $750—which tends to underscore the point I made earlier in this chapter about how great a buy this item is at the current retail price of $145.

"Swan with Wings Spread" (#5231), first issued in 1984 and still retailing at $145, which I call a great retail bargain—especially since, through a fluke of communication, this item was previously assumed to have been retired and commanded prices of $500-$750 at two of the exclusive Lladró auctions held in the early 1990s! Sculptor for this figure of extraordinary beauty and appeal was Francisco Catalá. A companion piece features a floating swan with wings closed, "Graceful Swan" (#5230), just retired in year 2000 at a last retail of $110. (Photo by William B. Bradley, Jr., from the author's own collection.)

Back in those days, auction sponsors didn't have the benefit of official retirement lists from the company; those are a recent development. What used to happen is that auction sponsors would have to rely on authorized dealers to tell them when something had dropped from the retail lists. In most cases, that meant the item was retired for all collecting intents and purposes. In a few cases, though, items everyone assumed to have been retired did appear again on retail lists a couple of years or more down the road, to the embarrassment of the secondary market. (It should be borne in mind here that the "mother company" is based in Spain, has its own production and marketing priorities, and cannot be expected to be cognizant of what Americans are doing on the secondary market.)

To avoid this confusion about recently-retired items, Lladró now issues, on an annual basis, formal lists of items due to be retired that year. Lladró buyers should beware seller attestations that an item is retired unless they can verify that status. Internet auctions, for instance, on a daily basis feature active items that sellers assume must be retired just because their aunt "bought it in Spain twenty years ago."

Understanding "Book Value"

While those of us who are passionate about it have every assurance that Lladró will be recognized as one of the great antiques of tomorrow, it must be admitted that the work is still too young for posterity to have issued any edict about it. What this means is that the secondary market will remain volatile and unstable for some years to come.

These days, it sometimes seems every buyer fancies himself a dealer. The ease with which people can buy and sell collectibles on the Internet has exponentially increased the number of "amateur dealers" selling Lladró, all of whom hope to get what's known as "book value" (i.e., the values in the price guides) for their particular items.

The supply of retired Lladró is still healthy enough, however, that even many of the most avid collectors will not pay a price premium to get items unless they are distinguished by rarity or some other factor leveraging their desirability. In other words, the market for retired Lladró is still a buyer's market in many parts of the country—especially with the advent of eBay™ and other Internet auctions, which have both expanded the pool of available retired figurines and made them more affordable through price competition.

Some book prices are based on quotes from dealers and brokers who deal largely or exclusively in Lladró and who charge top dollar for the advantages they can provide to a Lladró buyer: a large inventory of retired items, the reputation of the Lladró broker/dealer standing behind assurances about condition, a network of contacts for finding rare or elusive items, and a buyer-friendly sales transaction. Other price guides may be based on the appraisals of experts with a generic expertise in antiques and collectibles, but without any particular affinity or appreciation for Lladró. Such price guides may "low ball" values so much that collectors are left throwing up their hands and groaning, "I wish I could buy Lladró this cheap!"

Another thing one needs to understand about book values is that, based as they are either on asking prices or on appraisals, they do not necessarily represent actual selling prices, which may be negotiated to a point quite a bit lower than the ones in the book. (That's why the books are called "Price Guides" and not "Price Contracts!")

From a buyer's point of view, unless the item in question is rare or very difficult to find, you can almost always buy the Lladró you want much cheaper than "book"—provided you are willing to wait what may sometimes be years to find that particular item and provided you are willing to trust your own eyes to assure condition. From a seller's position, unless you are consigning your item through a well-known broker with a large network of potential buyers, you may not be able to realize anything approaching the values for it in the price guides.

"Sleepers" on the Generic Secondary Market

Many people are under the mistaken impression that there are no great buys on Lladró at traditional secondary market sites such as antique shops. While it is true that most antiques and collectibles dealers are by now savvy enough about Lladró not to give it away, collectors can still find some wonderful Lladró "sleepers" at antique shops.

I have even met one or two dealers who knew pretty much what they had but who were not used to carrying Lladró and were made nervous by its delicacy relative to some of their other inventory. "I just want to move it out of here before it gets broken," one of them told me before I obligingly helped him with his problem!

Sometimes a dealer simply doesn't know what he has, and that's where the bargains get truly incredible from a buyer's perspective. One has to wait for these and be willing to put up with weeks of scouring before making the find, but if you like antiquing anyway, the task shouldn't be too onerous.

The best buys I ever got on Lladró were on retired core collection pieces. I bought a not too badly damaged example of the extremely rare "Hunting Dog" (#308.13, pictured here) for $20. (See Chapter 6 for more about this particular piece.) At that price, I could well afford the $200 charge for a top-of-the-line restoration.

"Hunting Dog" variant, #308.13, a rare "decimal-point" serial number from around 1963, sculpted by Fulgencio García. The one in Lladró catalogs has long-necked goose in mouth; according to Lladró USA, this quail version may be even older. It bears the old impressed core collection mark LLADRÓ ESPAÑA and has a current book value of over $2000. I regard this as my once-in-a-lifetime find; while I will certainly remain vigilant for such rarities in the future, I recognize this extraordinary occurrence for what it is and do not expect to have such luck again—at least not on the generic market. (Photo by William B. Bradley, Jr., from the author's own collection.)

Much more recently, I walked into an antique shop that I frequently visit on the off chance it might have a Lladró among the knickknacks. One gets tired of doing this after months of failing to hit pay-dirt, and I was about at that point, pulling in at the last minute after I'd made the initial decision to drive by.

And there, in the midst of a shelf of unmarked figurine refugees from-a-dime-store-close-out, was a matte-finish "Girl with Hat" (#1147, pictured here). This piece was retired in 1985 and is not that easy to find. She can command $275-$300 among sellers who recognize her identity. I picked this one up and saw the green felt attached to the base, a material often adhered to cheap wares. A flick of my fingernail revealed that the felt was, in this case, the self-adhesive variety that peels easily away. Verifying the presence of the Lladró mark. I checked the price tag, tamped the felt down again, and ambled as nonchalantly as I could to the counter. "Nice piece," the shop owner commented, turning it over and adding, "Not marked, though." I felt almost guilty as I paid my $18 (yep, eighteen dollars) and slunk gleefully out to my car.

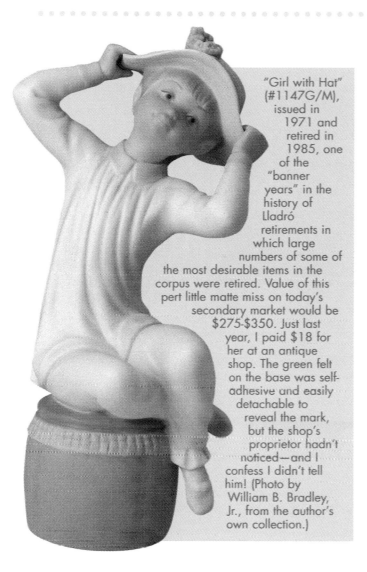

"Girl with Hat" (#1147G/M), issued in 1971 and retired in 1985, one of the "banner years" in the history of Lladró retirements in which large numbers of some of the most desirable items in the corpus were retired. Value of this pert little matte miss on today's secondary market would be $275-$350. Just last year, I paid $18 for her at an antique shop. The green felt on the base was self-adhesive and easily detachable to reveal the mark, but the shop's proprietor hadn't noticed—and I confess I didn't tell him! (Photo by William B. Bradley, Jr., from the author's own collection.)

Two of a series of three popular polar bears from the core collection. Left to right: "Seated Polar Bear" (#1207G) and "Attentive Polar Bear"(#1209G). I should buy the missing bear now if I want to be sure to get him! He is #1208G, called simply "Polar Bear," and is seated back on haunches with front paws raised. Issued in 1972, these are still active and, at a retail price of only $75 each, are among the most affordable items in the core collection. (Photo by William B. Bradley, Jr., from the author's own collection.)

Best Lladró Buys on the Retail and Secondary Market

- Older, long retired pieces
- Items that had a short retail run
- Small limited edition items (e.g. eggs, Christmas ornaments, and the like)
- Larger and older limited editions bought early in their retail run
- Items with lots of detail, including flowerwork in mint condition, at prices that aren't inflated for the decorative enhancements in question
- Older items offered near or under their last retail price
- Items with legitimate older marks that may not be recognized by dealers or unsuspecting collectors

"Sleepers" aside, some buys on the secondary market are better than others, from both an artistic and a monetary perspective. One factor to consider is how long the item was on the retail market. Certain of the lower ticket items—the three polar bears (#s 1207-1209), the six child angels (#s 4537-4541) and the little duck figures (originally sold separately as #s 4551-4553, but recently sold as a set, #7909)—have all been on the retail market for more than thirty years. The first thing this illustrates is that they are enormously popular. However, it also means that there are potentially thousands of them that could be floating around on the secondary market in any given future year. What that means in turn is that the market for them will always be, at least theoretically, a buyer's market, even after they retire. (This doesn't seem to stop some Internet auction buyers from bidding them up above retail, however, especially in the case of the three ducks!)

What About Society Pieces and Large Limited Editions?

As collectors, we may be accustomed to assume that, if something is a limited edition, it is *de facto* desirable. However, many market observers feel that the whole concept of "limited edition" has been so badly overused all across the collectibles market that it has essentially lost its meaning. It is worth remembering that for every Lladró limited edition that is sold out between one marketing brochure and the next, there are several others that take years to become fully subscribed. The fabulously gorgeous "18th Century Coach" (#1485) is still open as of this writing, even though it was issued in 1985 with an edition size of only 500. It's also a mighty long way from its substantial issue price of $14,000 to its whopping current retail of $31,000—a retail appreciation of more than 120%.

Collectors of large limited editions who find themselves winners are those who had the foresight and the financial wherewithal to purchase these items early in the company's history; appreciation on large limited editions has been most rapid and most consistent for those early pieces. For example, "Antique Auto" (serial #1146) was issued in an edition of 750 in 1971 at the then hefty price of $1000. It was fully subscribed by 1975, at which time it was retailing for $1750. Years later, prices for it at Lladró-only auctions sponsored by Rostand and Thalheimer ranged from $7,000 to $10,500—and, give or take a thousand dollars, these prices have remained fairly consistent across the secondary market ever since.

"Antique Auto" (#1146G) is one of Lladró's earliest and most famous limited editions. Issued in 1971 in an edition size of 750, it was fully subscribed in 1975. Its last retail price was $1750—a mere pittance compared to its much later Lladró auction prices of $7,000 to $10,500! (Photo courtesy of Lladró USA, Inc.)

An analysis of trends in the exclusive Lladró auctions shows that later-released limited editions often did not fare as well, sometimes even failing to achieve winning bids as high as their last retail prices. In general, the more expensive the item is at retail, the more vulnerable it is to equity loss on the secondary market, at least in the short- to mid-term. This dynamic applies to very expensive open issues as well as to large limited edition groupings; every item seems to have a kind of invisible price ceiling above which appreciation will

not venture. After all, even wealthy collectors like a bargain at auction. So if you're going to pay every cent that a Lladró will ever be worth, make sure you're willing to stay married to it.

The limited edition grouping called "The Hunt" (serial #1308) is a good case in point. Given its price tag of $3750 at the time of issue in 1974, it is not surprising that it took ten years to become fully subscribed, even though its issue size was the same as that for "Antique Auto." "The Hunt" was already retailing at $6300 by the year of its retirement in 1984. Even though it had been several years off the retail market by the time of the Rostand and Thalheimer's auctions, the highest price it was able to command was $6750—a scant $450 over its last retail price. If the consignor had originally bought the piece at or close to the time of issue, he or she would have realized a healthy profit. If, on the other hand, the consignor bought it at the end of its retail run, he or she probably lost money on it by the time the auction commission was subtracted from the winning bid.

This cautionary example also illustrates the importance of broad thematic appeal as a factor in appreciation. Thematically, "Antique Auto" is a grouping that can capture the attention of a wide spectrum of collectors. Strictly from a quality perspective, "The Hunt" is also a marvelously well-executed tableau; however, as a scene of scarlet-coated foxhunters riding to hounds, it has a more limited thematic appeal than does "Antique Auto."

It took ten years for "The Hunt" (#1308) to sell out of its edition of 750, from 1974 to 1984. This one was never a steal on the retail market, at an issue price of $3750 and a last retail of $6300. It couldn't jump a fence higher than $6750 at one of the Lladró-only auctions, and secondary market prices since have generally been in the $6900-$7300 range—not a lot of margin for a seller who bought it at that last full retail almost twenty years ago. (Photo courtesy of Lladró USA, Inc.)

Another factor to consider in the acquisition of large, complex limited editions is the display challenge they pose. Few people who could afford to buy one would risk acquiring "18th Century Coach" or "Cinderella's Arrival" without knowing where they planned to display it and without casing it under glass. Since these things don't come with their own cases, the likelihood is that the collector will have to have one custom-built. Some collectors haven't the space, others haven't the patience, and most of us haven't the money. Historically, smaller figures and limited editions often have a better appreciation ratio relative to their size and initial cost, and they don't present the space and display challenges of more elaborate compositions.

While it is not the most expensive item in the Lladró corpus (a distinction which belongs to "18th Century Coach"), "Cinderella's Arrival" has the merit of being the most expensive at the time of first issue: $25,950. The price has gone up a bit since the first issue in 1994; today, a buyer will have to pay $26,400 to get one of the 1500 in its edition size. A tableau like this poses the challenge of how to display it so that there's space left for you in the room. (We should be so lucky!) (Photo courtesy of Lladró USA, Inc.)

As for Lladró Society pieces, figurines that command the most inflated prices are the two earliest ones, "Little Pals" (#7600, pictured on page 50) and "Little Traveler" (#7602, pictured on page 49). This is consistent with trends across the collectibles field: the first issues in a members-only series typically command the highest prices because there were relatively few collectors around with the vision to a) join the Collector's Society as charter members and b) purchase the first members-only pieces on the retail market.

Unless the item can stand on its own artistic merits, later members-only pieces don't appear to appreciate more rapidly than especially popular open-issue figurines available to everyone else. Later Lladró Society pieces are among the Lladró figurines that tend

to be "carried" by their flowerwork. Flowerwork aside, there are only so many girls in long, swishy skirts one can view before they all start to look the same. As with any piece that has flowerwork, the operative question on purchase decisions is whether the piece would retain its artistic appeal even without the flowerwork.

"Afternoon Promenade" (#7636) was the Lladró Society figurine for 1995. Its last retail price in 1996 was $240. Its secondary market price is in the $300 to $350 range—not better than desirable general-issue figurines retired that year. (Photo courtesy of Lladró USA, Inc.)

The 1998 Society piece, "It Wasn't Me!" (#7672, pictured on page 51) is a good example. The piece has lots of flowerwork, but take away the flowers and the figure of the puppy and an overturned pot would still retain its charm. Not surprisingly, the piece rarely appears at Internet auction, even though the flower-laden Lladró Society figurines either side of it (those for 1997 and 1999) are regularly featured there.

At the risk of spreading heresy, I have heard at least a few collectors say there are other Lladrós they'd rather spend their dollars on than many of the Lladró Society pieces. A strong factor militating against this perspective, however, is the strength and durability of aspiration many collectors have to acquire a complete set of all the Lladró Society annual figurines. Also it remains to be seen what, if any, impact Lladró's decision to suspend the Society as of the year 2000 will have on future secondary market value of the Society pieces.

Condition on the Secondary Market

There are several reasons why Lladró items end up on the secondary market: because the original owner has died, because the owner is "upgrading" a collection, simply because the owner is tired of collecting, or because the owner is not a collector at all and only has one or two pieces of Lladró he doesn't particularly care to keep. Sometimes whole Lladró collections will make their way to antique shops via estate auctions. All these circumstances can mean some wonderful figurines available at modest prices on the secondary market.

However, much of what's actually available on the secondary market consists of damaged Lladró. One source for these damaged goods is serious collectors who won't have damaged pieces in their own collections but who don't feel right about just "tossing them out." This is *caveat emptor* territory. Sellers do not always declare damage (although they should!), and if the piece has been carefully repaired—even if inexpertly—the damage may not be evident to an unsuspecting buyer until some time after purchase.

Some collectors are so preoccupied by condition that they will even have a piece x-rayed to detect invisible restorations. Personally, as long as damage is truly invisible (and I have pretty sharp eyes!), I don't especially care that it's been professionally restored and would not go to inordinate lengths to assure that it hasn't been, nor would I turn my nose up at a great item declared as invisibly restored.

With almost any porcelain- or china-producing company that uses applied flowerwork as a decorative technique, it will be difficult to find mint-condition flowerwork on the secondary market. This is most true of nineteenth century or earlier Staffordshire and Meissen figurines. Some collectors may not mind minor damage to flowerwork on a very old piece that has lots of flowerwork on it, feeling that such condition goes with the territory of age and resale. In general, collectors of old Meissen are more forgiving of minor flower damage than are collectors of old Staffordshire. Most serious Lladró collectors, however, will be bothered by damage to Lladró's far more recent vintage flowerwork, and those to whom it is important should inspect that aspect of a figurine with particular care.

For more about the impact of damage and restoration on value, see Chapter 6.

Original Boxes

Let me just say it plainly at the outset: Original boxes are irrelevant to Lladró values. Occasionally, one may encounter buyers so eccentric they will insist on having the box, but this does not suffice to establish a norm. My position is supported by the Lladró company itself, as evidenced in a response by the then Lladró Society Director to a Letter to the Society published in the Fall 1989 issue of *Expressions*: "Time and time again we have noted that it is not necessary to keep the original Lladró box as a valued part of the collection."[5]

However, my position is also supported by common sense. It seems pretty silly to pass up a rare or important mint-condition Lladró just because it doesn't have its original cardboard. To see just how inappropriate it is to obsess about original boxes on fine porcelain, imagine yourself going into an antique store and asking, "Does that extraordinary eighteenth century Meissen grouping over there in the display case come with its original packing materials?"

As a matter of historical perspective, collector preoccupation with original boxes is a late twentieth century phenomenon. (That is, after all, why there are so few original boxes available on any merchandise retailed earlier than the second half of the twentieth century.) Generally speaking, your great grandmothers didn't keep the packing boxes on their sets of Limoges china or their Imari vases, and they would have thought it silly of anyone to suggest that they should.

On the practical side, too, many of the older Lladró boxes are in deplorable condition—having been used for the purpose for which they were intended: to take the barbs and slings of outrageous handling so that the figurine itself won't have to. The battered condition of these

"Baby on Floor" (#5101G), part of a sequence of small babies with pacifiers or bottles sculpted by Salvador Debón (#s 5099-5103G). Issued in 1984 and retired in 1987, their short retail run makes them a de facto time-limited edition, accounting for their value on today's secondary market at $275-$350. This one did not have its original box—so ask me if I cared! (Photo by William B. Bradley, Jr., from the author's own collection.)

containers begs the question of what they could possibly be worth. The largest of the boxes also take up an incredible amount of storage space. I know of at least one collector who finally gave up trying to accommodate them and sold all his empty Lladró boxes at Internet auction.

But here comes the *coup de grace* for collector preoccupation with box acquisition: At one of the Rostand-Thalheimer's auctions, a company representative was heard to announce that none of the three Lladró brothers keep the original boxes for items in their own collections. The spokesman went on to describe the boxes as merely a "necessary shipping instrument." And there you have it, ladies and gents, straight from the horse's mouth: Your Lladrós can live without their original boxes.

My misgivings about "value added" notwithstanding, I will admit that original boxes do have a practical, if not monetary, value. The safest way to transport or store Lladrós, especially figures with delicate protruding parts such as hands and flowerwork, is in their original boxes, many of which have internal foam moldings or cardboard cut-outs to keep the figure stationary. Having said that, I should also note that some of the earlier cardboard inserts are sufficiently complicated to require a degree in mechanical engineering to figure them out. The inserts are also susceptible to weakening over time, at which point they will fail, without the help of external reinforcements such as tape, to keep the figurine stationary within the box.

Signed Pieces

The growth of "signing events" is, like the fetish for original boxes, a late twentieth century phenomenon; in earlier centuries, the mark was the signature, and no one ever thought of chasing down the company's owners for an autograph.

Because autographing of collectibles is such a recent historical phenomenon, it is difficult to assess the long-term value of a Lladró family member's signature on a given piece. In the final analysis, this question will be determined, as such questions always are, by whether future collectors are willing to pay a premium for an autographed piece. So far, it does not appear that collectors are willing to pay more on the secondary market for an autographed Lladró than they would for the same piece unautographed.

A number of factors will need to be considered in future valuation of signed pieces:

- The number of signing events held for Lladró (the answer to which, by the way, is "legion").

- The number of pieces signed by a given member of the family, such that the signature of one may be "rarer" than that of the others.

- Whether the signature is that of a founder or a second-generation family member.

By the way, one of the more practical uses I have discovered for the Don Quixote embossed Lladró Society plaque that was given to all new members in their new member packets is the comparative use that can be made of the signatures. Scripted signatures, especially in Europe, contain many loops and flourishes which can make them individually difficult to decipher. The signatures of the three brothers on this plaque can help to identify founding-generation signatures on other signed pieces and to distinguish them from those of second-generation family members.

Two plaques for Lladró Society Members. Left: the 1999 membership premium, entitled "Art Brings Us Together" (#7677), worth about $35-$45. The white one on the right with the embossed figure of Don Quixote is the more familiar and was offered to all new members of the Lladró Society when they joined. The one pictured, which has the Lladró brothers' signatures in black, is worth about $25. Charter members received a piece with the signatures in blue, worth about $75 today. (Photo by William B. Bradley, Jr., from the author's own collection.)

The best advice I have for collectors on this question is to regard an autograph of a Lladró family member as a potential value-added feature of a piece that can be acquired at an otherwise reasonable price. Pending the ultimate judgment of posterity, collectors should assume only that an autographed piece is worth as much as the same piece not autographed.

"Angelic Melody" (#5963G), an "Angel Symphony" tree topper issued in 1993. Value today: $225-$250. The base of this particular example happens to be signed and dated (11/93) by Jose Lladró. (Photo by the author, from her personal collection.)

Glaze or Matte?

The first Lladró figurines I ever collected had the high-gloss glaze for which Lladró is famous. There's just something alluring about that shiny surface! As I continued collecting, however, I found myself more and more drawn to the matte finish figurines, and now, consistent with my thematic interests, I buy all the mattes I can find.

From the earliest days of factory production, many, if not most, of the glazed figures had matte versions as well. In 1991, however, the company made the decision to retire most of its existing matte corpus as well as to make far fewer mattes in the future. The reason for this decision was entirely practical: outside Europe, matte Lladrós usually did not sell very well relative to their glazed counterparts. For this reason, the matte figures often retired sooner than their glazed twins, even prior to the massive retirement of matte pieces in 1991.

This trend is only somewhat contradicted by evidence that, at least through the late 1980s, there was enough collector demand for matte figures that the company agreed to make even more mattes to meet that demand.[6] Apparently, matte collectors are passionate and vociferous, but not especially numerous, and collector demand for matte figurines fluctuates, tending perversely to peak in those periods when the company is making the least number of them.

One of the reasons demand for matte pieces tended to be spiky and sporadic was the limited selection of matte figurines available relative to offerings in glaze. In other words, because the glazed part of the corpus had more figurines to choose from, more of the glazed figures were seen and, hence, bought. This in turn would have served to reinforce the impression that collectors preferred the glazed figurines. (Similarly, many genuinely rare items across the antiques and collectibles market cannot parlay their rarity into collector demand, simply because collectors don't know enough about them to ask for them.)

The company has still retained some of its more popular items in matte; a notable instance is the set of six child angels (#s 4537-4541), whose retail sales have remained strong more than thirty years after their first issue. I've often thought those angel babies are so alluring they could have been modeled in grade school paper mache and people would still buy them!

Some secondary market dealers and brokers may price earlier-retired mattes above their glazed counterparts by virtue of their relative age. Others, offering the same retired figurine in both glazed and matte finishes, will price the matte figures lower in view of the mattes' lack-luster retail record.

Still, the decision by the company to retire much of the matte corpus has created a secondary market demand for matte figurines. For one thing, some collectors prefer the mattes. Also, it is likely that the company hadn't anticipated the impact of its 1991 en masse matte retirement decision on the collectors of sets, notably the Bethlehem Nativity set (#s 4670-4680, shown on facing page), originally made in both finishes. This eleven-piece set is affordable when the modestly priced figures are purchased individually as cash flow allows; purchased as a set, however, the outlay is about $1000. Therefore, many collectors build on the set from year to year rather than trying to buy it all at once. The decision to retire the matte figures for this set precipitated a crisis among those collectors who had already begun but not yet completed the matte Nativity set. Today, collectors are still searching for them; for some reason, the matte "Shepherdess with Rooster" figure (#4677) is especially difficult to find.

Famous group of six child angels (#s 4536-4541G/M) sculpted by Fulgencio García, currently retailing at $95 each and produced still in both matte and glaze. Two of those pictured are in the matte finish. (Photo by William B. Bradley, Jr., from the author's own collection.)

To appreciate the relative merits of the two types of finish, one must first of all understand how they function aesthetically. To quote the company, "Shine is more spectacular, matte is more direct and its charm lies in the material itself."[7] In other words, there is nothing between a matte-finish Lladró and the heart of a viewer. Matte has a naked impact, where the effect of the glazed figure is mediated by the allure of the glaze itself.[7]

On the other hand, a glazed finish brings out the color in a figurine; the subtle pastels in Lladró's palette will appear even more muted in a matte finish. Mattes may be too understated for collectors either consciously or subliminally troubled by the neutrality of Lladró's preferred palette—especially collectors immersed, as most of us are, in an era and a culture defined by its insatiable pursuit of sensory stimulation.

Aside from artificial production inducements to consider the matte figures "rare," I will risk a prediction that Lladró mattes will, at some future point, be considered even more valuable than their glazed counterparts, despite their lagging performance now. Artistic subtlety and understatement are hallmarks of the best of Lladró, and the matte finish is arguably more consistent with that subtlety than is a high-gloss glaze. This is not to say that the glazed figures will not continue to be popular in the future, but only that posterity may well give matte pieces a slight edge of superiority on purely aesthetic terms.

"The Belén [Bethlehem] Nativity," one of two Lladró Nativity sets sculpted by Juan Huerta. This one was issued in the mid- to late 1960s and is still open today in its glazed version. The matte version of the set was abruptly retired in 1991, along with much of the matte corpus for the core collection, and this has sent collectors scurrying to try to complete matte sets, (Photo by William B. Bradley, Jr., from the author's own collection.)

The eBay™ Effect

t is still too early to predict the ultimate impact that Internet auctions—and the bargain prices for which many people are willing to sell their Lladró on those sites—will have on the long-term resale value of Lladró figurines. Opinion on this question from those who have already weighed in is divided; some pundits say, "eBay™ is ruining the Lladró secondary market," others that "eBay™ will have no long-term effect on the Lladró secondary market." The first perspective seems to give Internet auctions too much power, the second to give them too little.

"Angel Wondering" (#4962G/M), part of a series of four (#s 4959-4962) sculpted by Salvador Debón. This matte version was retired in 1991 along with most of Lladró's matte corpus and is worth $175-$275 today. Glazed versions are still retailing at $130. (Photo by William B. Bradley, Jr., from the author's own collection.)

It will be immediately clear to collectors who make it a point to update their price guides annually that the Internet craze has had little or no impact on book price. Nor, at this writing, is there any substantial evidence that the buyers' prices for which Lladró is going at Internet auctions have had much affect on the prices of the same items being offered on the Web sites of more traditional secondary market dealers.

From a buyer's point of view, it is a legitimate question why one should pay the highest prices for Lladró in traditional sales venues when one can get the same items for half as much at Internet auction. Collectors' Information Bureau's executive director, Peggy Vitri, very astutely likens the eBay™ phenomenon to a stock market correction in response to inflated stock prices.[8] To the extent that some Lladró has been subject to the collectibles market equivalent of stock market speculation, the comparison is quite apt and the lessons to be learned by the burned are pretty much the same.

It is reasonable to expect that e-auctions will eventually have some modifying effect on secondary market prices for all collectibles, and not just for Lladró, at least over the short- to mid-term—whether or not "book value" ever gets around to reflecting that impact. The Internet exponentially expands the pool of available merchandise, so that items aren't as hard to find anymore as they were when shoppers were restricted to live venues within a certain radius of their homes. Lladró secondary market prices are not immune to the phenomenon of price inflation, as we saw in the "Olympic Puppet" example previously cited. Prices like that are ripe for challenge by a phenomenon such as the Internet auction.

A recent counterbalancing tendency has been asserting itself in eBay™ auctions, however, and that is for sellers to establish reserves—or in some case, even opening bids—at prices for which the same Lladró might sell elsewhere on the secondary market. In other words, there is evidence that sellers are getting wise to the bidding habits of many e-auction bargain trawlers and are "protecting their investment" accordingly. The days of acquiring Lladró at "steal" prices at e-auction may soon be over.

My analysis of Lladró offerings on eBay™ over the past couple of years has led me to several other conclusions about Lladró buying and selling trends on that site. First, what tends to turn up on eBay™ is the current issue stuff; retired items are usually recently retired, and the same items tend to reprise over and over again as eBay™ itself becomes a force and testing ground for determining prices. In other words, solid e-auction selling prices for particular items tend to drive others of their kind out of the collecting woodwork.

"Small Dog" (#4749G, AKA "Butterfly Dog" in a literal translation from the Spanish) is obviously of the Papillon breed (which name, of course, is the French word for "butterfly!"). Issued in 1971 and retired in 1985, he stands a mere 3" tall. Value: $225-$250—but I bought it at Internet auction for a lot less! (A larger "Papillon Dog" (#4857), issued in 1974 and retired in 1979, is valued at $550-$600.) (Photo by William B. Bradley, Jr., from the author's own collection.)

Second, buyers are often willing to pay above retail prices for small current issue items even as they resist paying anything approaching "book" for larger, retired items. One reason for this paradox is the ease of eBay™ purchase relative to Lladró's tightly-controlled authorized dealership system, which leaves many rural and suburban collectors without ready access to retail figurines. Another reason people would pay a premium for small current-issue Lladrós is that, even at twenty to thirty dollars above retail, these smaller items are relatively inexpensive compared to most other Lladró figurines. In fact, considering the number of current-issue Lladrós available through Internet auctions, a case could be made that, if eBay™ is harming any Lladró market at all, it is authorized retail, not the secondary market.

My third conclusion is that there is a plethora of Lladró Society "members-only" pieces offered for sale on eBay™. If there is one place where I think eBay™ really has done some damage to the Lladró secondary market, it would be here. During the month of April 2000 alone, there were over 100 Lladró Society annual figurines available for bid just on eBay™, including several examples of the first and heretofore "rare" "Little Pals." Lengthy scrolls of retired Lladró Society figures on the Internet tend to strip away the illusion of exclusivity which was meant to constitute the lion's share of their appeal in the first place.

It has occasionally been alleged that Lladró has been subject to market speculation by people who bought up special issues, not so much because they liked them, but because they expected to "make a killing" off them on resale. The flooding of eBay™ with Society members-only pieces appears to support that claim. Buying up Lladró for investment purposes is a dicey business, and the company itself has consistently warned collectors against stratospheric investment expectations for their collections. The best advice is and has always been, "Buy it because you like it"—not because you think it's an alternative to a stock portfolio.

Finally, eBayers tend to be younger, novice collectors whose taste in Lladró is pretty much conditioned by what they have seen in retail sales brochures and catalogs or in commercial ads in collectibles magazines. This may lead to a somewhat blunted taste palate that doesn't always appreciate the older factors that first made Lladró famous—e.g. subtle treatments, pastoral themes, and stylized and elongated forms. Although I rarely buy at Internet auction because of the limitations of the genre already mentioned, I have purchased through eBay™ at least two mint-condition older, retired Lladrós, managing to cop them at bargain prices against very little bidding competition.

"Sweet Dreams" (#1535G), issued in 1988 and open today at $240—although I once saw it bid up to $357 at a June 1999 eBay™ auction with 45 bids! (Photo by William B. Bradley, Jr., from the author's own collection.)

Still, the live secondary market should take heart. There are several reasons why the majority of buyers in the market for retired Lladró will always prefer live to virtual shopping. In the first place, condition is paramount. Unless e-sellers can attest, "I know it's mint because it's been in my own collection for the past twenty-five years," the buyer will be at risk for flawed condition that may not be evident either in a digital photo or to the eye of the casual seller.

Just as importantly, many collectors have had the experience of thinking they wanted a particular figure, based on what they'd seen of it in photographs, only to be fairly unimpressed when confronted with the item in three dimensions. Conversely, a figure they'd have thought they wouldn't care for at all seems to capture their fancy when they finally see the item in someone's shop; there's just nothing to beat the thrill of coming upon a solid Lladró sitting on a real shelf in a live antique store or estate sale.

Help in Identifying Retired Items

The best help in identifying retired items from the core collection is a picture catalog. Fortunately, the company itself has obliged by publishing the *Collector's Catalog* (in four volumes) and *The Lladró Authorized Reference Guide*; the latter is updated about every two years (most recent issue, year 2000). These publications are available through any authorized dealer or Lladró USA (see appendix for contact information).

For the core collection, the most comprehensive Web site at which a collector can match a title and serial number with an actual picture is the one for "A Retired Collection" (www.lladrolady.com). However, if all you have is an item with no clue to its serial number or title, even that user-friendly site won't be as much help in identifying your piece as thumbing through a picture catalog would be.

You will not find price guide lists of pictureless titles and accompanying serial numbers to be of much help. Lladró has several themes to which it returns over and over again, often calling them all by the same title. There are, for instance, several core collection items all named "Girl with Lamb" (#s 1010, 4505, 4584, 4834) and there are even more named "Girl with Turkey(s)" not to mention the girls with ducks!

"Little Girl with Turkeys" (#1180G) with an original blue backstamp. Issued in 1971 and retired in 1981, it is worth $400-$450 on today's secondary market. I bought this wonderful older item at Internet auction against relatively few bids—mostly, I think, because novice collectors didn't recognize it. (Photo by William B. Bradley, Jr., from the author's own collection.)

In the identification and price lists included in this book, I have tried to overcome this difficulty by adding brief descriptions that note distinguishing characteristics of each piece listed. Since this book cannot provide anything approaching a comprehensive listing of everything Lladró ever made, collectors will still find Lladró's own pictorial guides indispensable for identifying items in their core collections.

Notes to Chapter 5

1 "Primer on the Secondary Market," *Expressions* 6:2 (Summer 1990): 4-6.

2 Collectors are advised to confirm these prices with other knowledgeable sources, such as authorized dealers either in your area or online, as pricing information in *Lladró Reference Guides* is not always accurate.

3 As reported in "Retired Lladró Harlequins," *A Work of Art* 6:2 (Spring 1995): 11.

4 As reported in "The Mystery of Classic Spring and Classic Fall," *A Work of Art* 5:1 (Winter 1993/94): 21.

5 "Letters to the Society," *Expressions* 3:3 (Fall 1989): 17.

6 The Letters Column of *Expressions* 2:4 (Winter 1986) announced that, "beginning with the upcoming year," the company was responding to collector demand by assuring that "every" new introduction would be produced in both matte and glaze. As late as spring 1988, *Expressions* ran an article entitled "Matte vs. Glaze," which again referenced increased collector demand for matte, although only about 75% of new introductions were actually produced in matte for 1987 (*Expressions* 4:1).

7 "Matte vs. Glaze," 4.

8 As quoted in Susan K. Elliott's regular column "Internet Savvy," *COLLECTOR'S mart magazine* (June 2000), 26.

"Feeding the Ducks" (#4849G/M), issued in 1983 and retired in 1995 (matte in 1992). The sculptor was Alfredo Ruiz. Value today: $350-$400. When I found this piece on the secondary market, it was pretty dirty. Moistened Q-tips™ are great for getting into those little tight spots around the ducks and in the vegetable basket. (Photo by William B. Bradley, Jr., from the author's own collection.)

Chapter 6

RESTORATION: WHEN'S IT WORTH DOING?

Luckily, fine porcelain is not as delicate as it looks. It will often absorb a good deal of banging around without being the worse for wear. The "Letters" columns of early *Expressions* magazines are filled with tales of Lladró having survived hurricanes and earthquakes essentially or nearly intact—in some cases after being found lying amid stony rubble.

Among serious collectors, evident damage nearly always has a negative impact on value. "How much damage is damage" varies with the perspective of the viewer. A minor flake in the porcelain at the lip of the base, where it can't be seen when displayed, will not bother some collectors at all, whereas a flake on the visible surface will be less tolerable to most. Hairline fractures may not seem like a big deal to a secondary market dealer not used to handling Lladró, but they are a big deal to serious collectors. In general, novice collectors are more tolerant of minor damage than are veteran collectors.

My best advice is to buy merchandise in the best condition you can afford. That means that if you have $200 to spend on a Lladró, it is better spent on a simpler item in mint condition than a more elaborate one with damage.

Defective items can result in two ways: through manufacturing defect or through breakage. Lladró destroys most of its defective merchandise at the factory site; however, some minor defects do occasionally slip through Lladró's quality net. These are usually nearly undetectable and may include a pinprick hole in the glaze, for example, or a minor firing crack. A firing crack is distinguishable from a later damage crack by the appearance of the crack itself; the firing crack will have jagged edges and will tend to separate, whereas the damage crack will typically have a straight–line appearance, often referred to as a hairline crack, and the edges of it do not separate.

Minor production defects will be acceptable to many collectors; the more obvious they are, however, the more they will detract from the figurine itself. I have cheerfully purchased retired and hard-to-find items with minute production flaws, but I have also reluctantly passed up at least two retired figurines with firing cracks large enough and at vulnerable enough positions on the figure that I felt the structure was at high risk for future damage.

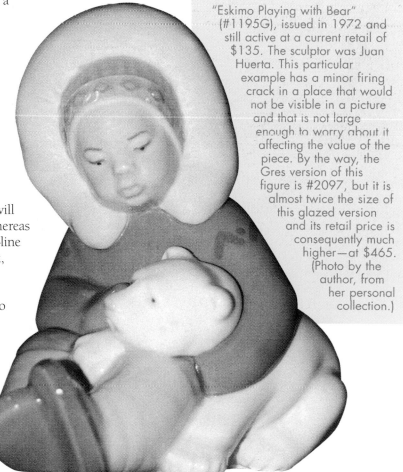

"Eskimo Playing with Bear" (#1195G), issued in 1972 and still active at a current retail of $135. The sculptor was Juan Huerta. This particular example has a minor firing crack in a place that would not be visible in a picture and that is not large enough to worry about it affecting the value of the piece. By the way, the Gres version of this figure is #2097, but it is almost twice the size of this glazed version and its retail price is consequently much higher—at $465. (Photo by the author, from her personal collection.)

PLACES TO CHECK CAREFULLY FOR DAMAGE
OR REPAIR BEFORE BUYING SECONDARY MARKET
LLADRO

- The point where head joins neck

- The point where neck joins torso

- Separately articulated hands and fingers

- Flowerwork and lace work

- Any other small projecting parts

It is usually not worthwhile to buy damaged pieces of Lladró with the intention of having them restored. Only in the case of a very rare piece can a professional restoration recoup not just the aesthetic value, but also 100% of the financial value because every collector who wants it cannot find the rarest pieces—in any shape at any price. However, a rare piece is precisely that—rare! The general rule of thumb is that a professional restoration, especially if the work is detectable with the naked eye, restores only about 75% of the value as long as the same piece in mint condition is readily available.

The Art of Porcelain Cleaning

It is a well-known fact that most porcelain figurines get damaged while someone is cleaning them. (I once heard a horror story relating how a cleaning lady inadvertently toppled an entire curio cabinet of expensive Lladró, breaking it all into smithereens.) It follows, then, that your best insurance against damage is care in cleaning.

Large feather dusters and cloths are verboten! An article entitled "Handy Hints" in the Winter 1993/94 issue of *A Work of Art* suggests that you use a hand-held hair-dryer to blow the dust off your Lladró. It also highly recommends the basting brush—one never before used, of course! The authors found the bristles "soft, but strong enough to remove almost any residue."

Particularly if you are an inveterate antique store haunt like me, you will find that many of the Lladrós you find in that sector of the secondary market will be quite dirty. Once I bought a figurine so filthy I could

barely tell if it was damaged or not. In such an instance, not cleaning the figurine is not an option, and a basting brush isn't likely to cut it for the worst grease and grime. For that, you'll need water.

Never immerse your figurines in the dishpan! For one thing, it increases the possibility of dropping and breakage. But the other problem is that all Lladrós are equipped with those little holes in the base that are placed there to allow the steam to escape during the firing process so they don't blow apart in the kiln. The same aperture through which steam escapes is the aperture through which water will enter the figurine if you immerse it. Even if you think you got it all out, you may well be dismayed to find water damage on your curio shelves the next time you dust.

For Lladró cleaning jobs that require a little soap and water, the best utensil I've discovered is a Q-tip™. Yes, that's right. Just get a little cup of water with a drop of some grease-cutting dish detergent in it, stick the end of the Q-tip in the water, and you're good to go into all those tight little corners and crevices that a regular dusting won't touch.

There are potions available on the retail market that take off that troublesome glue that too often adheres to the surface of porcelain once the price tag is removed. But slathering the little area with vegetable oil or lemon juice works just as well, and it's cheaper. (I've never had the nerve to try this on my mattes; even though they're not supposed to be porous, I don't want to be the one to find out they hate lemon juice. I do not hesitate to use a little mild dish soap and water on them, though, applied via my trusty Q-tip™.)

Various Types of Restoration

Professional restoration is a costly undertaking. In the case of most current issue Lladró, it will usually be cheaper to buy a new piece than to restore the damaged one.

There are various types of restoration. The best and most expensive is "invisible restoration," so called because it is undetectable either by the naked eye or under black light. Black light will cause glue around repairs to fluoresce. (Black light use takes a certain amount of experience, as certain paints as well as specks of dust will also fluoresce.) Because an invisible restoration is done not with glue but with liquid porcelain, it does not fluoresce. Invisible restoration is, however, detectable by X-ray; some collectors obsessive about condition and who have access to medical imaging technology will subject figures to it just to be sure they haven't been invisibly restored.

The second kind of restoration is a careful cementing of the broken parts and some restoration of the paint and surrounding glaze. This type of restoration will remain evident to the naked eye of anyone searching carefully for it.

By the Way...

Lladró uses liquid porcelain rather than glue to attach accessory parts to a figurine or grouping, so whenever you see glue on a Lladró, the glued part has been either repaired or repositioned. Recently, for example, I found an old, matte "Girl with Mandolin" (#1026) on the secondary market. Retired since 1978, this figure would be a great addition to anyone's collection. The price was right, too, at $249 for a figurine that can easily go for twice or more that price. When I gave the figure my most thorough physical examination, though, I noticed that the mandolin's body was actually glued to the girl. A second look showed me there was also glue around the hand where it met the neck of the mandolin.

The piece had obviously not been broken, yet the presence of glue indicated to me that, at some point, the mandolin had come loose and been skillfully, if not professionally, reattached. A quick consultation with the picture of this figure in my *Lladró Collection Reference Guide* (a copy of which I carry with me in my car at all times) confirmed my suspicion. The angle of the mandolin against the girl in the piece I'd examined was wrong; it had been reattached. Though another collector might not mind a little glue as long as there were no visible breaks, I passed on her. If I'm going to pay over $200 for a figurine, I want it to be undeniably mint.

The final, and least costly form of restoration involves merely a careful gluing of broken parts, with the break neatly repaired but clearly visible. Whether or not such restoration is acceptable to a collector will depend on the collector's own financial resources and standards for condition.

To help collectors decide whether to restore a given piece, I thought it would be helpful to share three scenarios from my own experience: one a no-brainer for restoration, another probably worth doing, and a third clearly not worth doing.

Scenario One: Do It!

One day, in a Vermont antiques mall, I found a damaged Lladró figurine of a setter dog with a bird in its mouth. The dealer knew it was a Lladró and had so indicated on the tag, but she'd marked it "as is," probably thinking to herself that, damaged as it was, she'd be lucky to get $20 for it. It was fairly early on in my collecting experience, so I had to go out to my car to look the figure up in my [then] *1996 Lladró Collection Reference Guide*, whereupon I saw that it was the rare "Hunting Dog," #308.13 (pictured on page 188). Unable to believe my luck, I hurried in to buy the piece.

The two breaks, at the base of the tail and across one hind leg, were clean and all the parts were present and accounted for, despite the crude, messy, and obviously amateur job of cementing them. (I have always blessed that unknown person for keeping all the parts together!)

I proceeded to get a price quote on invisible restoration from a professional experienced in Lladró restoration. The quote necessitated several hours of driving from my home in Vermont, as the restorer would not give me a quote over the phone. When I got there, he gave me the princely estimate of $780 and nine months to complete the work. I confess I was tempted even at that; after all, I told myself, the piece has a "book value" of over $2,000.

Then I asked myself, "What are you, nuts?" The more I thought rationally about it, the less sense this quote made to me. I decided to get a second opinion, and chose restorer Jodi Leak of Leak Enterprises in Lakeview, Florida, who had been recommended to me by a trusted secondary market broker. Her price? $200! Restoration given that quote and excellent references was a no-brainer.

LESSON ONE: DON'T LET JUST ANYONE DO IT!

Look for a *qualified* restorer who will not take advantage of you on price. Get recommendations and references from people you trust!

Finding a qualified restorer may not be as easy as you think. Trade journals for antiques and collectibles are filled with classified ads guaranteeing to teach the art of restoration to all comers in a few easy lessons. That should give us all pause. The adage that you get what you pay for applies. There is a world of difference between a mail-order certification of competence in restoring porcelain and years of apprenticeship and painstaking experience in actually doing it.

One skilled professional restorer, Christine Cunningham of Orford, New Hampshire, pointed out to me that Lladró is especially difficult to work on because the colors often flow into one another naturally—i.e. there are no obvious breaks where one color leaves off and another begins. Repainting a damaged section of Lladró is thus not a matter of simply "coloring within the lines." Lladró restoration requires a special skill in blending the new pigment into the surrounding colors.

Scenario Two: Probably Worth Doing

My second scenario involved purchase on the secondary market of an expensive current edition item at a substantial price reduction off retail. The item in question was "Kittens in a Basket with Flowers" (#1444, pictured here), first issued in 1983.[1] This piece features three mischievous kittens in a handled basket filled with flowers.

"Kittens in a Basket with Flowers" (#1444G), found on the secondary market at a great price with some minor damage to the flowerwork. The company keeps flowerwork supplies on hand for current pieces in order to supply them for restoration purposes. In the end, I had a piece restored to its full retail value of $615, which is more than I could have afforded to spend to buy it on the retail market. (Photo by William B. Bradley, Jr., from the author's own collection.)

The flowerwork and the difficulty in manufacture that would be posed by the thin porcelain basket handle make this an expensive piece to buy at $615 retail. (A related piece, #1441, featuring three puppies in the flower basket, retails even higher, at $645.) The item I purchased was being offered at $255 by a dealer who knew little about Lladró and had some minor damage to the flowerwork. Because I knew that Lladró regards flowerwork restored professionally using factory-supplied parts as constituting a return to pristine condition, I figured the sale price was a real bargain.

After I bought it, I got a quote from the same restorer who'd done my Hunting Dog; the quote for the flowerwork came in surprisingly high, at $170. (Apparently, it's a real pain working with all those tiny petals and stamens!) Still, for a total outlay of $425, I would have a Lladró whose retail value would, under ordinary circumstances, be beyond my means. While the total cost of acquisition plus restoration was more than I had ever paid for any individual Lladró in my collection, the "pain" was spread out over time, as restorers typically only ask for a 50% down payment up front, with the remainder due upon completion of the work. All things considered, I still felt it was probably worth doing. After restoration, I still have almost $200 in equity in the piece when I compare my total outlay to the current retail price.

Close-up showing detail from "Kittens in a Basket with Flowers" AKA "Purr-fect" (#1441G). Hand painting creates variable expressions in the faces of kittens from model to model. Retails at $615. (Photo by William B. Bradley, Jr., from the author's own collection.)

LESSON TWO: FOLLOW YOUR NOSE!

If a quote smells too expensive, shop around. But beware of bargains in porcelain repair—whether on your teeth or on your Lladró!

Scenario Three: Just Not Worth It

have just described to you virtually the only two circumstances under which a restoration of Lladró is worth doing: 1) the piece is truly rare or 2) a currently active piece is expensive on the retail market, whereas a damaged piece can be restored for less using Lladró supplied parts.

Here's an example of a different scenario altogether. I did reflect a long time on this decision because the piece was one I'd have loved to have in my collection. It was being offered in the same antiques mall at which I'd purchased my "Kittens in a Basket." The piece, long retired, was called "Blue Creeper," and features a small bird poised on the stock of a large, lush, pale pink, peony-like flower. At $150, it was an absolute steal! But what was this? There seemed to be something broken off from the flower stalk. Sure enough, consultation with the picture in my *Lladró Collection Reference Guide* showed there was a whole stalk, leaf, and bud missing from the piece.[2] (Well, that explained the price!)

Another example of a restoration not worth doing. This piece is marked "Made in Spain," but otherwise unattributed, although the face is very Lladró-like. She has a missing hand in addition to the damage to an accessory rooster in basket. At a minimum, the restorer would have to resculpt the hand from scratch—without a picture of the original to go by. Whenever a restorer has to reconstruct missing pieces, the expense is usually prohibitive. Nothing was ventured, here, but nothing lost, either: I bought the damaged piece for a buck at an antique mall. (Photo by the author.)

Because this was a retired piece, I suspected that Lladró would no longer have the petal and leaf parts to supply to a restorer; a call confirmed my fear. Not only that, but the stalk itself was not an accessory part; it was integral to the model—meaning the restorer would actually have to sculpt it.

Well, if simple placement of company-supplied petals was going to cost $170 in the case of my previous venture, I couldn't begin to imagine what it could cost to have a restorer rebuild an entire Lladró flower stalk, complete with leaf and bud, from scratch. I didn't even bother to get a quote in this instance. Total outlay— acquisition cost plus restoration cost—would be a minimum of $350 for a piece that is considered desirable but not rare. At the time, this would have been close to the cap on secondary market value for a mint example of the same piece. That, however, was precisely the trouble: because the item wasn't rare, the "75% rule" would kick in. In other words, were I to succumb to this temptation, I would have, after all my outlay, a piece worth no more than about 75% of the cost of the same piece in mint condition.

When I did the math and forced myself to be realistic, I realized that I'd have to pay more to buy this piece and have it restored than it would ever be worth. Besides, I couldn't imagine, given the distinctiveness of Lladró's famous flowerwork, that a restorer, no matter how good, could make the reconstructed part look entirely natural and integral to the rest of the piece.

I concluded, reluctantly, that the work just wasn't worth doing. Even then, the little birdy occasionally tempted me for weeks afterward until one day, some other person with less exacting condition standards than I finally bought the beauty and put me out of my misery.

LESSON THREE: GET REAL!

Don't let sentiment or romanticism force you into investing more in a damaged figurine than it will ever be worth.

This is not to say there aren't restoration considerations more important than money. If your favorite great aunt gave you that figurine, you may, indeed, want to invest more in it than you might ordinarily. Still, let rationality play some role in your decision. If the piece is a Lladró that is still being made, and you can replace it with a mint clone, isn't that also a tribute to Aunt Esmeralda? There, there now, you already feel badly enough about breaking it, don't you? It's probably not necessary to punish yourself by paying $200 more than the retail price just to have the very one she touched restored to some semblance of its original grace.

Protecting Your Investment

One of your collecting priorities, if you intend to have more than a few pieces of Lladró, should be insuring your collection. You'll need insurance if you're ever faced with substantial restoration or replacement costs for your Lladró collection.

Many people mistakenly assume that regular renter's or homeowner's insurance covers loss of or damage to a collection. Chances are, you'll need a fine arts rider on your insurance in order to have your Lladró collection covered in a disaster. The extra cost will be nominal for the peace of mind it provides. Don't wait for a disaster before finding out your "regular insurance" doesn't cover your collectibles.

Here's a horror story that serves as object lesson. Someone once told me how her oldest and dearest friend was moving from one area of the country to another. Since this lady would have to stay in temporary quarters until her new house was ready, she had put all her fine antique furniture and other valuables in a locked storage facility—without insuring it.

As ill fortune would have it, her storage unit was robbed. What was most astonishing about the theft was that the thieves took only her Lladró collection, leaving all her high-end antiques behind. The fact that the thieves had such good taste in stealing the thing she herself most valued was small consolation for her lost collection and her lack of financial resources to replace en masse what she had gathered over a period of years.

Whether or not you live in an area prone to crime— and these days, who doesn't?—just about everyone lives in an area susceptible to one type of natural disaster or another. If your part of the country is vulnerable to earthquakes, floods, hurricanes, or tornadoes, all the more reason: If you can't secure it, insure it!

Some Parting Words from a Collector to Collectors

A surprising number of longtime collectors with whom I've spoken are troubled by various aspects of Lladró collecting today, including the sheer profligacy of new issues. (One always wonders whether it's possible for artists to be too prolific and thereby lose their artistic edge.) To such concerns, I would simply say it is not necessary to be a Lladró company "groupie" to love the best of its work, nor is it necessary to admire everything Lladró has ever created in order to go on enjoying the works one loves. The field is plenty wide open and exciting for those who learn how to glean the wheat and leave the tares behind.

Also, Lladró collectors sometimes have to put up with the turned-up noses of other people who think a fine collectible has to be old to matter. You know the type: "[Sniff] Oh, Lladró…That's new, isn't it? [Sniff! Sniff!]"

Honestly! I sometimes wonder how these folks think fine antiques ever got to be that way. The humble truth is that every antique becomes one because people thought it was worth acquiring when new and then handing down through the generations. So, all you Lladró collectors, celebrate your collections with proper pride!

"Two Women Carrying Water Jugs" (#1014G/M), a classic older Lladró in the distinctive, elongated style inspired by El Greco. The lines and form are spectacular. First issued in the late 1960s, the piece was retired in 1985 at a last retail price of $350. Lladró exclusive auction prices ranged from $475-$750, and the matte version of it can go as high as $800-$900 on today's secondary market. (Photo courtesy of Lladró USA, Inc.)

My collection's insured with a fine arts rider to my homeowner/renter insurance policy. Is yours? (Photo by the author, courtesy of Caren Reed and Reed's Antiques and Collectibles of Wells, ME.)

Notes to Chapter 6

1 My preferred title for this piece is a literal translation from the Spanish. The punning in the English title, "Purr-fect" is a little too kitschy for my taste.

2 As you can see, the *Lladró Collection Reference Guide* is useful not only for the identification of figurines but for the identification of damage in figurines with which the collector may be unfamiliar. The pictures in the Guide are awfully small, but they can usually tell you when a part's missing or if it's been reattached in a different position.

References

Coady, Cliff. "Lladró adds line to fill price gap," HFD-the Home Furnishings Newspaper, March 23,1992.

Collector's Information Bureau. Collectibles Price Guide & Directory to Secondary Market Dealers. Iola, WI: Krause Publications, 2000.

Elliott, Susan K. "Internet Savvy," COLLECTOR'S mart magazine, June 2000, p. 26.

Expressions. Lladró Society. Tavernes Blanques, Valencia, Spain. Published quarterly.

Hammer, Janet Gale. Newsletter. *A Retired Collection* (web site: lladrolady.com). Longboat Key, Florida. Published quarterly.

Lewis, David and Joan and Brad Welch, Eds. *A Work of Art 1-6,* 1990-1996. Ceased Publication.

The Lladró Authorized Reference Guide. Moonachie, NJ: The Lladró Society, 1996, 1998, 2000.

Lladró; the Art of Porcelain. Barcelona, Spain: Salvat Editores, SA, 1981.

Lladró; the Magic of Porcelain. Barcelona, Spain: Salvat Editores, SA, 1989.

Lladró Collector's Catalog. Vol. 1-4. Valencia, Spain: The Lladró Society, 1994.

"Lladró's 22 Latest Figurines Part of Bid to Broaden Image," HFD-the Weekly Home Furnishings Newspaper, December 7, 1987.

McAllister, Liane. "Valencia: Spanish Ceramics Show Growing Pains And Pluses," Gifts and Decorative Accessories (January), 1997.

Rinker Enterprises. *The Official® Price Guide to Collector Plates,* 7th ed. New York: The Ballantine Publishing Group, 1999.

APPENDICES
Core Collection Marks

1. Impressed "Lladró España" mark, used c1960-1963. (All photographs of marks by William B. Bradley, Jr. unless otherwise noted.)

2. Impressed "Lladró, Made in Spain" mark, used c1965-1970.

3. First blue backstamp with logo, used from about 1971 to 1974. Note the absence of the accent over the o.

4. Second core collection backstamp adds accent and trademark sign, but no copyright. Used from about 1974 to 1977.

5. Third backstamp adds the copyright acronym DAISA without a copyright date. Used from around 1977 to 1984.

6. Fourth backstamp adds copyright date. Used from about 1984 to 1989. At around this time, the four-digit serial number also began to be added to the base, as in this picture.

7. Contemporary backstamp introduced in 1990, with revised logo and typeface. The LHF33 is an example of one of Lladró's codes and is important for collector information purposes.

8. LCS stamp on base of a "Members Only" piece.

9. Example of a "special events" stamp.

A List of Important Lladró Resources

The following list is not exhaustive; it includes a number of resources with Web sites which, over the years, I have found consistently enough helpful to have bookmarked as favorites on my own computer. All of these collectors and companies have a stable presence in the Lladró field. However, things change fast in the Internet world; should you have any trouble reaching them with the Web and e-mail addresses given, just type the business names into the search field of your favorite search engine, and they should pop right up!

Lladró USA
1 Lladró Drive
Moonachie, NJ 07074
1-888-448-3552
www.lladro.com

The company's Spanish headquarters maintains a Web site in several languages including English. This is a good source of information on latest developments, including new series and retail issues and latest retirements.

The site also has a list of retail authorized dealers from which you can locate the one nearest you.

Janet Hammer
A Retired Collection
550 Harbor Cove Circle
Longboat Key, FL 34228-3544
http://lladrolady.com
e-mail: Janet@lladrolady.com

Janet is widely recognized as the foremost secondary market broker of Lladró in the United States and maintains what is probably the most comprehensive secondary market Web site on earth. What Janet doesn't know about Lladró, nobody does, and if she can't find a given item, it can't be found! Her database is enormous and her network of contacts extensive. She is consistently cordial and helpful. For many collectors in the U.S., Janet is Lladró, and she is widely known simply as "the Lladró lady."

Barbara Bennett
832 Oaklette Ave.
Chesapeake, VA 23325
(757) 545-0028
www.bzweb.com/lladro
e-mail: mylladro@home.com

Barbara is a longtime Lladró collector/dealer. Her Web site is user-friendly, and Barbara herself is a pleasure to deal with. Her inventory list is not long, but she has some great stuff on it.

Collector's Showcase
477 Milford Road, PMB #295
Swansea, MA 02777
(888) 245-9001
www.collectorsshowcase.com
e-mail: collectorsshowcase@msn.com

This brokerage has a fairly extensive database of retired Lladró, arranged in a large-type, alphabetical, user-friendly format. It gives quantities available with price ranges where more than one is listed.

European Imports & Gifts
7900 N. Milwaukee Ave.
Niles, IL 60714
(800) 227-8670
www.europeanimports.com
e-mail: europeanimports@europeanimports.com

I have found this Web site invaluable because it includes not only a large inventory of retired core collection items but also what may be the only significant database of recently retired NAO on the Internet.

Debra and Dennis Landis
www.debnden.com
e-mail: den@debnden.com

Collectors Deb and Dennis Landis sponsor this very helpful Lladró informational Web site that includes photos of legitimate marks and counterfeits (the posting of which is a real public service to collectors!) as well as links to retail and secondary market Web sites.

Francisca Madden
"La Dulcinea"
6432 Grassy Point Cv.
Memphis, TN 38135
(901) 382-8760
http:/member.aol.com/lladrodulc/dulcinea.htm
e-mail: LladroDulc@aol.com

A native of Spain now residing in the U.S., Francisca has a secondary market business named "La Dulcinea" (after Don Quixote's beloved). It is accessible by Web and is a lovely place to visit for a variety of secondary market figurines.

Nadal Collectibles (Nadal Imports)
PO Box 10374
Burbank, CA 91505
(818) 768-9924
www.nadalporcelain.com
e-mail: fnadal@1stnetusa.com

Not to be confused with the Lladró competitor company located in Spain, Nadal Collectibles in the U.S. is a dealership/brokerage specializing in retired Lladró. Collectors Francisco and Mercedes Nadal came to the U.S. in 1965 and opened their business at the urging of friends. An extensive database of retired items is available at their Web site.

Sanchez Collectibles
1555 East Glendale Avenue
Phoenix, AZ 85020
(602) 395-9974
www.primenet.com/~sanchcol/lladronr
e-mail: sanchcol@primenet.com

Sanchez Collectibles, owned by Clark and Charlotte Sanchez, is a large secondary market company handling exclusively Lladró and Swarovski Crystal. Collectors will find a large inventory of current and retired Lladró at their Web site. There is also some solid information on the Norman Rockwell and Ford Car series which collectors of those items will find particularly useful.

Wendy Still
(916) 784-0732
www.wendyslladro.com
e-mail: still4@aol.com

Wendy Still is another Lladró collector who has broadened her interest to include sales of retired Lladró. She has a growing inventory of retired pieces available for sale.

Yesterday's South
POB 565097
Miami, FL 33256
1-800-Doulton
www.yesterdayssouth.com

This is a secondary market dealership with exclusive focus on rare and retired Royal Doulton and Lladró. Its Lladró database is not as extensive as some others are, but it does contain some hard-to-find items.

"Diana, Goddess of the Hunt" (#6269) was first issued in 1996 and is a very recent retirement in year 2000. Her last retail price was $1250. (Photo courtesy of Lladró USA, Inc.)